The World of Homer

Andrew Lang

The World of Homer

The present edition is a reproduction of previous publication of this classic work. Minor typographical errors may have been corrected without note, however, for an authentic reading experience the spelling, punctuation, and capitalization have been retained from the original text.

ISBN: 978-1-64799-615-4

PREFACE

In 1895 I published Homer and the Epic (pp. 424), containing a criticism of Wolf's theory, if theory it can be called, which is the mother of modern Homeric criticism. I analysed, book by book, the Iliad and the Odyssey, observing on the modern ideas of interpolation and the modern objections to many scores of passages which, as a rule, I defended from charges of "lateness" and inconsistency.

I added chapters on the Lost Epics of Greece, on Archeology, and on the early Epic poetry of other ages and peoples which offers analogies, more or less imperfect, with Homer.

On the whole my conclusions were identical with those of Signor Comparetti, in his preface to his learned book on the Finnish Kalewala. He says:

"The anatomical and conjectural analysis which has been applied so often and so long ... to the Homeric poems and other national epics, proceeds from an universal abstract principle, which is correct, and from a concrete application of that principle, which is imaginary and groundless."

The true principle, recognised since the end of the eighteenth century, separates the "personal" and learned Art Epics, like the Æneid and the Gerusalemme Liberata, from those which belong to the period of spontaneous epic production, "when Folk-singers fashioned many epic lays of small or moderate compass." (Perhaps Folk-singers is hardly the right term. Such songs of exploits as the Borderers "made themselves," as Bishop Lesley said in 1578, were not "epic lays," but ballads like "Jock o' the Side," and "Archie o' Cafield," and "Johnie Cock," despite its name the most romantic of all.)

"These epic lays were called 'national' or 'popular,' not only by virtue of their contents, sentiment, and audience, but mainly because the poetry which takes this form is natural, collective, popular, and hence 'national' in its origin and development." (By "collective" I understand the author to mean, not that a whole country-side automatically and collectively bellows out a new ballad, but that the original author uses traditional formulae in verse wherever he can, and that his ballad is altered in the course of recitation by others, so that any version which has been obtained from recitation is, in fact, one of many variants which have arisen in course of time and recitation.)

"The baseless application of this principle is to regard the national poems not as creations of a single poet, but as put together out of shorter pre-existing lays (either by a single person at one time, or by several in succession), until the final fashioning of the poem. And this process is conceived of as a mere stringing together, without any sort of fusion, so that a critical philologist, thanks to his special sharpness and by aid of certain criteria, would be in a position to recognise the joinings, and to recover the lays out of which the poem has been made up.

"With this preconceived idea people have gone on anatomising the Epics; from Lachmann to the present day they have not desisted, although so far no positive satisfactory and harmonious results have been won. This restless business of analysis, which has lasted so long, impatient of its own fruitlessness, yet unconvinced of it, builds up and pulls down, and builds again, while its shifting foundations, its insufficient and falsely applied criteria, condemn it to remain fruitless, tedious, and repulsive. The observer marks with amazement the degree of intellectual shortsightedness produced by excessive and exclusive analysis. The investigator becomes a sort of man-microscope, who can see atoms but not bodies; motes, and these magnified, but not beams."

Comparetti proceeds: "No doubt before the epic there existed the shorter lays; but what is the relation of the lays to the epic? Is the epic a mere material synthesis of lays, or does it stand to them as a thing higher in the scale of poetic organisms,—does it move on a loftier plane, attaining higher, broader conceptions, and a new style appropriate to these?" Notoriously the epic infinitely transcends in scale, breadth of conception, and grandeur of style any brief popular lays of which we have knowledge. It never was made by stringing them together.

So much for the little lay theory. "But there remains the nucleus theory" (the theory of "the kernel"), "for example of an original Achilleis" (the Menis) expanded by self-denying poets into an Iliad. Comparetti does not believe that a poet would fashion lays "to be inserted in a greater work already constructed by others, nor that he would have done this with so much regard for other men's work, and with such strict limitation of his own, that the modern erudite can recognise the joinings, and distinguish the original kernel and each of the later additions."

Here Wolf anticipated Comparetti, he did not believe that the additions could be detected.

But Comparetti does not reckon with his host. The astute critics tell us that the later poets did not compose "with so much respect for other men's work"; far from that, the poet of Iliad ix. calmly turned the work of the poet of Iliad xvi. into nonsense, we are told (see infra, "The Great Discrepancies"). Again, the critics will say that a later poet did not "fashion lays to be inserted in another man's work." He merely fashioned lays. Much later other men, the Pisistratean, or Solonian, or Hipparchian Committee of Recension, took his lays and foisted them into the middle of another man's work, making every kind of blunder and discrepancy in the process of making everything smooth and neat.

Comparetti goes on: "The difficulty is increased when we have to do with epics which seem in all their parts to be composed on a definite plan, which exists in the final poem, not in the supposed kernel. The organic unity, the harmony, the relation of all the portions, which are arranged so as to lead up to the final catastrophe, are such as to imply the agreement and homogeneity of the poetic creation in a common idea, and, moreover, resting on that idea—a limitation of the creative processes."

Comparetti, I fear, forgets that his "man-microscopes" see none of these things; "they see the mote, not the beam." Finally, granting the pre-existence of a mass of poetic material, "He who could extract from this mass the epics which we possess, and not a kind of Greek Mahabharata, would have produced, at all events, such a work of genius that in fairness he must be called not merely the redactor, but the author and poet."

How true is all that Comparetti says of "this restless business of analysis, which has lasted so long, impatient of its own fruitlessness, yet unconvinced of it! It builds up, and pulls down, and builds again, while its insufficient and falsely applied criteria condemn it to remain fruitless, tedious, and repulsive."

"Our little systems have their day." "They have their day, and cease to be." The little system which explained the Iliad as a mass, or rather a concatenation of short lays, "has had its day." The system of a primal "kernel" (Books i., xi., xvi., and so forth)—a kernel more archaic in language than Books ix., x., xxiii., xxiv.—is also perishing, "stricken through with doubt." The linguistic analysis of Miss Stawell (Homer and the Iliad, 1909) and, in America, of Professor Scott, has fatally damaged the linguistic tests of books for earliness and lateness.

The most advanced German critics find that Book i. of the Iliad is no longer that genuine kernel which, with certain other passages, represents the primal Menis, or "wrath of Achilles," as opposed to the later accretions of three or four centuries. Das ist ausgespielt! The "kernel" hypothesis is doomed. Its cornerstone—Book i. of the Iliad, is, by the builders of new theories, rejected; it is now one of the latest additions to the Iliad.[1] Only to one point is

---

[1] Vinzler, Homer, p. 597 ff.

criticism steadfast. The Iliad must be a thing of rags and tatters; and it is torn up by the process of misstating its statements and finding "discrepancies" in the statements misstated.

Again, as even Comparetti's "man-microscopes" could not well help seeing that the epics, though not good enough as compositions for them, still are compositions; have, in a way, organic unity, harmony, adjusted relations of all the portions, some critics tried to account for the facts as the result of the labours of the Pisistratean, or Solonian, or Hipparchian Committee of Recension at Athens, in the sixth century B.C. But so many critics of all shades of opinion have rejected this hypothesis, even with scorn, as "a worthless fable," "an absurd legend," part of Homeric mythology (Blass, Meyer, Mr. T. W. Alien, D. B. Monro, Nutzhorn, Grote, and many others), that it can scarcely be restored even by the learned ingenuity of Mr. Verrall.[2]

In defect of the late Recension, which is wholly destitute of historic evidence, a poet, a Dichter, has to be sought somewhere, and at some period of the supposed "evolution" of the Iliad. He may lawfully be sought, it seems, at any period of the history of the poem, except at the point where, in fact, the poet is always found, namely at the beginning. The search for the poet will never find him anywhere else. He cannot be made to fit into the eighth or seventh or sixth century; it is useless to look for him at the Court of Croesus! A poem purely Achaean had an Achaean author.

None of the many critical keys fits the lock. The linguistic key breaks itself, it cannot break the wards.

Archaeology is used as a test of passages very early and very late; and the archaeology is also wrong, demonstrably fallacious. The archaeologists themselves, Mr. Arthur Evans and Mr. Ridgeway, will have none of Reichel's key. Whatever archaeology may prove, it does not prove what Reichel and his followers believed it to demonstrate. If I succeed in convincing any separatist critics that the costume and armour in the Iliad are much less like the costume and armour of Ionia in the seventh century B.C. than like those of Athens at the end of the sixth and beginning of the fifth centuries, these critics will probably be grateful. Here, they may perhaps say, is proof of our late Athenian recension, by which the actual Athenian dress and armour of 540-480 were written into the ancient poems.

I would agree with them if the members of the Committee of Recension had excised the huge Homeric shields, introduced cavalry in place of chariotry, iron instead of bronze weapons;

---

[2] See Appendix B, "The Supposed Athenian Recension."

excised the bride-price in marriage law, introduced the rite of purification of homicides by pigs' blood, and generally, in a score of other ways, for example by introducing hero-worship, had brought the Iliad "up to date." But as I cannot easily conceive that only armour and costume were brought up to date, I suppose that the whirligig of time and fashion had reverted in Athens to hauberks of scales in place of the uniform use of back-plate and breast-plate, and had also deserted the Ionian and early Hellenic cypassis, the Aegean loin-cloth or bathing-drawers for the longer and loose Homeric chiton.

If each critic would publish his own polychrome Iliad, with "primitive" passages printed in gold, "secondary" in red, "tertiary" in blue, "very late" in green, with orange for "the Pisistratean editor," purple for the "diaskeuast," and mauve for "fragments of older epics" stuck in the context, and so on, the differences that prevail among the professors of the Higher Criticism would be amazingly apparent.

One writer of a book on Homer has accused me of neglecting "science" in favour of mere literary appreciation, and of "trying to set back the hands on the clock of criticism." Really I want to clean and regulate that timepiece, which reminds one of

"The crazy old church-clock
And the bewildered chimes,"

in Wordsworth's poem.

Never were chimes more bewildered, verdicts more various, and contradictions in terms more innocently combined than in the higher criticism of Homer. It is necessary and right that men's opinions should alter, in consequence of reflection, and of the increase of our knowledge of prehistoric Greece, through the revelations of excavators on the ancient sites of a rediscovered world. It is natural that Homeric critics should sometimes contradict themselves and each other. But they contradict each other so constantly and confidently that, clearly, their conclusions are not to be called conclusions of science.

That in one book a critic should reject, let us say, the hypothesis of the "Pisistratean recension" of the epics, and, in his next book, accept it, is nothing. Reflection has caused him to change his opinion. But when, in one book, in one chapter, perhaps in one page, a critic, without perceiving it, bases his argument on contradictions in terms, then his house is founded on the sand, and needs no tempest to overthrow its pinnacles and towers.

Through indulgence in fantastic theory-making, and through disregard of logical consistency, Homeric criticism has become, as

Blass vigorously put the case in his latest work, "a swamp haunted by wandering fires, will-o'-the-wisps."

In 1906, in Homer and his Age, I again studied the Homeric Question, with particular reference to fresh archaeological discoveries, and to the contradictory methods, as I reckon them, which critics have employed in the effort to prove that the Homeric epics are mosaics, composed in, and confusing the manners and usages of, four or five prehistoric and proto-historic ages.

I do not now reprint either of my earlier books on Homer. Further study appears to have made many points more clear than they were. It is especially clear that "the Ionian father of the rest," as Tennyson calls Homer, is not Ionian; that the early Ionian settlers in Asia respected Homer's matter, which is Achaean, and did not intermingle with it any traits of their own very different beliefs, rites, tastes, morals, usages, armour and costume.

By the term "Ionian" I here mean to speak of the works composed in the Ionian settlements in Asia, probably in the eighth to seventh centuries B.C., and of the non-Homeric beliefs, rites, usages, costume and armour of the same people and period. Most of these beliefs, usages, and rites also mark historic Hellas, and very probably existed in the early populations of Greece before the dominance of Homer's Achaeans.

On the chronological period, as determined by archaeology, in which the Iliad and Odyssey were composed, I am fortunate in having the support of Mr. Arthur Evans, the chief authority in this matter; while Mr. T. W. Allen, our leading textual critic, is persuaded of the fact of Homeric unity. Where language is concerned (as has been said), the linguistic Appendices to Miss Stawell's Homer and the Iliad (1909), with the minute and elaborate studies of Professor Scott of the North-Western University, Illinois,[3] seem to me to overthrow the separatist conclusions as to the presence of an earlier stage of language and metre in some books; a later, or "Odyssean" stage in other books of the Iliad. I have seen scarcely any public criticism in reply to Miss Stawell and Professor Scott on these essential points, in which I have not scholarship enough to pretend to be a judge.

Meanwhile my friend, Mr. Shewan, has in preparation a comprehensive criticism of the separatist arguments, especially those drawn from language and metre; a work which, I venture to think, it will not be easy, and will not be fair, to ignore.

---

3 "Odyssean Words found in but One Book of the Iliad" (Classical Philology, vol. v. p. 41 ff.). "The Relative Antiquity of the Iliad and Odyssey tested by Abstract Nouns" (Classical Review, vol. xxiv., p. 8 ff.).

All my writings on the Homeric question are, necessarily, controversial. The reaction against the suggestion of Wolf, against a critical tradition of a century's standing, has begun in earnest. But the friends of that tradition are eminently learned, and occupy the highest places in scholarship and education. Scholars as eminent, who differ from them, as a rule, are content to keep their own opinions, and remain silent. If the views of the reaction, of the believers in Homeric unity, in the epics as the wonderful legacy of the brief prehistoric Achaean age, are to prevail, the opposing ideas must be assailed, and if possible confuted. In all controversy the constant danger is the tendency to misunderstand opponents. As a rule, A. supposes B. to be holding this or that position. A. assails and captures it, but B. was holding quite another position. A. has misunderstood his case. Critics of works of mine, on other subjects, have often missed my meaning, and I am therefore constrained to suppose that I may have, in like manner, misconstrued some of the opinions of others, which, as I understand them, I am obliged to contest. I have done my best to understand, and will deeply regret any failures of interpretation on my part.

Mr. Gilbert Murray, whose opinions I am obliged to oppose in the course of "the struggle for existence," has, with very great kindness and courtesy, read my proof sheets, and enabled me to give a less inaccurate statement of his position. On one point where I had misapprehended it, I have added an Appendix, "The Lost Epics and the Homeric Epics."

I owe more than I can easily express to the kindness of my friend, Mr. A. Shewan, of St. Andrews, who read and corrected my first proofs (any surviving errors are due to my own want of care), and who has lent me books and papers from his Homeric collection.

Mr. R. M. Dawkins, Head of the British School of Athens, has had the goodness to read my chapters on Homeric, Ionian, and historic armour and costume, and I have quoted the gist of his letters on points where he differs from my conclusions. The topic of female costume is peculiarly difficult and disputable.

A. LANG
September 9, 1910

CONTENTS

APPENDIXES

CHAPTER I

HOMER'S WORLD. THE FOUR AGES

"Homer's world," "the world that Homer knew," these are familiar phrases; and criticism is apt to tell us that they are empty phrases. Nevertheless when we use them we think of that enchanted land, so clearly seen in the light of "the Sun of Greece"; in the light of Homer. It is a realm of splendid wars, of gleaming gold and bronze, of noble men and of the most beautiful of women, which shines through a rift in the mists that hide the years before it and the years that followed. Can what appears so brilliant, so living, so solid, have been unreal, the baseless fabric of a vision; of a dream, too, that Homer never dreamed, for there was no Homer? The Homeric picture of life, the critics tell us, displays no actual scene of past human existence, and is not even the creation of one man's fantasy. It is but a bright medley and mosaic of coloured particles that came together fortuitously, or were pieced together clumsily, like some church window made up of fragments of stained mediaeval glass. "Homeric civilisation," says a critic, "is like Homeric language; as the one was never spoken, so the other was never lived by any one society."[4]

It is the object of this book to prove, on the other hand, that Homeric civilisation, in all its details, was lived at a brief given period; that it was real. This could never be demonstrated till of recent years; till search with the spade on ancient sites that were ruinous or were built over anew in the historic times of Greece, revealed to us the ages that were before Homer, and that succeeded his day. By dint of excavations in the soil we now know much of the great Aegean or Minoan culture that was behind Homer; and know not a little of the Dark Ages that followed the disruption of his Achaean society.

In studying Homer, and the predecessors and successors of the men of his Achaean time, we find ourselves obliged to take into account Four distinct Ages, and the culture of two or perhaps three distinct peoples; the pre-Homeric population of the Aegean coasts and isles; the Homeric Achaeans: and the historic Greeks, who appear to descend from, and to hold of both the pre-Homeric and the Homeric strains of blood and civilisation.

---

4 Church Quarterly Review, vol. xi. p. 414. It is easy to recognise the anonymous writer.

Turning then to what we shall style the Four Ages, we observe first, that which is called the "Late Minoan," namely the bloom, in Crete and on the mainland, of a civilisation even then very ancient, having its focus, and chief manifestation, in the isle of the Hundred Cities. Here the art is most graphic, a revelation of the life; the palaces are most numerous and most magnificent; the towns are most tranquil, being unwalled, as the palaces are unfortified; while the arrangements, as for sanitation; and the costume of the women at some periods, are quite modern in character. Separate bodices and skirts, heavily flounced, were worn; through all varieties of fashion the dresses were sewn and shaped. Men did not, as a rule, wear the Homeric smock or chiton, but loin-cloths or bathing-drawers. Brooches or fibulae, like safety pins, were not in use.

This culture had also in a less remarkable degree affected the mainland of Greece. It was an Age of bronze, for weapons and implements, with this peculiarity, that, while arrow tips were often of stone, beautifully chipped flint, or of keen black glass-like obsidian, iron was known, a few large finger-rings of iron occur in graves; the metal being rare and strange. It was an Age of linear writing, on clay tablets, or in ink with pen or reed. The dead, perhaps occasionally embalmed, were buried in shaft tombs hewn deep in the rock; or in "beehive"-shaped sepulchres with chambers, often sunk in the side of a hill. With the dead were laid their arms of bronze, golden ornaments, crystal and ivory, and silver, and cups and vases of peculiar fashion, fabric, and decoration.

Concerning the language or languages of the people of this First Age, nothing is known with certainty, as their writing has not been deciphered. We know that they were and had long been in touch with Egypt, and the highly civilised Egyptian society. Egyptian objects are found in the ruins of Cretan palaces; Cretan pottery is abundant in the soil of Egypt; and their envoys, in Egyptian wall-pictures, bear ingots and golden cups of their fashioning, as presents or as tribute to Egyptian kings. Their palaces, about 1450-1400 B.C. (?) were sacked and consumed by fire, but their culture, and even their writing, continued to exist with dwindling vitality. Of the religion we speak later.

Then comes the Second Age, the period represented in the Homeric poems. Greek is their language, whether the people of the Cretan culture on the mainland of Greece had previously spoken Greek, or a cognate language, or not. Iron had ceased to be a rare metal used only for rings; it was now employed for tools and implements, occasionally for arrow-heads, and was an article of commerce; but bronze was the metal for swords, spears, and body armour; and stone was no longer used for arrow points; leather no longer, as previously, sufficed for shield coverings, bronze plating was needed. The dead were not now buried merely, they were cremated, as often in ancient central and northern Europe, and as in these regions the bones were placed in urns of gold, bronze, or pottery, wrapped in linen, and bestowed in a stone-built chamber, beneath a mound or cairn of earth, on which was set a memorial pillar.[5]

Treasures do not appear to have been buried with the dead, as a rule. A new costume, a northern costume, had come in, not sewn and shaped, as in the previous age, but fastened with pins and fibulae, "safety pins," such as were in use in northern regions, in the basin of the Danube, Bosnia, and North Italy. This is the costume and these are the pins and brooches described by Homer.

The Third Age, subsequent to the Homeric, is a dark period; illustrated by the vases and other objects found at ancient "Tiryns of the mighty walls"; and by the contents of the cemetery outside of the Dipylon gate at Athens; in Cretan sites and elsewhere. The nature of the civilisation (called "the Dipylon") will be described later. It is the fully developed age of iron for weapons and implements; riding of horses is superseding the war-chariots, common to both preceding periods; art is represented by both decadent Minoan work, and rude vase-paintings of human existence. The dead, with humbler treasures, are more frequently buried than burned; cairns are not raised over them; the costume of women appears to have been, occasionally at least, a survival from or revival of that of the First Age, the separate skirt and bodice.

The Fourth Age is the archaic or "proto-historic" period of Greece. It is represented by objects found in the soil of Sparta of the ninth to seventh centuries; by objects of the eighth to seventh century used by Ionian settlers in Asia, as at Ephesus; and by "proto-Athenian" "post-Dipylon" vases and other archaic remains in

---

5 It does not follow, in my opinion, that the change in burial customs necessarily implies the advent of a new and strange "race" on the scene. Mr. Ridgeway writes that the discovery in the Roman Forum of "graves exhibiting two different ways of disposing of the dead—the one class inhumation, the other cremation, of itself" is "a proof of the existence of two races with very different views respecting the soul." ("Who were the Romans?" Proceedings of the British Academy, vol. iii. p. 7. (Tiré à part.) The word "race" has the vaguest meaning, but the Tasmanians are usually supposed to have been a fairly unmixed "race." Yet they buried, as do the Australian tribes, in a variety of ways, cremation, inhumation, tree burial, and in other fashions, and all sorts of beliefs about the soul co-existed. (See Ling Roth, The Tasmanians, pp. 128-134.) Methods of burial do not afford proof of varieties of "race."

art; while, later, come the Black Figure vases of the early sixth century, to which succeed the more accomplished painters of the Red Figure vases (late sixth and early fifth centuries). In this period male costume was often more of the first or Aegean, than of the second or Homeric Age.

Now, according to the majority of critics of Homer, the life, with all its details, which he describes, is not that of a single age, our second, but is a mosaic of all Four Ages. "The first rhapsodies were born in the bronze age, in the day of the ponderous Mykenaean shield—the last in the iron age, when men armed themselves with breastplate and light round buckler. The whole view of life and death, of divine and human polity had changed."[6]

If this be true, the Homeric world as depicted in the poems existed only in fancy; it is a medley of four periods extending over some six centuries or more, and the Homeric picture must be a mere chaos as regards costume, manners, rites, armour, tactics, laws, geographical knowledge, domestic life, and everything. Is it such a chaos? The critics say that it is, and seek for proof in the poems. They find anachronisms and inconsistencies as to armour (but not costume), as to rites, as to marriage laws, as to houses, as to tactics, as to land tenure; but the inconsistencies and anachronisms at most are petty, and, we are to argue, at most represent such minute variations from the norm as occur in all societies, savage or civilised.

For the Homeric period, except in the case of the fibulae marking the change of costume in the Second Age, we have little evidence except in the Homeric poems themselves. No Homeric cairns with their characteristic contents have been discovered by modern scientific experts, a point to be discussed later. But for our Fourth Age we have literary evidence, that of the remains and epitomes of the Cyclic poems, composed in Ionia, about the eighth to seventh centuries, by the poets of the Ionian settlers in Asia, who were dominated by Attic, not Achaean traditions. These poems, we are to show (see "The Cyclic Poems") differ immensely, in descriptions of rites and of religion, and in the characters of heroes, in their pseudo-historic legends, and in geographical knowledge, from the pictures given by Homer. The Ionian armour, too, and round or oval blazoned bucklers worn on the left arm, as displayed in archaic and early Black Figure vases, are widely different from Homeric armour, and from the huge Homeric shield, unblazoned, suspended by a belt or baldric.

The Fourth Age, in fact, is represented by its own epic poetry,

---

[6] Leaf, Iliad, vol. ii., 1902, p. x.

and by its own art; and its representations of armour, religion, rites, personages, and traditions, are never intruded into our Homeric epics. The two ages stand apart. The Homeric world is not that of the Fourth Age. There is no mosaic, except in the epic poetry of the Fourth Age, which imitated the Homeric poetry, but is full of conspicuous anachronisms in essential points.

Though the details of life in the Second and Fourth periods,— the Homeric or Achaean and the Ionian, stand conspicuously apart, modern criticism, we have said, represents them as inextricably mingled in our Homer, and naturally thus confused, for what is most ancient in our Homer is said to have been worked over and recomposed by the poets of Ionia; in Ionia, we are told, Homer had a second birth, and our Homer is half-Ionian.

The critical case is well stated thus: "There is, on the whole, a striking resemblance between the life of Homer's heroes in its material aspects and the [Aegean] remains" [of our First Age] "which have been discovered at Tiryns, Mykene, and elsewhere. The two cultures are not identical, but, beyond doubt, the Homeric resembles in the main the Mykenaean rather than that of the "Dipylon" (so far as we know it), or the archaic Greek. The ancient tradition is on the whole truly kept in the Epos. Yet in many points we can see traces of apparent anachronisms," whether the departure from the "Mykenaean" be "due to a later development of that culture itself, or to an unintentional introduction of elements from the very different conditions of later Greece."[7] In the Epics carried to Asia, says our author, "much of the old was faithfully preserved, though adapted to new hearers, much being new added." "We meet with so many inconsistencies so closely interwoven that the tangle may well seem beyond our powers to unravel."[8]

When novelties were intentionally added the purpose was to please listeners later by many centuries than those for whom the original poets sang; to please the active commercial citizens of Ionia, who had not the polity, nor the armour, nor the war-chariots, nor the weapons, nor the costume, nor the beliefs, nor the burial rites, nor the marriage customs, nor the houses, nor the tactics, nor the domestic life, and had more than the geographical knowledge of the people who listened to the original minstrel. Each of the novelties supposed to have been introduced to gratify new hearers, each novelty in armour, weapons, tactics, would only produce in the Iliad an unintelligible and chaotic blend, such as, the critics tell us,

---

[7] Leaf, Iliad, vol. i. pp. xiv, xv.

[8] Ibid., vol. ii. p. x. Much of the "new," we must remark, was added, on this theory, not "unintentionally," but consciously and purposefully.

actually was produced—a tangle which we cannot unravel. The fighting scenes, in particular, thanks to the retention of old armour and tactics, and the simultaneous introduction of novelties to please practical readers, must have passed all understanding, and, as we are told, they make nonsense. No practical hearers in that case could have endured the confusion, a point to be demonstrated in detail.[9]

Let us remember, too, that the novelties said to have been introduced were of the pettiest kind. The Iliad and Odyssey retain a non-Ionian polity: non-Ionian burial rites; non-Ionian marriage customs (in which a change is detected in one case); non-Ionian houses; non-Ionian shields, non-Ionian armour, non-Ionian military tactics; while truly and specially Ionian rites and beliefs and geographical knowledge are all absent. Why should poets who were innovating have left the whole Homeric picture standing except in certain minute details of corslets, greaves, bride-price, and upper storeys and separate sleeping chambers in houses?

It is our opinion, therefore, that the details of life in the poems are all old and all congruous; while we find the "much new" abundantly present, not in Homer, but in the fragments and summaries of the contents of the "Cyclic" Ionian Epics, dating from the age (770-650 B.C.) when the novelties are supposed to have been most copiously foisted into the Iliad and Odyssey—in which, as a matter of fact, they never appear. Far from altering the old epics, I hope to show that the Ionians laboured at constructing new epics, the "Cyclics"; partly for the purpose of connecting their ancestors with ancient heroic events in which, according to Homeric tradition, their ancestors played no part; partly to tell the whole tale of Troy.

The task of these Ionian poets was later taken up by the Athenian tragedians, and a non-Homeric, we may say almost an anti-Homeric tradition was established, was accepted by Virgil and by the late Greek compiler, Dictys of Crete; and finally reached and was elaborated by the romancers of the Christian Middle Ages.

It is not easy to do justice to this theory except in a perpetual running fight with the believers in the Ionian moulders of the Homeric poems into their actual form with its contents. Now few things are more unpleasant than a running fight of controversial argument, the reader is lost in the jangle and clash of opinions and replies, often concerned with details at once insignificant and obscure. Into such minutiae I would not enter, if they were not the main stock of separatist critics.

On the whole, then, it seems best to describe, first, as far as we

9 See "Homeric Arms and Costume," and "Homeric Tactics," infra.

may, the age preceding that of Homer, and then the Homeric world, just as the poet paints it, without alluding to differences of critical opinion. These are discussed later, and separately.

CHAPTER II

HOMERIC LANDS AND PEOPLES

Homer conceives of his heroes as living in an age indefinitely remote: their epoch "has won its way to the mythical." They are often sons or grandsons of Gods: the Gods walk the earth among them, friendly, amorous, or hostile. From this fact, more than from the degeneracy in physical force which Homer often attributes to his contemporaries, we see that the mist of time and the glamour of romance have closed over the heroes.

But this might happen in the course of a pair of centuries. In the French Chansons de Geste of 1080-1300, Charlemagne (circ. 814), a perfectly historical character to us,—has become almost as mythical as Arthur to the poets. He conquers Saracens as Arthur conquers all western Europe; he visits Constantinople; he is counselled by visible angels, who to some degree play the part of the gods in Homer.

Perhaps two or three centuries may separate Homer from any actual heroic princes of whom traditions have reached him. Modern research holds that the Achaeans of Homer, by infiltration and by conquest, had succeeded to more civilised owners of Greece.

But Homer has nothing to say about a conquest of Greece by the Achaeans, Danaans, Argives, and the rest, from the north, except in two cases. He speaks of combats with wild mountain-dwelling tribes in Thessaly, in Nestor's youth. Nestor knew "the strongest of men who warred with the strongest, the mountain-dwelling Pheres,"[10] shaggy folk, says the Catalogue, whom Peirithous drove out of Pelion in northern Thessaly, and forced back on the Aethices of Pindus in the west.[11] It appears, from recent

[10] Iliad, i. 266-268.
[11] Iliad, ii. 741-744.

excavations, that the age of stone lingered long in these regions, and the people were probably rude and uncultivated, like the Centaurs.

The recent excavators of Zerelia, north-east of the Spercheios valley, the home of Achilles, write that their discoveries in the soil "clearly point to the fact that in prehistoric times the cultures of North and South Greece were radically different. This probably indicates an ethnological difference as well."[12] Before the period when "Late Minoan III." pottery occurs in Thessaly, the people used stone tools and weapons, and knew not the potter's wheel. It may not, therefore, be too fanciful to regard Nestor's tales of fights with a wild mountain race as shadowy memories of actual Achaean conquests in Thessaly, where Aegean culture arrived very much later than in Southern Greece.

Secondly, Homer twice speaks of regions as "Pelasgian," in which he represents the actual inhabitants as Hellenes and Achaeans, not Pelasgic. These regions are the realm of Achilles in south-west Thessaly; and Epirus.[13] But the actual Pelasgians whom Homer knows are allies of Troy; they dwell on the North Aegean coasts (where Herodotus found living Pelasgians), or reside, with Achaeans, Dorians, True Cretans, and Cydonians, in Crete. These facts indicate Homer's knowledge that, in some regions, Achaeans had dispossessed "Pelasgians," whoever the Pelasgians may have been. Again, Homer makes Achilles address the "Pelasgic Zeus" of Dodona in Epirus, in which he locates Perhaebians and Eneienes.

It thus appears that he supposed the Achaeans to have driven out Pelasgians from Epirus and Thessaly, at least, if not from southern Greece. It may well seem to us strange that as the Achaean settlement in Crete, or at least in parts of Crete, must have been comparatively recent when Homer sang, he never mentions so great an event. But reasons for and a parallel to his silence are not hard to find. If, as many authorities hold, the great Cnossian palace had fallen, and the Cretan civilisation had sunk into decadence before the Achaeans arrived in the island,[14] they might meet with but slight resistance; great feats of heroism might not claim record. Again, the Norman Conquest gave rise to no Anglo-Norman epic. The invaders already possessed their epic tradition, that of Charlemagne, borrowed from "the Franks of France," while they presently, in the twelfth century, took up and expanded the epic traditions of the Welsh and Bretons, in the Arthurian cycles of romances. In the same way, for all that we know, the Achaean epics may have a basis

---

[12] Proceedings, British School of Athens, xiv., 1907, 1908, p. 223.

[13] Iliad, ii. 681-684, xvi. 233-235.

[14] Mackenzie, "Cretan Palaces," in Brit. School of Athens, xii. pp. 216-258.

in the traditions of the earlier and more civilised populations usually styled "Pelasgians." The manners, however, of the Iliad and Odyssey are Achaean, as the manners of the French romances of Arthur are not Celtic, but feudal and chivalrous.[15] Homer, in any case, conceives of his own race as at home in Greece and Crete, and he has nothing to say about Greek settlements on the Asiatic coast. To him the inhabitants of Miletus are not the Ionian colonists. "Carians uncouth of speech" dwelt by the banks of the Meander, and the Asiatic allies of Priam are people "scattered, of diverse tongues."[16] For purposes of convenience all parties to the war understand each other's speech.[17]

In Odyssey, xix. 172-177, Homer gives an account of populous Crete, with ninety cities, and a mingling of various tongues, "therein are Achaeans, and True Cretans high of heart, and Cydonians, and Dorians in their three divisions, and noble Pelasgians." Did they vary in language, or in dialect and accent merely? We cannot know, we cannot be sure that "True Cretans" were the pre-existing Aegeans. The Cydonians dwelt beside the Jardanus; Jardanus is also a river-name in Elis. Mr. Leaf thinks of the Semitic yârad, "to flow" (Jordan), but we have other such river-names, Yarrow, and the Australian Yarra Yarra; the word may be onomatopoeic, expressing the murmur of the water.

Homer, in any case, does not despise the Asiatic allies of Troy as "barbarous," does not think them alien wholly, as the poets of the Chansons de Geste regard the Saracens,—worshippers of Mahound and Apollon. The Asians have the same gods and rites as his own people; Glaucus and Sarpedon are as good knights and live in precisely the same sort of polity as Aias or Achilles. Homer does not think of the strife as between Hellenes and Barbarians, that is a far later idea never interpolated into the Epics. All men are children of the Olympians.

It would appear that Homer sang before the northern invasion, usually called "Dorian," caused the Achaean and Ionian migrations from the Greek mainland, and the Greek settlements on the Asiatic coast (950-900 B.C.?). He never alludes to these events, but it may be said that he deliberately conceals them.

The account which Homer gives of the Achaean heroes and

---

[15] The parallel has been brought to my notice in detail by Mr. J. W. Mackail; it had already occurred to me in a general way.

[16] Iliad, ii. 867, ii. 804.

[17] In the line just cited, and in the Carians Βαρβαροθώνω of Iliad, ii. 867, we cannot positively know whether Homer is thinking of different languages, or of differences in accent and dialect.

their realms is to be found in the Catalogue of the Ships in Book ii., a passage of three hundred lines. It is, perhaps, not very probable that this long list was usually recited at popular gatherings, and there is much dispute as to its date and purpose. We relegate to an appendix some remarks on the debated questions. Whether the Catalogue, or most of it, was part of the original Iliad or not, most of it was certainly composed at a time when the condition of prehistoric Greece was well known, when a lively tradition of its divisions still existed; moreover, it is the work of a poet, and Milton deemed it worthy of imitation in Paradise Lost.

The Catalogue was omitted from many manuscripts of the Iliad, probably because it was thought tedious reading. But to us there is poetry in the very names of "rocky Aulis," and "Mycalessus of the wide lawns," and "dove-haunted Thisbe," and "Lacedaemon lying low among the rifted hills." The author wrote "with his eye on the object," and the doves of Thisbe have survived many empires and religions, still floating round their old domains and uttering their changeless note.[18] "Pleasant Titaresius" still mingles his clear waters with the chalk-stained Peneius, and Celadon brawls as when Nestor heard its music.

The Catalogue enumerates all the Achaeans; Boeotians, Phocians, Minyans; light-armed Locrian slingers; the Abantes of Euboea, fond of close combat; the Arcadians, whose dialect was nearest akin to Homer's own language, but who take no part in the action; the Epeians of Elis, once foes of Nestor's Pylians; the far-off Aetolians, no longer led by golden-haired Meleager; the Cretans of Cnossos, under Idomeneus, grandson of Minos; his neighbour Tlepolemos of Rhodes, of the blood of Heracles, and probably a Dorian, though the Dorian name is not uttered; and some of the Sporades. There are, too, the south Thessalian Achaeans and Hellenes, the Myrmidons under Achilles; the men of Philoctetes, who lies sore hurt by a serpent's bite in the Isle of Lemnos; the descendants in Thessaly (not a Homeric name) of the Lapithae; the Pethraebians from "wintry Dodona"; the men of Argos and Tiryns of the mighty walls, under Diomede; the men of Lacedaemon under Menelaus; the Athenians (much suspected of interpolating their own mention), Odysseus of the western and Aias of the eastern isles (Ithaca and Salamis); and the host of Agamemnon, lord of Corinth, Sicyon, and Mycenae, himself the Over Lord of all.

Taking the Catalogue as it stands, the princes of whom Agamemnon of Mycenae was Over Lord come from the Greek mainland, from southern Thessaly and Aetolia to the southernmost

---

[18] Leaf, on Iliad, ii. 502.

point of the Morea, and the islands as far south and east as Crete, Carpathos, and Rhodes.

Now, as Agamemnon is the Over Lord, and Idomeneus of Cnossos in Crete is one of his thanes, so to speak, the poet clearly regards the Greek mainland as the centre of an Achaean dominion, of which Crete is a great dependency. He shows no idea that Crete had been the centre of another power, and the focus of another civilisation, held by a people who, since the age of stone weapons and implements, had developed its culture without interruption, and had sent its arts to the mainland of Greece. To Homer, Mycenae is the centre; the prince of Cnossos is a great feudatory of Agamemnon.

The poet is much interested in Crete; not only does the Iliad dwell on the prowess of Idomeneus the prince of Cnossos, and of Meriones; but in the feigned tales of Odysseus, when he returns to Ithaca, he represents himself as a Cretan adventurer. Homer avoids the Athenian tales about Cretan tyranny, about the Minotaur, and the prowess of Theseus in aid of the freedom of Athens. These things are not touched upon, as they certainly would have been had Athenians freely interpolated the poems. Homer entirely ignores all Athenian and Ionian traditions.[19]

This is not the place to ask whether Achaeans from the mainland were the men who took and sacked the palace of Cnossos in Crete about 1400 B.C., or whether the spoilers were "Pelasgians," that is, people living on the mainland in Cretan conditions of culture, driven from the mainland by the Achaean irruption; or whether the palace was wrecked during an internal revolution before the Achaeans came to the island.[20] Homer undeniably regards Idomeneus as an Achaean and a descendant of Minos; and Minos as a son of Zeus.[21] Rhadamanthus of his blood, is "the golden-haired," like Menelaus, Meleager, and some other heroes.[22] We are not here concerned with discrepant traditions, and with the

---

[19] Save in the interpolated name of Theseus, twice, and in doubtful parts of Odyssey, xi.

[20] These various views are held, or have been held, by Mr. Evans, Mr. Ridgeway, Dr. Mackenzie, and others (Monthly Review, 1901, pp. 121-131; Times, Oct. 31, 1905; Annuals, British School of Athens, xi. p. 14; ibid. xii. 216 et seqq., xiii. 423 et seqq.). In Dr. Mackenzie's ample arguments, cf. Hogarth, Ionia and the East, pp. 32, 33, the Pelasgians were the sackers of Cnossos. The evidence is mainly archaeological, and might be argued over endlessly.

[21] Iliad, xiii. 450.

[22] These views are suggested by Professor Ridgeway in a paper read to the British Academy; see Athenaeum, June 5, 1909.

idea that Minos is an Aegean as Pharaoh is an Egyptian name of kings in general. That may be so; Minos may have been a figure in Cretan legend before the Achaeans came thither; if so, they adopted him as their own. We are only stating Homer's view of the relations between Crete and the Achaean power on the mainland.

Homer's Catalogue of the Asian allies of Troy is brief, and contains only about sixty lines. There was a Trojan Catalogue in the Cypria, a lost Ionian epic poem of the eighth century, and as the Ionian colonists in Asia knew the country of their settlement well, it is likely to have been copious. Beginning, in Homer's Trojan Catalogue, with the Dardanians under Aeneas, who may be said to represent "the Orleans branch" of the Trojan royal family, we next hear of the Trojans under Pandarus, who, in fact, broke the solemn oaths of truce, and sealed the doom of Ilium (Iliad, iv.), but who somehow as "Sir Pandarus of Troy" acquired another kind of ill fame among our mediaeval poets. He dwelt by the Aesepus. "At the extreme north of the Troad, where the Hellespont opens out into the Sea of Marmora," lived Adrastus and Amphius. Asius led forces from Sestus and Abydus, on both sides, European and Asian, of the Hellespont: there were also Pelasgians, apparently from the European side. There were, from Europe, Thracians and Cicones; the chief Thracian contingent arrived later (see Iliad, Book x.). The Cicones, with whom Odysseus has trouble when first he leaves Troy, in the Odyssey, are also European, as were probably, in origin, the people of Troy itself. European are the Paeonians, the Paphlagonians, again, are Asiatic; the Alizonians are remote and unrecognisable. Then we have Asiatic Mysians and Phrygians, and Maeonians from near Sardis, and under Mount Tmolos inland. The Carians of Miletus (later an Ionian city) follow, the Meander is their river; last come the Lycians under Sarpedon (whom legend connects with Crete), and Glaucus; another Glaucus was son of Sisyphus of Ephyre (Corinth), in Argos, and was father of Bellerophon. Bellerophon, again, was sent to his death in Lycia, by Proetus, who had married a Lycian princess. The Lycian Glaucus of the Iliad is a grandson of Bellerophon (Iliad, vi.).

According to this story, Greeks freely passed to Lycia and intermarried with Lycians. Only the Carians are described as "barbaric" in language. Homer knows not, we said, the distinction of Hellenes and Barbarians; the Greeks did not know it till the struggle of their Asiatic colonies against Lydia and Persia produced the sense of "racial" repulsion. In Homer any Greek prince going to Asia is courteously treated, perhaps settles there like Bellerophon, or makes hereditary guest-friendships, like the ancestors of Glaucus and Diomede.

The distinction which Homer does know is that between god-fearing men, with cities, laws, and rulers, on one hand, and men who are like the Cyclops, lonely, and lawless (Od. ix. 112-115). The Cyclops is not so godless as he boasts himself to be; he does pray to his father Poseidon, but he is wholly lawless, and each man is king in his own family. The cannibal Laestrygones, even, have a king and a city, though their manners are disgusting. Homer cannot easily, we see, conceive of men whose polity and cities are not like those with which he is familiar. He may have heard vaguely of far northern tribes abiding by their fiords in the land of amber, the land of the nightless summer and of the sunless winter. Such tales would come with the amber from the Baltic coasts, for which merchants bartered the bronze swords and vessels of their own civilisation. He had certainly heard of "the proud Hippemolgoi," drinkers of mares' milk, nomad Scythians north of the Danube, living like Tartars on koumiss.[23] If he has heard of any empire in the Asian hinterland, he may speak of it as one of the two Ethiopian realms; but here all is mythical.

Egypt, too, appears in the tales of Odysseus when he represents himself as a Cretan adventurer, a raider in the lands by the river Aegyptus. Helen has been in Egypt, and received the drug nepenthes from the wife of the king, just as she has been in Egyptian Thebes, and carried treasures thence (Od. iv. 130 ff.). Achilles[24] knows the wealth of Egyptian Thebes, and its hundred gates, and countless charioteers. Sicily is known to the Odyssey, a poem of Ithaca and the west, and of "perilous seas in fairy lands forlorn"; it is not mentioned in the Iliad, a poem of the east and the Asian shore. The Phoenicians are familiar as traders (Iliad, xxiii. 743), and are much better known, as is natural, to the sea-poem, the Odyssey. The appearance of the Phoenicians in the Odyssey, when they sell jewels to the women and kidnap the child Eumaeus, has been spoken of as work of the seventh century B.C.; a scene of

---

[23] Iliad, xiii. 5, 6, and Leaf's note.

[24] Ibid. ix. 381. Mr. Leaf attributes the lines to "some person with a dull chronological mind," who remembered that Thebes in Greece had been left in ruins by the war of the Epigonoi. "He forgot, however, that Egypt is elsewhere unknown to the Iliad." If a place is unknown because no one has occasion to mention it, unknown is Thebes to the Iliad. But to say that a poet familiar with Crete never heard of Egypt; that Egypt was rediscovered between the dates of composition of Iliad and Odyssey, is arbitrary. We might as well say that Shakespeare, who never mentions tobacco, never heard of the weed, or that no Biblical author ever saw a cat (out of the Apocrypha).

contemporary life in that late age. But Mr. H. R. Hall, writing on early relations between Greece and Egypt, as depicted in Egyptian wall-paintings of the eighteenth Egyptian dynasty, represents commerce between the Aegean peoples of Greece and Crete as filtering through "Phoenician channels." The Phoenicians were active navigators and were merchants then and afterwards, that is, from the sixteenth century B.C. onwards. A fresco in an Egyptian tomb of the early date shows the arrival of "beaknosed" Phoenicians "in voluminous and multi-coloured robes," one of them carrying "a small Mycenaean amphora," at the Theban quays.[25] This being so, it is not so easy to bring down the Phoenicians of the Odyssey to the seventh century B.C. The Sidonians make the goods which the Phoenicians transport, but the Phoenician slave of the father of Eumaeus declares that she comes from the town of Sidon, and the Phoenician sailor knows her parents (Odyssey, xv. 415-433). No very clear distinction seems to have been drawn between Phoenicians and Sidonians.

These Semitic peoples were persistently credited, till lately, with all the finer works of art and craft which Homer mentions. The discovery of the art of Minoan Crete has made this unqualified attribution impossible.[26] Certainly Homer conceives of the Semites as doing a large trade, and as kidnapping children in the Greek seas; but their own art was imitative, and it is unlikely that, in Homer's time, the characters of their alphabet had ousted those of Aegean civilisation. It is curious that the place in which Phoenicians exercised most influence, Cyprus, was also the place where the Phoenician alphabet was so long in supplanting the native syllabary, akin to the unread documents of Minoan Crete.

We may thus conceive Homer's ancestors, by 1400 B.C., as men far from savage or barbarian,[27] who then succeeded to an Aegean civilisation much more luxurious and artistic than their own; and, centuries later, when Homer sang, the glow of the Aegean culture still flushed the sky: its art was known to the poet.

---

[25] B. S. A. viii. 174.
[26] See Hogarth, Ionia and the East, pp. 83-86.
[27] Ibid. pp. 112-115.

CHAPTER III

HOMERIC POLITY. THE OVER LORD

As Homer conceives the period of his heroes, they live in a perfectly well known stage of society, illustrated in later northern Europe by the French Chansons de Geste; by the most ancient Irish stories in prose mixed with verse; and even to some extent by the Arthurian romances. Every prince has his castle and town or towns, his lands, pasturage, tilth, and orchards; he is, in the Irish phrase, a righ. He is surrounded by the γέροντες,—in Irish the flaith, the gentry or squires, who held "rich lands remote from towns," and possessed war-chariots.[28] The princes and gentry with war-chariots alone take notable individual parts in the fighting, whether they fight mounted or dismounted. It is the gentry who offer a rich demesne, vineland and tilth, to Meleager, imploring him to take part in their war.[29] It appears to me that the gentry themselves held land in severalty, perhaps contrary to the old letter of the law, and in possession rather than in property.

The question of Homeric land tenure, as of all early land tenure before written records, is very obscure. There existed "common fields" certainly; but were they common property, each freeman having no more than his strip; separated, we know, from that of others by a longitudinal "balk" or boundary? We hear of men wrangling across the balk, "with measures in their hands, in a common field, striving for their right within scanty space."[30] Such quarrels were common in the Scotland of the eighteenth century, under the "run-rig" system of common fields; but then the men were tenants. They may have been free-holders in Homer's time, each with his assured "lot" (κλῆρος)[31] The Irish tribal free man had a right to one of these lots, which were redistributed by rotation, but

[28] Iliad, xxiii. 832. All this passage, the conclusion of the funeral games, is regarded as a late addition. It may be, but the poet preserves the distinction between the uses of iron for implements, and of bronze for weapons, which pervades both Epics. When a warrior like Achilles offers a mass of iron for a prize, "we rather expect from him," says Helbig, "an allusion to the military uses of the metal" (Das Homerische Epos, pp. 330, 331, 1887). But Homer does not regard iron as a military metal.

[29] Iliad, ix. 574-580.

[30] Iliad, xii. 421-423.

[31] xv. 498.

many lots came gradually into the hands of each of the flaith, squires, (γέροντες), who were rich in cattle, and let out the cattle to poor lease-holders, for returns of rent in kind. A mail in Homer might have no lot,[32] and yet employ hinds, and be a cultivator. He must have been a tenant farmer.

In the Iliad, apart from the demesnes allotted to great men by the γέροντες, we only hear of personal property, gold, iron, cattle, and so on. In the Odyssey (xiv. 211) we read of men in Crete who each possessed several lots; and in so old a civilisation nothing is more probable. One is inclined to suppose that the majority of freemen held each his lot, while some had lost their lots; that many who had been land-holders came to hold as tenants merely, under rent in kind paid for stock to the γέροντες, who were rich in ploughing cattle; and that some γέροντες, and all princes held demesnes and a large share of the unfenced pasturage, worked by slaves and hinds. This is quite a practicable condition of affairs; there were all grades of wealth, some men were, as Odysseus feigned to be, wandering tramps. By the time of Hesiod lots of land were purchaseable,[33] but we do not hear in Homer that lots could be bought and sold.

It does not seem that these variations of conditions, in a society where the rich and the very poor certainly coexisted, are proofs that ideas and practices of various later ages have been brought into the Epics by the insertion of lays of various dates. In savage and barbaric societies on a very low level, even in Australia, we find the most various social rules coexisting, and tribes with maternal and with paternal reckoning of descent live side by side. In Melanesia the conditions of native land-tenure vary greatly, some are "primitive" others not so.[34] When we reflect on facts so certain, it seems strange that the hints of varieties in the condition of land-tenure in Homer are regarded as a proof that the poems are a patchwork of the usages of four changing centuries.

We do not, of course, know anything about land-tenure in the early Ionian settlements in Asia, where, if anywhere, novelties would be interpolated. Probably, as was usual and natural in the foundation of a colony, each freeman was assigned his lot. But as the cities became full of seafaring traders and sailors, some men thus occupied would part with the lots which they could not cultivate, and these would be bought by capitalists. Now Homer never mentions the purchase of lots. Athenian tradition held that

---

[32] Odyssey, xi. 490.

[33] Opp. 341.

[34] Codrington, The Melanesians.

their colonists were led by the Codrids, descendants of kings not Athenians, descendants of the sons of Neleus of Pylos, Nestor's family. This legend was probably invented for the purpose of introducing Attica into the Achaean cycle of history, in which Attica, as far as Achaean traditions inform us, had no part. Indeed we cannot know whether or not princes like these of Homer long ruled the Ionian cities. Colonists are usually impatient of monarchy.

Returning to the Homeric Over Lord, the princes do not hold land from the Crown, so to speak. The Over Lord is primus inter pares by right divine, not by election. In late forms of the Trojan tale, Agamemnon is only an elected general; this idea may be derived from the Ionic poem, the Cypria. In Homer, Agamemnon is commander-in-chief by birth; but the princes, in formal council, or on the field, deliver their advice, which may or may not be accepted. Agamemnon usually gives way to it. The Over Lord's rights are not strictly defined, except by traditionary custom. Like Charlemagne in the later Chansons de Geste, like Fion MacCumhail in his cycle, even like Arthur, the Achaean Over Lord is not the favourite of the poets and romancers. They much prefer, in Homer's case, the princes; in the mediaeval romances they prefer Diarmaid, Cuchullain, Oscar, Lancelot, and the rest, to the Over Lord. Except in the case of Arthur, who himself tends to become a fainéant, the Over Lords are always capricious, arbitrary, unjust, always encroaching, and are apt to be rebuked or even reviled, by their more energetic subordinates. Agamemnon is in a position between that of the Charlemagne of the Chanson de Roland, and the dotard of the later chansons. His divine right is always recognised; his bursts of insolent temper are easily checked; his nervousness as a commander-in-chief brings on him rebukes to which he instantly yields, and is partly redeemed by his personal prowess and skill with the spear. When the Over Lord's insolence and injustice are beyond bearing, the injured prince may blamelessly "renounce his allegiance," return home or remain without taking part in battle or council. Nobody blames Achilles for his mutiny, least of all does Athene, till he, in turn, exceeds his rights by refusing atonement and apology.[35] It seems that Achilles would actually have lost consideration had he returned to action without receiving gifts of

---

35 Iliad, ix. "When Achilles is justly angered with Agamemnon at first none can blame him (ix. 523); but if he persists after Agamemnon has sued for forgiveness, then there will be nemesis; people will be indignant. He will know he is doing wrong." So Mr. Murray writes (Rise of the Greek Epic, p. 81).

atonement,[36] as Meleager did in his day. This is the chief point of the long exhortation of Phoenix.[37]

When reconciliation did occur, it was regulated by minute etiquette (as in Iliad, xix. 171-183); there is an oath, a banquet, the gifts of atonement are publicly brought into the midst of the Assembly, ἐς μεσσην ἀγορήν, and exhibited: none of these points may be omitted in the customary mode of giving satisfaction, ἵνα μή τι δίκης ἐπιδευὲς ἔχηισθα.

These transactions Odysseus forces on the reluctant Achilles, as one who "knows better" than he.[38]

There is nothing superstitious in the manly and constitutional attitude of the princes towards the king. He is not a god of vegetation, who is slain or sacrificed yearly or at longer intervals; if ever such a mortal king god of vegetation existed anywhere. In the Odyssey (xix. 107-114) we hear that, under a godfearing king, who reigns over strong men and a large population, and maintains just dealings, the crops, whether of grain or fruit-trees, and the flocks are fertile, while the sea yields fish abundantly, "through the king's good government." Here is a trace of belief in the prosperity of a good king, the gods reward him, and his people prosper. But there is no hint that the king, as the embodiment of a god, controls the weather.

The Achaean attitude towards the Over Lord is stated by Nestor,—"Think not, son of Peleus, to strive with a king, might against might, seeing that no common honour pertaineth to a sceptred king to whom Zeus apportioneth glory." "I have beside me," says Agamemnon, "others that shall do me honour, and above all Zeus, lord of counsel." He inherits his sceptre "that over many islands and all Argos he should be lord." He rules by right divine, but there are recognised limits to his authority. This is a well-known form of polity in early civilisations, and, so far, Homer, from first to last, thoroughly understands his world. He never lets his Over Lord fall into the decadence of Charlemagne in the Chansons de Geste. It may be a later, it was certainly a more hostile spirit, as regards the Over Lord, that reached the Cyclic poets (circ. 760-660), who dwell

---

[36] Iliad, ix. 605.

[37] ix. 434 et seqq.

[38] They weary the critics, who are not at the Homeric point of view. "It is quite conceivable that the whole idea of the Reconciliation is an afterthought ... it is not only consistent with the character of Achilles, but materially adds to the movement of the story, if we suppose that on hearing of the death of Patroklos he set out to avenge it without more ado" (Leaf, Iliad, vol. ii. p. 317).

on the tyranny suffered by Palamedes and Philoctetes, Palamedes being the inventor of alphabetic writing. Pindar and the Greek tragedians followed, and exaggerated such traditions.[39]

Homer retains the true sense of the position of the Over Lord, no tincture of the ideas of later ages appears in the Epics. Now, is it not a point worth considering that the Epics, though the critics take them to have been open to interpolation even in their oldest passages, down to 540 B.C. or thereabouts, never contain the word τύραννος or any of its compounds? The τύραννος, the "Tyrant," was originally the person who unconstitutionally seized power in one of the republics, usually oligarchic, that succeeded to the Homeric kingships. We place the early "tyrants" in the eighth century and onwards. To the Athenian tragedians a Homeric king was a "tyrant." Yet despite the assumed facility of interpolation into the Epics, even at a much later date than the eighth century, no late poet foisted into our Epics the word τύραννος, nor the ideas which it denotes. This abstinence is irreconcilable with the supposed freedom of late interpolating poets in uncritical ages. The Epics are perfectly consistent in their view of the divine right, but limited power, of the Over Lord. He may display illegal arrogance (ὕβρις), but he is never a τύραννος. The word, and the ideas connected with the word,—usurpation by an individual of despotic power over members of a free commonwealth,—were familiar to Greeks on both sides of the sea in the eighth century. Interpolators of that period could hardly have kept the word τύραννος out of their additions of new matter, but it appears to occur for the first time in the Hymn to Ares: "tyranny" (τύραννίς) is familiar to Archilochus.[40]

Thus, in the important matter of polity, we see that the Homeric picture of society is coherent, represents a well-known social and political state of affairs, is drawn with minute knowledge of the rights and duties of all concerned, and bears no trace of interpolations made under the later conditions known to Ionian poets in Asia. But some epics of these poets display a grudge against the Over Lord and his House, which is un-Homeric, and is exaggerated by the Athenian tragedians.

---

[39] See infra, "The Story of Palamedes."

[40] 25 Bergk.

CHAPTER IV

HOMER'S WORLD IN PEACE

Though Homer describes a military aristocracy he is remarkable for his love of peace and hatred of war. His war-god, Ares, is a bully and a coward; his home is Thrace; and he is never mentioned with sympathy. It seems to follow that Homer's people are conceived as long settled in tranquil homes; and, though Achilles says that "cattle are to be had for the raiding of them" (Iliad, ix. 406), actual fighting to recover captured cattle is thrown back into the youth of Nestor. Young adventurers, however, expend their energy, like the Icelanders of the sagas, in "going on viking," "risking their own lives, bringing bane to alien men." The great war against Thebes is a memory of an earlier generation; as are the combats with the wild and shaggy hill tribes, and the war between Meleager and the Couretes. When war is in hand it has no more spirited singer than Homer; he has a special word (if correctly rendered) for "the joy of battle" (χάρμη), but it has often been remarked that his men are not very resolute and stubborn fighters. They are not like the Spartans or the Macleans, with their traditional rule of never retreating.

War may be a duty, in the eyes of Homer, but it is not a pleasure; and this is the more singular as, in early societies, the bard, who, like Ian Lom,[41] does not fight himself, is fond of provoking men to battle. Though Odysseus, in his feigned tales of himself as a Cretan adventurer, speaks of piracy, and of raids on the coasts of Egypt, and though casual homicides are lightly mentioned, the Homeric is a peace-loving world. The wild justice of the blood-feud, after a fatal blow struck in anger, exists, and, as a rule, the slayer goes into exile, to some friendly prince, and thus avoids the feud of the dead man's kin.

On the Shield of Achilles was depicted a scene at the Althing (to use the Icelandic expression): "The folk were gathered in the assembly place; for there was a strife arisen, two men striving about the blood-price of a man slain; the one claiming to pay full atonement, expounding to the people, but the other denied him, and would take naught." The people are taking sides, and shouting, the heralds restrain them, the γέροντες (the probi homines or

---

[41] The bard of the Macdonalds in the year of Montrose.

prud'hommes) sit listening, on stone seats in the sacred circle.[42] The public sense had enabled the slayer to remain at home, if the kin of the dead would accept the blood-wyte, and allow the feud to be pacified. As Aias says to Achilles, "a man accepts recompense of his brother's murderer, or for his dead son; and so the manslayer for a great price abides in his own land...."[43] Probably it was usual to accept the blood-price if a man had been slain openly, sword in hand; but when a premeditated murder was committed, actual revenge was desired. There was nothing reckoned mean or contemptible in the pacific arrangement: in heroic Iceland it was hard indeed to induce men to accept it.

These are the manners of a settled people, who will bear much for the sake of peace, and of a people free from superstitious dread of the blood curse, and ignorant of the filthy rite of purification by the blood of swine, which was a regular piece of ritual in historic Hellas, and is familiar to Aeschylus,[44] the Ionian epic poets, and to Apollonius Rhodius. Certainly the rite was unknown to Homer, who mentions many homicides but says nothing of purification or of pollution. This point is later studied in detail. The life of the heroes in peace is the life of all early aristocracies who do not idle, and do not intrigue in a Court. The women spin and embroider, like Penelope and Helen, and keep their eyes on household affairs, and on their poultry, mainly geese. Nausicaa sees to the washing of the linen. The men hunt hares and boars, and attend "days of law" in the legal courts, and take part in funeral games. As yet we hear of no periodical games, such as the Olympian, Isthmian, and Pythian, though the legends of historic Greece pretend that these were founded in pre-Homeric times.

The princes also looked well to their lands. Odysseus alone is mentioned as a skilled ploughman, carpenter, and shipwright, as some of the Icelandic heroes are swordsmiths, but we see little of any prince but Odysseus in peaceful life. There are professional artisans, whose services are highly valued, carpenters, potters, bronze-smiths, and weavers.

The women meanwhile are amused by the visits of Phoenician pedlars, who bring goods and gauds of every kind, and steal a child or carry away a serving maid if they have the opportunity, as in the case of Eumaeus. After supper the minstrel of the prince chants lays, like Demodocus in Phaeacia. As Spenser observed in Ireland, and as the Brehon laws declare, the minstrel was highly honoured

---

[42] Iliad, xviii. 497-504.

[43] ix. 632-634.

[44] Eumenides, 273.

and trusted; the minstrel of Agamemnon is charged, during the war, with the care of Clytemnestra. These poets did not accompany the host to the war, where Achilles solaced himself by singing to the harp "the renowns of men."[45]

Such is the general picture of Homer's world in time of peace, as far as the days and works of the princely class and the gentry are concerned. They are richly equipped with cups of gold, and furniture inlaid with ivory and silver, even in the house of Odysseus. This was but the dwelling of a king of a rocky isle. Entering the hall of Menelaus, Telemachus bids his companion, the son of Nestor, marvel at the gleam of bronze, gold, electrum, silver, and ivory.[46] Apparently the home of Nestor in Pylos was not so rich and lordly. The house of Menelaus is a picture of a dwelling rich in such treasures as have been found in the Royal graves of Mycenae and in the palace of Cnossos in Crete. In the house of Odysseus we hear of no bathroom and bath, in which the girls of the house bathed princely guests and gave them change of raiment.[47] Weapons adorn the walls (in the house of Odysseus only), unless this be a later addition to the picture.

In the Homeric hall, each guest had his own little table and his chair. The prince and his wife sat in the centre, beside the fire, under the chief pillars. Honoured guests sat by them; the beggar was placed on the threshold, with his mess of meat. As in heroic Ireland, where the rules were very minute, some portions of the flesh were more honourable than others. In the lost Thebais, Oedipus curses his sons, Eteocles and Polynices, because they send him, not the shoulder, but the haunch (ἰσχίον)[48] This is a very archaic touch.

Homer's world is aristocratic. The poet, none the less, has his eye on the folk; on the honest poor woman who carefully weighs her wool; on the aged female thrall who is busy all night over her task of grain-grinding, and prays that the wooers who have broken her strength may now eat their latest meal. He is keenly interested in the work of artisans, such as the currier and shield maker who wrought the great shield of Aias; in the fisherman with his nets, or line and bait; in the diver for oysters; in the woodmen with their

---

45 Iliad, ix. 186, 189.

46 Odyssey, iv. 70-75.

47 Ibid. iii. 464-469. The word for bath, ἀσαμίνθος, is thought, like other words with the same termination, to be of the language of the Aegean race, whoever they may have been: the termination is common in place-names, and names of flowers.

48 Kinkel, Epicorum Graecorum Fragmenta, p. 11.

axes; in sowing and ploughing, and the relative merits of oxen and mules as plough-beasts; in the quarrel between two farmers over their boundary balk in the common field; in the lot of the hind of a landless man, the hardest lot of any; in gold-workers and spinners; shepherds, hunts-men, herdsmen; in the potter who "sitting by his wheel maketh trial of it whether it run"; in the virtues of a swineherd, a slave, who is noble by birth, like Eumaeus; in all seafaring men down to the pursers and stewards; in the laughing girls that gather in the vintage, while a boy makes sweet music, and sings the song of Linus with delicate voice; in the ploughman who has a drink of wine at the end of the furrow; in the gardener with his orchard, the watering of a plot as it is done to this day in the East; the fruit trees that Odysseus as a child was given "for his very own"; in the smith's warm forge where masterless tramps sleep at night; in the beggar men with their wallets, who crouch on the outer part of the threshold; in the old cadger who goes on the errands of the wooers; in the little girl that runs till she is weary by her mother's side, and catches at her skirt, praying to be taken up in her arms; in the children who build castles with the sea sand; in boys who, "always fond of mischief," stone the wasps' nest, and make the angry wasps a common nuisance; or cudgel the stubborn ass that is too strong for them; in all poor wayfarers who wander under the protection of Zeus; in all suppliants who, having slain a man, embrace the knees of the prince to whom they flee. All mankind are as interesting to Homer as the gallant youths at the bridal dance who wear "daggers of gold in baldrics of silver"; such bronze daggers with gilded blade-centres as were found in the tombs of Mycenae and elsewhere.

It is plain from Homeric descriptions of palaces, and of works of art, that his age had not lost touch with or memory of the Aegean culture. Whether some great Aegean or Mycenaean palaces with friezes of cyanus (dark blue glass paste), and of metals, were still in a habitable state, in Homer's days, or whether only the tradition of their glory survived,—as memories of Roman buildings dwell in the early Anglo-Saxon poem on the Ruined City of the Romans in England,—it is clear that plenty of Aegean artistic work in gold and other metals, cups and sword hilts, was preserved, and known to the poet. The Achaeans did not invade merely to destroy, like the Anglo-Saxon invaders of Romanised Britain. Far more civilised and refined than these rude hordes, they could appreciate and preserve as well as burn and break,—in an hour of furious sack,—the treasures of the more civilised race. But these treasures they could not imitate and reproduce, apparently (they are often spoken of as the work of the god Hephaestus), and the ancient Aegean art waned and passed under new and crude influences.

Much as Homer delights in works of art, and vividly as he describes them, and describes the toil of weavers, carpenters, shipwrights, ploughmen, reapers, and vintagers, he never shows us a painter at work on wall or vase, nor a mortal hand delineating, in any material, men and women; except when Helen is weaving a great purple web, and embroidering thereon, or interweaving therewith, "many battles of horse-taming Trojans and mail-clad Achaeans."[49] This art implies some knowledge of drawing and painting: from the Homeric age we have no relics of this art; but such webs might, like the Bayeux tapestry, last long, and might be imitated, and it may have been from such old Aegean fabrics or copies of them that Homer took his idea.

CHAPTER V

MEN AND WOMEN

In all modern times Homer has been admired for his noble, tender, and chivalrous sense of what is due to women; for his pictures of the perfect mother, Thetis; the perfect wife, Andromache; the perfect maiden, frank, stainless, and kind, Nausicaa; for the woman of immortal charm, Helen; while, when he does touch on the less lovable humours of women,—on the nagging shrew, the light o' love, the rather bitter virgin,—he selects his examples from the divine society of the Gods.

It is an instance of the high and noble taste of the poet and his audience, that he dwells most on the best and most charming of the women in old traditions, and is manifestly reluctant to tell of any evil deed, or any cruel sorrow of a lady. Yet legend was full of women fierce and revengeful as Brynhild; such women as Medea, who slew her own children; Ino, who hated her step-children; Althaea, who, to avenge her brothers, burned the brand that was the life-token of her son, Meleager of the golden hair. There was hateful Eriphyle, bribed by the gift that drew her lord to his doom; there

---

[49] Iliad, iii. 125-127.

was hapless Epicaste, wedded to her son, the slayer of his father; there were unhappy Chloris, and unhappy Tyro, mother of Pelias and Neleus by Poseidon, and victim of a feminine revenge. But this part of the tale is Ionian or Athenian, not Homeric. In Homer a woman is not dishonoured, but more highly esteemed, because she has been loved by a god. In Attic traditions she is cruelly punished by her own kinsfolk.

The wicked and ill-fated ladies who remind us of heroines in ancient German epos, are scarcely mentioned, or not at all in the Iliad (where they could only appear in digressions), and the poet merely touches on their fortunes when Odysseus meets them in Hades. From the guilt and the misery of the "far-renowned brides of ancient song," Homer averts his eyes. Even to Clytemnestra, though her sin cannot be hidden, he allows the bon naturel which Mary Stuart justly claimed for herself. We are reminded of the tenderness of Chaucer for the fault of Cressida, "Ne me list this sely womman chyde."

Homer himself never blames Helen, he regards her with the affection and pity of Hector and Priam: it is the Trojan women and Penelope, her cousin, who speak frankly of Helen and the ruin which she wrought. In the Iliad she does not, "where'er she came, bring calamity"; she is penitent, she longs for home, and her lord, and her one child, the little maid Hermione. She scorns the cowardice of her lover, and, in the third Book of the Iliad, the poet plainly declares that she is. the unwilling victim of Aphrodite. In the Odyssey, wherever she appears, she brings beauty, grace, charm, and quiet, and her appointed home is in the temperate meadows of the Elysian land.

Homer does not dwell on the passion of love; he could not do so in an epic of war, and in an epic of a man seeking to win, on the sea, "the return of his company." But each epic turns on and is motive by love; the Iliad springs from the lawless love of Paris and Helen; the Odyssey from the wedded love of Odysseus and Penelope. The Wrath of Achilles, too, arises on account of his lost love. In the instance of Paris, love has turned to the most tragic end: the passion of Helen is changed into bitter contempt and inconsolable regret.

The loves of youth and maiden, the whispered oaristys "from rock and oak," are seldom the theme of Greek poetry; in the Epics they would be as out of place as in the Chanson de Roland. The loves of Troilus and Cressida were, to Chaucer, the central interest of the Trojan leaguer; no such place could they hold in Homer: he has an infinitely larger and nobler topic. Yet he who listens may hear "The awakened loves around him murmuring," in the lines that, through the din of battle, just mention some old amour of gods with mortal maidens, of mortal men with fairies of the woods and hills.

Considering the warlike nature of the Iliad, the parts played by women, by Helen, Andromache, Hecuba, and the touches that bring forward the wifely tenderness of Theano, are almost surprising; while the whole poem is dominated by the maternal love of Thetis, that magical figure of sorrow, foreboding, and affection, without which the character of Achilles would be jejune, and bereft of occasions to display its fond of tenderness and melancholy. Of course we are told that all these women are "late," and formed no part of the original lay of the Wrath: that is to be expected of critical sagacity.

The magnificent passages on Helen, Andromache, and Hecuba; the humorous descriptions of Hera; Athene, her divine father's darling, and of Aphrodite; the unnatural hatred of Althaea; the caprice of Anteia; the pathos of the dirges of Briseis for Patroclus, of Helen for Hector; the remorseless jealousy of the mother of Phoenix, when his father loves a mistress among her maids, all supply "the female interest" in the Iliad.

There is not so much "female interest" as in the Volsunga Saga, but women occupy the same position, are regarded with the same deference; they are free, on earth and in Olympus, they give their counsel and even carry their point, as in the Icelandic sagas. In the Odyssey, Arete and Nausicaa appear exactly in the fashion of Wealtheow, Hrothgar's Queen, and her daughter in Beowulf,[50] they grace the company and still the quarrels of men.

The whole view of women is what we may call "northern"; it is the view of the sagas, of the English and the Teutonic epics; and is remote from the spirit of the partly orientalised poets of Ionia. But for the bequest of ancient heroic tradition the poets of Athens could not have created their noble heroines. Attic life, Ionian life, could not produce such women; and Aeschylus and Sophocles fall back on memories of heroines who are not Ionian and are not Attic, in the great majority of cases. Christian Europe at various times, in the age of the chivalrous romances, and in comedy generally, fell far below the old northern and Achaean view of the women's part. To chivalry, adultery was a duty, to our European comedy it was a jest: marriage was a bourgeois business. But even to historic Greece the sanctity of the marriage-tie was a serious matter: adulterous intrigues are not the theme of Greek poets and comedians, as they have been ever since our Middle Ages. Lancelot, and still more Tristram, would

[50] Beowulf, 611-628, 1162-1174, 1215-1231.

have been stigmatised as Paris is by Hector; and Guinevere and Iseult would have heard more reproaches from their own sex, than Penelope and the Trojan women bestow on Helen. The Gods are a sinful and adulterous generation, in the mythical view; but in the religious view they warn Aegisthus against his sin and its consequence.[51]

Turning to the legal position of women, we do not know much about the civil penalty or fine for adultery (μοιχάγρια), but Menelaus, the soul of honour, is eager to avenge himself in the duel. The fine for adultery may have been the equivalent of the bride-price paid by the bridegroom. Hephaestus, in the song of Demodocus, demands the return of the bride-price which he gave for the faithless Aphrodite, the ἔεδνα.[52] The bride-price, often mentioned, is a well-known institution, obsolete in historic Greece but familiar to the poet. In very rare cases in Homer, a man may receive a bride without paying a price for doing some great public service: in some circumstances the father will even give a dowry with the bride.[53] In the most notable passage where dowry (μείλια) is mentioned by the poet, he plainly shows his knowledge that the giving of dowry is an exception to the general rule; for he mentions the rule—the wooer pays the bride-price ἔεδνα, but in his sore need of Achilles, Agamemnon offers his daughter "without price" (ἀνάεδνον), and plus such gifts as no man ever endowed his daughter with.[54] This is no proof that the poet of Book ix. lived in a later age than that of the bride-price. He merely recognises what, in an age of bride-price, must have been the fact, that in unusual circumstances, when the alliance of a man was of crucial importance to the father, he would buy instead of selling his daughter's marriage. People were never such pedants as not to infringe a custom, not sacred but a secular bargain, when strong need came on them.

In another instance the husband was King Priam, whose alliance was worth buying by the aged father of the bride. "Circumstances alter cases," as critics often forget, and such rare divergences from the usual rule are not proofs of late interpolation. The Icelanders gave dowries with their daughters, but when Njal was especially eager for a bride for his foster son, he offered to reverse the process and give ἔεδνα, bride-price.[55] In the case of the

---

[51] Odyssey, i. 36-43.

[52] Odyssey, viii. 317-320.

[53] Iliad, xxii. 51, ix. 146-158.

[54] Iliad, ix. 146 et seqq.

[55] Story of Burnt Njal, vol. ii p. 81.

marriage of Penelope (a very peculiar instance, as there was no proof that she was a widow, and as it is not easy to see who "had her marriage"), we hear of bride-price "such as is meet to go with a dear daughter." This return of the price, or of part of it, was familiar to the Laws of Hammurabi and of the Germans of Tacitus.[56] We may, with the separatist critics, suppose that the passages about returning the bride-price of Penelope when she goes to her second husband,[57] belong to a later period than the body of the Epics; or, more probably, that a variety of customs may coexist (that they may we have proved), and, in any case, Penelope's people were anxious to get her off their hands in one way or another, her situation being irksome and anomalous. Rare must be the examples of interpolated details, when a case so anomalous as that of Penelope is seized on as proof of the presence of later social practices. The passages about Penelope are peculiar. In Od. ii. 53, Telemachus says that the wooers have no mind to go to the father of Penelope, who αὐτὸς ἐεδνώσαιτο θύγατρα. If we take this to mean "will endow her," the writer does not know the meaning of ἔεδνα; but I conceive him to say, "will fix the bride-price," or make the terms.[58] Compare Iliad, xiii. 384, ἐπεὶ οὔ τοι ἐεδνωταὶ κακοί εἰμεν, "we will not make hard marriage terms," that is, will not demand a heavy bride-price.

In Od. i. 278, ii. 196, Telemachus is bidden to take his mother to her father, "they will give the marriage feast and ἀρτυνέουσιν ἔεδνα, many such as should follow with a dear daughter." Mr. Murray says that the writer of these lines "mistook the meaning of estim because he had forgotten the custom" (R. G. E. p. 152). But even Aeschylus knew that ἔεδνα were gifts from the bridegroom (Prometheus, 559, quoted by Mr. Murray); and if the author of the passages in Odyssey, i. ii., did not know, he cannot have read the Iliad and Odyssey. This is so improbable, for even the author of the very "late" song of Ares and Aphrodite (Od. viii. 318) knew all about the legal nature of ἔεδνα, that we can hardly suppose the writer of the passages in Od. i. ii. to have fancied that ἔεδνα meant "dowry."

One thing is certain, that the prehistoric usage of bride-price almost uniformly prevails in the poems, with a trace of such variations in custom as actually occur, when circumstances or affection demand it, in every stage of human society. The bridal customs are not pedantically stereotyped in Homer, but variations

[56] Germania, R. G. E. p. 151, note 1, citing Ham. 160, 163, 164.

[57] Odyssey, i. 278, ii. 195-197.

[58] See Pierron, "qu'il s'entendra avec le prétendant." Merry and Riddell translate, "will accept gifts of wooing for his daughter." Leaf: "get the bride-price for his daughter."

in accordance with circumstances do not prove lateness or earliness, any more than such female names as Alphesiboea, Phereboea, Polyboea, and others, indicating that a daughter, on her marriage, will bring many kine into her family, "express the excuse which the parents made to themselves for venturing to rear the useless female child."[59]

Not even in Australian black society are girls more apt than male babies to be killed as bouches inutiles, they are far too valuable to their brothers or maternal uncles, being exchanged for other men's sisters or nieces as brides. The cattle-owning barbaric societies of Africa are not addicted to female infanticide, much less could Homeric society be with its wealth and its tenderness of heart. In Greek non-Homeric legend how often do we hear of a baby-girl being exposed? It is the boys who suffer, in the hope of defeating some prophecy. Homeric society is infinitely remote from that in which girls were too expensive and useless to keep.[60]

Homer is the last author in whom we can hopefully look for survivals of savagery, or of cruel and filthy superstitions. In the Epics there is not a harlot, common as they are in the ancient Hebrew books. It is not to be supposed that the ancient profession was unknown, but all such things are ignored in deference to a taste more pure than that of early Ionian society and of historic Greece from first to last. The tone of taste and morals is, in short, Achaean, like the poet himself;[61] Shakespeare, in Troilus and Cressida, makes Patroclus mimic Nestor; he

> *"coughs and spits,*
> *And with a palsy fumbling in his gorget,*
> *Shakes in and out the rivet,"*

in "a night-alarm." Shakespeare has read of the night-alarm in Iliad, Book x., but not there did he find, nowhere in Homer could he find "the faint defects of age" made matter of merriment. In Homer nobody coughs!

The Homeric idea of the family is symbolised in the wedding bed which Odysseus fashioned with his own hands, making it fast to the trunk of a living tree that it might never be moved.[62] and

---

59 R. G. E. p. 151.

60 No society is less affluent than that of the Australian tribes. But this does not provoke preferential female infanticide. See Spencer and Gillen, Native Tribes of Central Australia, pp. 51, 52, 264; Northern Tribes, p. 608; Howitt, Native Tribes of South East Australia, pp. 749, 750.

61 See Appendix, "The supposed Expurgation of Homer."

62 Odyssey, xxiii. 183-204.

adorning it with inlay of gold, silver and ivory. According to many critics, of whom Wolf is the earliest, the final books of the Odyssey are later than the rest, and the idea of a separate chamber for husband and wife is late. Other critics, when they find mentions of such a separate chamber (δάλαμος) in other parts of the Epic, explain them as late interpolations. They appear once again to forget that in no civilised society is there absolute uniformity of detail in all the arrangements of domestic life. An interesting example may be found in Scott's description of the hall and house of Cedric the Saxon,—the hall floored with "earth mixed with lime, trodden into a hard substance, such as is often employed in flooring our modern barns," the rafters "encrusted with a black varnish of soot" (the melathron), the walls "hung with implements of war," "the low irregular building," are like the house of Odysseus. There were "buildings after building."[63] Contrasted with these arrangements were the castles of the Normans, "tall, turreted, and castellated buildings."

"In the Iliad and Odyssey the houses are normally one-room halls. The master and mistress live in the megaron in the daytime and sleep there at night ... grown-up sons and daughters have separate 'halls' or thalamoi built for them close by."[64]

On this showing, Odysseus had chosen to adopt a different arrangement, it does not quite follow that the account of his house is late; it would be hard to prove that thalamos (chamber) and megaron (hall) are identical, we hear of no outside thalamos, like that of Telemachus, occupied by a girl, and the whole topic demands very minute criticism. But the question of Aegean and Achaean architecture is at present the subject of controversy among architectural specialists.

The happiness of wedded life has never been more nobly praised than by Homer in the famous speech of Odysseus to Alcinous. Adultery is laughed at only among the gods. Moreover, we never hear of lightness of behaviour in girls, except when a God is the wooer, and that is reckoned an honour, the woman is sought for in marriage by mortals. In Ionian tradition, as has been said, on the other hand, the girls beloved by gods are severely punished, like Tyro.

Fidelity is not expected from men when absent at a long siege, or lost in unknown lands, like Odysseus, who does not scruple to tell Penelope about Circe and Calypso. At home the fidelity of husbands depends on the characters of the pair. Laertes is fond of a fair

---

[63] Odyssey, xvii. 266.

[64] R. G. E. p. 153.

handmaid, but dreads the wrath of his wife, as the father of Phoenix, in a similar case, found that he had good reason to do. The bastards of whom we hear are probably sons of the captives of the spear, brought home as Agamemnon unadvisedly brought Cassandra. Theano, wife of Antenor, "nurtured his bastard, like her own children, to do her husband pleasure."[65] Teucer also, a bastard, was brought up by his father in his own house.[66] There was one law for the men, another for the women, and Dr. Johnson approved of this moral system in England.

The domestic relations are very pleasingly portrayed in the Iliad. Homer, to be sure, knows that family life is not always monotonously peaceful and affectionate. In the long speech of Phoenix (Book ix.) we see a son, Meleager, who has a feud with his maternal uncles and is under his mother's curse. This family feud, in which the wife and mother takes sides with her own kin against her husband or sons, is a common motive in the oldest Teutonic Epics, and even in the historic traditions of the Camerons.

But it is among the Olympians that Homer finds his blustering, teasing yet placable husband and father, Zeus; his shrewish wife, Hera; his rather spiteful daughter, Athene; and his lady of pleasure, Aphrodite, whose intrigues are a jest. The affection of Zeus for his daughter, none the less, is happily displayed, while among men the fraternal affection of Agamemnon for Menelaus is his most agreeable trait. Parents and children, except in the woeful adventure of Phoenix, are always on the best of terms, as in the households of Odysseus, Nestor, and Alcinous; and the petulance of Priam towards his sons, after the death of Hector, is excused by his age and intolerable sufferings. "With his staff he chased forth the men, and they went before the old man in his haste."[67]

In short, though wives were bought with the bride-price, it seems probable that the affectionate Homeric fathers allowed more latitude of choice to their daughters than has, in many periods, been permitted by ourselves in England, and no literature in the world displays a happier domestic life, a life more gentle, true, and loving than the old Epics of the mail-clad Achaeans.[68]

---

[65] Iliad, v. 69-71.
[66] viii. 281-284.
[67] xxiv. 247.
[68] Mr. Murray refers me, for female infanticide among Greeks, to a letter in Pap. Oxyz., 744: "Keep a male. Cast out a female child." These may have been the manners of late Egyptianised Greeks, but I am not dealing with them. See p. 40 supra under note 2.

CHAPTER VI

THE HOMERIC WORLD IN WAR

On the fringe of the horizon, in Homer's day as in our own, always hung the cloud of war. In war, men were as cruel as they have usually been. A successful siege of a city involved the slaying of its defenders, and the carrying away of the women, "to make another's bed, and draw water from another's well." Hector, when the broken oaths of the duel[69] make it certain that Troy must perish, looks for no better fortune to befall Andromache; may the earth be mounded above him before that day!

Though a truce is granted for the cremation and burial, with one common cairn, of the men who fall in a great battle,[70] it is not Achilles alone who would fain refuse burial, and rest in the House of Hades, to an enemy. Hector intends to give the body of Patroclus to the dogs of Troy, and to fix his head on the palisade above the wall.[71] The fury of Achilles, when he learns from Iris the intentions of Hector, has thus more excuse than is usually supposed. Homer himself found such deeds in the tradition; and though he regards them with horror, he cannot expurgate them. The insults lavished by Achilles on the dead Hector are ἀεικέα ἔργα, deeds of shame.[72] But the deeds of Hector would have been as shameful. The treatment of Hector was not sensational enough for the refined taste of the Athenian tragedians. Sophocles and Euripides make Achilles drag the wounded but living Hector.[73]

The tragedians here followed a tradition that was not Homer's; it may have come, Mr. Murray suggests, from the lost Cyclic poem Iliou Persis, the Sack of Ilios. The Cyclic poets of 750-650 B.C. are in all ways more superstitious and barbarous than Homer; theirs is the taste of a later age than his, and, as we shall see, they are usually followed by the Athenian tragedians. They preferred the "sensational" and the "harrowing," and did not shrink, in the Andromache, as in the Ionian Sack of Ilios, from the brutal murder of Hector's child, Astyanax. Homer's men are never child-

---

69 Iliad, iii. iv.

70 vii. 332-420.

71 xviii. 175-177.

72 Ferdiad, in the Old Irish Tain Bo Cualgne, also drags a dead man by his chariot wheels.

73 R.G.E. p. 118. Ajax, 1031. Euripides, Andromache, 399.

murderers. City sackings were as cruel as those of Cromwell in Ireland, of Monk in Dundee; our own dealings with Badajoz and Ciudad Rodrigo are more recent examples, and these were towns of our allies. But Homer's men do not, like the Assyrians, torture prisoners of war; such captives were starved, tortured, and literally caged, to extract ransom, during our Hundred Years' War with France; as Cromwell's prisoners, after Dunbar, were starved in Durham Cathedral. In Homer, ransom is sometimes accepted, in the earlier days of the siege. Achilles, especially, took ransoms and was merciful. Contrast the ferocity of Agamemnon, who refuses quarter, and slays a man to whom Menelaus was giving quarter.[74] Agamemnon actually cuts off the hands and head of one foe, and throws the head into the throng! He desires that not even the male child in the womb may escape! (Iliad, vi. 56-60). There are chivalrous passages, as when Hector and Aias exchange gifts after an indecisive passage of arms, and when Diomede and Glaucus recognise their ancestral friendship; but there are plenty of cases in which victors exult with cruel humour over their fallen foes, in the spirit of Arthur in Layamon's Brut. (1200 A.D.).

The dead, except in the case of Eetion on whom Achilles had ruth, were always stripped of arms and armour, if the victors were not impeded. The hut of Idomeneus held many such Trojan spoils. There are hints of a custom of tearing the tunics, or chitons,[75] but they are vague and unimportant. No doubt the act, when performed, was intended as an insult, but it is only alluded to twice or thrice: in one case the tunic is "of bronze," answering to the current term χαλκοχίτωνες, "bronze-clad."[76] The case is obscure.

A la guerre comme à la guerre. The morals of war in Homer are not unlike those of war everywhere in the matter of "atrocities." The siege operations were very inefficient. The Achaeans were not able to invest Troy, and they never dreamed of an escalade. Without

---

[74] Iliad, vi. 37-65, xi. 122-147.

[75] Iliad, xi. 100, ii. 416.

[76] Ibid. xiii. 439, 440. That the bronze tunic is a softening of the sense by a late interpolator is not very likely, for Homer, we have seen, represents a warrior as cutting off a dead man's hands and head; and if he does not shirk this, if no later hand corrects him, why should he strain at tearing a chiton? Miss Stawell ingeniously remarks that the chiton-tearing is a proof of the prevalent use of corslet? If men fought without corslets, the chiton "must always have been getting torn in the mêlée, whatever the warrior's fate. But the sign would have been unmistakable if the tunic was usually covered by the corslet and could not be torn until that was taken off...." (Homer and the Iliad, p. 211). But, I fear, Homeric warriors did not come to such close quarters as at Rugby football.

a scaling-ladder Patroclus "thrice clomb on the corner of the lofty wall," and was only thrust back by Apollo.[77] But scaling-ladders are never mentioned; a night attack is never contemplated. The famous Wooden Horse is the only hint of an approach under a wooden cover on wheels (the mediaeval "Sow"); and if it was anything of that sort, Homer did not understand its nature. The efficient fighting in the open was done by chariotry (the owners usually dismounted and fought in line or column); as in most ancient oriental countries, Scotland in Roman times, and Ireland in the Late Celtic period, perhaps as late as 300 a.d., also in early Britain. By the date of the Black Figure vases (sixth century B.C.) and in seventh century art, the painters often introduce mounted men: the "late poets" abstained from doing so, it appears, except the late unspeakable Stümper of the Doloneia, according to Reichel.

The tactics, as far as we can make a coherent picture of them, were peculiar, but not unexampled.

At the beginning of a pitched battle the knights (owners of chariots) dismounted, and formed a thick and serried line of infantry: behind them came the nameless host, concerning whose armour we have no information. The light-armed archers and slingers showered their missiles, and the combat might last for hours. At "the break of the battle," when one side had broken the enemy's line, the victors pursued either on foot, or, more generally, in their chariots which had been stationed behind them in the close combat; while the vanquished leaped into their chariots and fled, save the brave who retired face to the foe. After the break in the battle, the individual exploits of the mounted knights, the chariotry, fill the picture, till the beaten forces reach the wall of the Greek camp, or of Troy, when a rally occurs, followed by another battle in ordered ranks.[78]

As to the armour and weapons, Homer represents every man-at-arms as wearing a helmet, usually of bronze; and a huge shield, very long, like the three sorts of shield represented in Aegean art on the Mycenaean dagger blade showing lion hunters. Some shields in this art are in form like the figure 8, they belly out, and protect a man from neck to ankles. Others are merely doors, flat and oblong, of the same size; others are equally large, cylindrical, and partly protect the sides. All are hung from the shoulder by baldrics, not held in the hand, like the parrying bucklers of the eighth century and later. Homer thus describes such huge shields as these of Aegean art, with baldrics; but his language not infrequently conveys

---

[77] Iliad, xvi. 702, 703.

[78] See "Homeric Tactics."

the impression that some shields are circular; indeed, it is only by wrenching the sense of the Greek that any other meaning can be obtained. The details are considered later; meanwhile Homer's shields are neither those of the Dipylon period nor of archaic Greek art, and in their size and their baldrics correspond to those of Aegean representations. The substance of the shields is layers of ox's hide, covered with a plating of bronze. Warriors also wear corslet, metal girdle, and metal-plated kirtle: the corslet was thin, and could be pierced by arrows. The greaves to cover the shins were probably of bronze, laced up with wire, as in a pair from Enkomi in Cyprus, of the Age of Bronze, now in the British Museum. No thigh pieces are mentioned, though they are commonly shown in the art of the seventh to sixth centuries.[79]

For offensive weapons the men-at-arms use two spears with heavy heads of bronze, these are usually thrown; and a sword of bronze, commonly a heavy cut and thrust blade (never the long Elizabethan rapier of an earlier Minoan time), with a handle of ivory, inlaid or studded with gold or silver, in some cases. The sheath is similarly decorated. Only once do we hear of a battle-axe of bronze; and the dirk, sometimes of iron, is never said to be used in battle. These weapons have analogues in certain swords and daggers found in Aegean graves.

Archery is not so highly considered as when "the man Heracles" and the great Eurytus were bowmen. Odysseus, the heir of the mighty bow of Eurytus, left it at home, and fought as a heavy-armed footman. Pandarus, on the other hand, left his horses and chariots at home, and came to Troy trusting in his bow.[80] Teucer, Pandarus, Paris, and occasionally Meriones, are the bowmen, among the princes, and Paris and Pandarus are taunted for their weak and cowardly missiles; honour was to be won with sword and spear. The Scots archers, in the same way, were always anxious to come to hand-strokes with their sperths, or battle-axes; the Highlanders threw down their muskets, after one discharge, and went in with the claymore; the French never reconciled themselves to the long bow; the Spartans despised it. This was the Homeric sentiment: the bow was scarcely the weapon for a hero. The arrow-heads were of bronze.[81] In Mycenaean graves at Kakovotos (Old Pylos) in Elis, the stone arrow points are of very fine neolithic work.[82] When archery declined yet lower, in historic times, the

---

[79] For details and discussion, see "Homeric Armour and Costume."

[80] Iliad, v. 193-205.

[81] On stone and bronze arrow-heads, see Tsountas and Manatt, p. 209.

[82] Kurt Müller, Alt Pyhs, p. 292. Attische Mitteilungen, 1909. Cf. plate xv.

round or oval parrying buckler, carried on the left arm, came in, as a protection against spears and sword-strokes. This parrying buckler does not appear in Homer: efforts made to discover it are unsuccessful.

Thus Homer describes a given stage in the art of war: his pictures are not patchworks of "Mycenaean" fighting (about which we know nothing), and of civic Greek fighting in the age of civic heavy-armed foot.

CHAPTER VII

HOMERIC TACTICS

Homer is not a scientific military historian, but a poet. Consequently, in his accounts of pitched battles, he naturally dwells on the prowess of famous individuals in the single combat; the struggle of one hero against a group of assailants; the pursuit and the flight; more than he dwells on the long encounter of marshalled lines before "the break in the battle."

Let us consider the battle in Iliad, xi. The princes begin by giving their chariots to the charioteers, "to hold them in by the fosse, well and orderly," and "themselves as heavy men-at-arms were hastening about."[83] They are then marshalled in order, with the chariots behind them. Meanwhile Hector arrays the Trojans, being now with the front and now with the rear ranks.[84] The fight begins; "equal heads had the battle." The two forces meet like two bands of reapers shearing the corn of a field from either limit, and meeting in the centre.[85] This steady fight of lines of dismounted men-at-arms endures from dawn to midday, till, at noon, comes "the break in the battle," "the Danaans by their valour brake the battalions."[86] Agamemnon, on foot, rushes into the ruined ranks of Troy, and slays many Trojans in their chariots (which they would

---

[83] Iliad, xi. 49, αὐτοὶ δὲ πρυλέες σὺν τεύχεσιθωρηχθέντες. Cf. v. 744, πρυλέες "may mean either footmen or champions." Leaf.

[84] Iliad, xi. 59-66.

[85] xi. 67-69.

[86] θαλάγγαι, xi. 90.

naturally mount for the sake of speedier flight); there is a pursuit of the broken foe, "footmen kept slaying footmen as they were driven in flight, and horsemen slaying horsemen with the sword"; till the flying Trojans rally at the Scaean gate, while Agamemnon still slays the hindmost fugitives. A flesh-wound irks him, and he "retires hurt." Hector, by command of Zeus, has waited for this moment, and now leads a chariot-charge among the scattered Achaeans. Henceforth there is a series of individual encounters; Odysseus is alone and is surrounded; he fights hard; he calls for aid, and is rescued by Menelaus and Aias. Several Achaean princes are wounded, among others Diomede, Agamemnon, and Odysseus retire to their quarters for rest and surgical aid.

This is not scientific fighting: no general is apart, receiving news of the fight, sending supports where they are needed, husbanding the reserves, and so forth. The leaders actually lead, and their men are discouraged and give ground when the chiefs are put out of action, precisely as in the Highland armies of clans under Dundee or Montrose or Prince Charles, where so much depended on the success of the first onslaught. Homer's men have more faculty for recovering from a severe stroke. The Achaeans, after a long struggle of heavy dismounted men-at-arms, drive the Trojans to the city wall. The Trojans rally, and drive the Achaeans to their own fortifications, where there is a confused mellay at the fosse and under the wall.[87]

Polydamas very properly now advises the chivalry of Troy to dismount and fight on foot (πρυλέες) in dense columns, while their chariots are held stationary by their squires. Hector approves, and the dismounted Trojans form five columns of attack on a fortified position.[88] The Achaeans, scattered and disheartened, are mainly led and helped by the two Aiantes, but Poseidon rallies five or six young heroes of Boeotia, Aetolia, Crete, and Pylos.[89] They are confessedly both wearied and demoralised by the success of Hector in breaking down the gate.[90] They are actually weeping!

But now, encouraged by the god, they form a "schiltrom," a close clump of spears advanced and levelled, underlying and overlying each other.[91] (The spears of defenders and assailants, at the battle of Langside (1568), were so closely interlocked, that

---

[87] Iliad, xii. 3, μάχοντο ὁμιλαδόν. Cf. xii. 35, 36.
[88] xii. 66-107.
[89] Iliad, xiii. 81-124.
[90] xiii. 80-90.
[91] πτύσσοντο, xiii. 134.

discharged pistols and daggers thrown by the combatants lay on them!) Shield touches shield, the plumes of the helmets meet.[92]

As was natural, Hector's column was arrested by the "dark impenetrable wood" of Achaean spears,[93] and now the poet makes Poseidon, who has lost a grandson (xiii. 207) in the fight, stir up Idomeneus, who is at a distance from Hector's point of attack, and we have the day of valour, and the success of the Cretan prince, on the left of the Achaean fortified position. The Boeotians there, with the Athenians and "Ionian tunic-trailers," are hard pressed, but the Aiantes make a stout resistance, and the arrows of the Locrians are showered on Hector's column.[94] Polydamas advises Hector to retreat, but he hurries off and brings up reinforcements in good order. He then tries again and again to break through the schiltrom of the Achaean dismounted men-at-arms, and the two forces clash with cries of onset.[95]

Here we have a renewal of the steady conflict of men duly marshalled. Hector, however, is put out of action, sore smitten by a boulder from the hand of Aias; the Trojans give ground, are pursued, and fall back, till when Hector revives, Aias and the princes who joined him at the command of Poseidon, form a firm line of resistance.[96]

Again there is a dogged contest of marshalled forces, till Apollo causes a panic among the Achaeans, and their line is broken. "Then man fell upon man when the close fight was scattered,"[97] and we have a new set of individual valiances, among the bravest; but the Achaean host is flying in disorderly rout, "hither and thither in terror," through the ditch and within the wall.

It is in his chariot, to which he had been carried when stunned by the boulder, that Hector now calls for a chariot charge on the fosse and wall, which Apollo makes possible by levelling the wall into the dyke.[98] After mixed fighting, the spear of Aias is lopped in twain by the sword of Hector, and fire is thrown into the ship of Protesilaus. This is the moment that Achilles has prayed and longed for since the first book of the poem. Addressing Agamemnon, he then swore a great oath by the sceptre that "longing for Achilles shall come upon the Achaeans one and all, when multitudes fall

[92] xiii. 128-133.
[93] xiii. 144-148.
[94] xiii. 789-906.
[95] xiii. 833-837.
[96] xv. 299-301.
[97] Iliad, xv. 328.
[98] xv. 343-366.

dying before manslaying Hector."[99] In the same book he bids Thetis pray to Zeus to "hem the Achaeans among the sterns of their ships, given over to slaughter."[100] When the Embassy sought Achilles in Book ix., with the offers of Agamemnon, this dire need had not fallen on the Achaeans, and Achilles rejected their prayers. But he promised to fight if Hector, as he burned the ships, came to those of the Myrmidons.[101]

Hector never came so far; for[102] though Achilles kept the letter of his vow in Book ix., and did not arm, he sent Patroclus forth in Achilles' armour, at the head of the Myrmidons, and their charge on rear and flank drove the Trojans far from the ships and the wall.

This is a brief summary of the main movements in the engagement, up to the moment when Achilles let slip the Myrmidons. We see that, setting aside the interferences of gods, and the pardonable exaggeration of the prowess of favourite heroes, we have a set of as natural pictures of the flux and reflux of battle-tides as if we were reading about Waterloo. The character of the engagements is conditioned by the use of dismounted men-at-arms as heavy infantry, whether employed in lines of resistance, in squares or schiltroms of levelled spears, or in columns of attack. The fighting men in view are the gentry, stiffening "the host," the λαός of whose equipment we know little, while the archery of light-armed bowmen, such as the Locrians, is not without its effect. But the bows are short, and the arrow is drawn only to the breast, not, as by Egyptian and Assyrian archers, on the monuments, and by the archers of mediaeval England, to the ear. Chariots are not employed, in Homer, as on the Egyptian monuments, in charging squadrons, closely and neatly arranged, but in the flight and the pursuit, and to bear the prince rapidly to distant points of the field.[103]

The most obvious and closest analogy to Homeric warfare is that of the period (1300-1430 A.D.) when the Flemings and Scots had shown the powerlessness of charges of heavy cavalry against the schiltroms of spearmen, if these had not been broken up by "artillery preparation," by the long bow. Henceforth the English

---

[99] i. 241-244.

[100] i. 409-412.

[101] ix. 653-656.

[102] xvi. 1-155.

[103] Rapid retreat, xi. 359-360. Rapid pursuit, viii. 87-90, 340-349. Leaf on viii. 348. Cf. Caesar, Bellum Gallicum, iv. 33. Chariot in attendance to remove wounded hero, xi. 273, 399. Quick mounting and dismounting, xvi. 426, 427.

knights, squires, and "lances," or men-at-arms dismounted, their horses being held in reserve, and received the attacks of the heavy French cavalry on foot, with spear, sword, and axe. In case of defeat (which did not occur) or of pursuit, the horses were in readiness. Heavy armed infantry, like the hoplites of historic Greece, were developed later than Homer, and the heavy cavalry then became a separate arm. The changes occurred in the dim age between the date of the Iliad and Odyssey and the dawn of historic Greece. Chariots ceased to be employed in war by the Greek cities of Asia. The chief arm was the heavy drilled infantry, the hoplites. We catch our first glimpses of them on the Warrior Vase of the upper and later stratum at Mycenae, and on an old sculptured Mycenaean stele, later "plastered over and painted in fresco." In the former is a line of swordless spearmen on the march; on the latter, a row of swordless spearmen in the act of brandishing the spear. Their bucklers are worn on the left arm: they appear to wear hauberks, not corslets of plate, but one cannot be certain.[104] In these figures we see the germ of the infantry of historic Hellas. The war chariot becoming obsolete, civic cavalry were employed; the horsemen of Colophon were celebrated for dealing a fatal conclusive charge.

Nothing could be much less like Homeric than historical Ionian warfare, except in so far as Homer's dismounted men-at-arms resemble the heavy historic infantry, who never mount.

We have now given a brief sketch of Homer's idea of a general engagement in force. The clash of marshalled lines of heavy dismounted men-at-arms ends in the breaking of the phalanxes, and in the single combats, or combats of small knots of heroes, in which the poet and his audience take special delight.

We now criticise the modern criticisms of Homeric pictures of battles.

Herr Mülder, in 1906, and Mr. Murray, in 1908, discover that Homeric formations and fighting are a confusion of the methods of historic Greece—with drilled hoplites and cavalry,—and the "Mycenaean" system of "a battle of promachoi or champions."[105]

According to the English critic, in the Iliad "the men are, so to speak, advertised as fighting in one way, and then they proceed to fight in another."[106] As we have seen, they are "advertised as fighting in one way," that is, in ordered phalanxes of dismounted men-at-arms, and they do fight in that way, from dawn till noon; and then when "the phalanxes are broken," when "the battle is scattered,"

---

104 Ridgeway, E. A. G., vol. i. pp. 313-315.

105 R. G. E. pp. 141-143. Homer und die altjonische Elegie, pp. 32-41.

106 R. G. E. p. 143.

they "fight in another way"; there is flight, pursuit, and examples of individual valour; there is a rally, and the lines of men on foot re-form. What else could there possibly be? The charge of the Union brigade, at Waterloo, begins by "fighting in one way," a resistless charge of squadrons, and ends by "fighting in another way," in knots, with individual examples of flight, or of single prowess, when Piré's Red Lancers swoop down on the scattered and broken ranks. At Bannockburn you have the slow advance of the clogged English columns on a narrow front, you have the slow advance in mass of the Scottish spearmen, till "the phalanxes are broken" of England, and then comes the isolated struggle of Edward II., and the charge of d'Argentine,—alone.

It was always thus that men fought, before the invention of modern projectiles. It was thus they fought at Inkerman, nay, for a moment at Waggon Hill, as one who was in the thick of it informs me. Ian Hamilton and de Villiers, Albrecht and Digby Jones were among the promachoi.

There is no confusion of a "Mycenaean" and a historic mode of battle in Homer; and we have absolutely no evidence as to how a "Mycenaean" or Aegean general engagement was conducted: no Aegean work of art in which it is represented.[107]

There is no confusion of military styles in Homer; the trouble is caused when Herr Mülder chooses to say that there is confusion; that a fight of masses is promised (apparently by an Ionian interpolator), and that single combats are given (apparently by the older minstrel).[108] Both sorts of fighting are given in their proper places: the engagement of masses before, the individual valiances after "the battle is scattered," while in the clash of the massed forces, the conduct of prominent assailants and defenders is noted. Mülder's remarks arise from his eagerness to prove that not only the

---

[107] Mr. Murray writes: "It is in this way" (in phalanxes) "that people are said to be going to fight before each great battle begins. But strangely enough it is not at all in this way that they really fight when the battle is fairly joined, in the heart of the poem. In the heart of the poem, when the real fight comes, it is as a rule purely Mycenaean." We do not know how Mycenaeans fought in a general engagement. But people, in Homer, do fight as they "are said to be going to tight," when a schiltrom of spears is formed and is assailed, as in Iliad, xiii. 125-205. There the Trojan charge is checked by the hedge of spears. The general assault, the combined resistance, and the conduct of the most prominent men in defence and attack, is described, just as, at Waterloo and Culloden, historians describe the general conflict, and also the individual prowess of Shaw, Gillie Macbean, and others.

[108] Mülder, op. cit. p. 32.

armature is a muddle of anachronisms, which is not the case, but that the fighting, too, is anachronistic and self-contradictory.

The aged Nestor remembers and approves of a mode of fighting which, at Troy, has become obsolete, owing to the new system of dismounting the men-at-arms and arraying them in line or in column of attack. He says to his Pylians (Iliad, iv. 303 seqq.), "Neither let any man, trusting to his horsemanship and valour, be eager to fight the Trojans alone before the rest, nor yet let him draw back.... But whensoever a warrior from his own chariot can come at the chariot of the foe, let him thrust forth with his spear, even so is the far better way," the old way. "The style of fighting is not Epic," says Mr. Leaf. It is meant not to be "Epic"; it is old-fashioned, like Nestor.

We know "the old way" from pictures on Egyptian monuments, showing the charge of squadrons using the bow, and routing an irregular advance of Hittite chariotry, using the spear. But, under Troy, the combatants usually fight dismounted; always, in the opening of a general action. But though Nestor recommends the old chariotry tactics, Herr Mülder says that he is recommending the historic, "the modern method," and attributing it to the old military school of his youth (οἱ πρότεροι).[109] The general purpose is to prove that "edifying passages from the old Ionic hortatory writers seem to have been introduced into Homer."[110]

The tactics and military formations of Homer are as intelligible as those of Chandos and Henry v. They can only be misunderstood by critics under the suggestion of the idea that the Iliad is riddled with Ionian tamperings. The Ionians never touched the matter of the Iliad.

---

[109] Mülder, op. cit. p. 36.

[110] R. G. E. 133, note 1. Thus the hortatory eloquence of Poseidon (xiii. 108 fi.) is an echo of Callinus's stimulating appeal to the young to bestir themselves, when the country is at war. Callinus. fr. 1. Thus Poseidon cannot say "young men, don't be slack," without quoting an Ionian elegiac poet! (Mülder, pp. 12, 13). It is waste of time to discuss criticism of this sort, especially as, even if there were any borrowing, the Ionian elegy-maker must be reminiscent of the Iliad, as Tyrtaeus is in a familiar passage.

CHAPTER VIII

MEN'S DRESS IN HOMER. ARMOUR

As the following remarks are inevitably full of minute and complex detail, it may be well to say briefly what I wish to prove. According to the view of many critics, German and English, the "early lays" of the Iliad were composed when men wore smocks or chitons, like the Greeks of the historic ages. In war, on this theory, they wore no armour save the huge body—covering shields of Aegean art, but not the loin-cloth or the bathing-drawers which were the sole costume of the Aegean fighting man. The Homeric warrior of the "early lays" was thus accoutred; like the Aegean warrior, he had no body armour save the shield, but, by way of dress, he had the smock or chiton, not the loin-cloth.

On this theory the corslet did not come into vogue till the eighth to seventh century. Then it arrived with the zoster, or mailed belt, and the mitrê, or mailed kirtle. When these had been accepted, the huge early shield, slung by a baldric, was discarded for the round or oval parrying buckler, blazoned with a device, and carried on the left arm. The smock or chiton continued to be worn. Ionian poets interpolated their corslet, mitre, zoster, and greaves into passages of old lays that originally knew no such armour. The result was confused nonsense.

Against all this I am to contend that greaves, bronze corslets of plate, bronze girdles, and mailed kirtles were known in Aegean times long before the arrival of the Achaeans in Crete: proof is given from a work of Aegean art. Secondly, hauberks of metal scales were worn in very early post-Homeric times; and Homer minutely describes such hauberks, which clasped in front and back. Thirdly, the Ionian armour of the eighth, seventh, and early sixth centuries was not Homeric. Men wore, not hauberks of mail, clasping at front and back, but corslets with breast-plate and back-plate fastened at the sides; with these they wore neither mailed belt nor mailed kirtle. They wore not only greaves, but protective thigh-pieces (parameridia) unknown to Homer. But, about 530 B.C., these corslets of plate began to go out, and yield place to hauberks of mail, clasping at front and back; and with these were worn mailed belts and mailed kirtles, but no thigh-pieces. In Homer this is the usual equipment, though corslets of plate appear also to be known.

As to dress, the Ionian warrior of the eighth to early sixth century did not wear in active life the Homeric smock or chiton. He either reverted to the Aegean loin-cloth or drawers, or he wore a very tight curt jerkin, coming down no lower than the buttocks. It was when the mailed hauberk, mailed belt, and mailed flaps under the belt came in, that the smock or chiton also reappeared, and the tight curt jerkin or the loin-cloth went out.

Thus the Ionian minstrels did not bring into old lays armour which they did not wear, and the chiton which they did not wear they did not excise. Nor did any one, at any time, foist in the round Ionian parrying shield on the left arm: the Homeric body-covering shield hung by a baldric retained its place. Women, too, I am to argue, reverted on occasion to the Aegean tight bodice, small waist and skirt, or wore a chiton tight, comparatively short, and not, like the Homeric peplos, long, loose, and trailing. But these intermediate periods, between the Homeric and historic, left not a trace in the pictures presented by the Iliad and Odyssey.

Why was the new Ionian armour introduced, as we are told it was, while the un-Homeric features in dress were not introduced into the poems?

Coming to men's dress in Homer, we do not know exactly how long the ordinary Homeric chiton was. If the word τερμιόεις means "reaching to the feet," it would apply well to a shield of the huge Mycenaean make, and to a chiton, and it is used of both.[111] But some take it to mean "fringed," which cannot apply to the Mycenaean shield, or to chitons as represented anywhere except perhaps in the Warrior Vase (sub-Mycenæan) of Mycenae. No brooches are mentioned as fastening chitons, and it rather appears that these resembled the very short-sleeved, rather loose, and not girdled sewn smock of the lowest figure in the Mycenaean "siege vase." Eumaeus the swine-herd belts his chiton with a girdle when he goes out to his work.[112] Probably, therefore, it reached the feet, and had to be "kirtled up." Now the curt jerkin of seventh to sixth century art needs no tucking up, it merely covers the buttocks. The material was linen, if the name chiton be derived from a Semitic word for linen.

When we read that the tunic of Odysseus was "shining like the skin of a dried onion, so soft it was, and bright as the sun," it is not quite clear whether it was as tight, or as bright, as the onion skin; and perhaps its brilliance suggests that it was of silk, rather than of linen, unstarched.

A person who comes fresh from Homer to the study of Greek archaic art, of the latest eighth, the seventh, and the sixth centuries, cannot but be struck by the fact, rather neglected by writers on

---

[111] Iliad, xvi. 803 (the shield); Odyssey, xix. 242 (the chiton).
[112] Odyssey, xiv. 72.

costume, that the men are not wearing the Homeric chiton, which needs to be kirtled up in active life. On the other hand, "on the earliest vases the men are often nude, with the exception of a loin-cloth or pair of tight fitting bathing-drawers."[113] This is the usual pre-Achaean dress of men in Minoan art. In archaic Greek art, men often wear either a very tight jerkin, covering the trunk, or, "on the earliest vases," the men have reverted from the Homeric chiton to the Aegean loin-cloth and bathing-drawers. Either this is the case, or the men, in fact, never wore the chiton in the "earliest" lays; the chiton, like the armour, as we are told, must have been introduced by the "tunic-trailing Ionians." Yet these Ionians, or any Greeks of the eighth to seventh centuries, in their art are represented as wearing loin-cloths, bathing-drawers, or curt tight jerkins needing not to be girdled up, except in cases of reverend seignors, in a house of repose, and at festivals. (See fig. 1.)

Fig. 1.—Sacrifice to Athene—B.F. Archaic Vase-Painting

One or other or all of the tight curt men's garments—loin-cloth, bathing-drawers, or jerkin, reaching from the shoulders to just below the buttocks—was called in Ionia the cypassis, a term as much unknown to Homer as the article itself.

The κυπυσσις is mentioned by Alcaeus (611 B.C.) and prayed for by Hipponax, an Ephesian poet contemporary with Croesus: in art we find it represented from the eighth to the sixth century.[114] Such a dress, with a very broad belt, is a male costume common for archers and men at work, in the Assyrian art of the eighth to seventh centuries and in Aztec art![115]

It is a good dress for fighting men; its fashion changes, and finally it divides down the front, below the belt, with embroidered borders, in Assyrian and archaic Greek art. In some cases it does not suffice for decency. This is not the Homeric chiton, especially if that reached to the feet, and needed to be girdled when a man went

---

[113] Walters, History of Ancient Pottery, vol. ii. p. 200.

[114] See Studniczka, Geschichte der altgriechischen Tracht, p. 21, and notes.

[115] See Layard, Monuments, in many plates.

about active work. At peaceful festivals, Ionians wore the "trailing chiton," in active life the un-Homeric tight curt garment.

We may understand, I think, that between the age when the Homeric poems were composed, and the eighth century B.C., men's costume had greatly altered. The Homeric chiton did not cease to exist, but it was worn by men merely on festive occasions, and by old men; while the dress in active life reverted towards the Aegean costume, the bathing-drawers, or even loin-cloth; or more usually became the short tight jersey, covering the trunk and the upper part of the thigh. This is a natural reversion. The Achaean invaders from the colder north had practically worn smock and plaid, chiton and chlaina. In the warmer south they found the tight and curt cypassis more suitable. In the sixth to fifth century the chiton gradually reasserts itself, as we see in the late black figure, and still more manifestly in the red figure vases. The chiton is a more graceful, decent, and civilised dress than the short tight cypassis.

Either this was the course of evolution, or "late" poets inserted the chiton as worn both in peace and war into every part of the Iliad and Odyssey; though, in fact, they saw only old men, or men on formal occasions, wearing the chiton. Or they applied the word "chiton," in poetry, to the tight curt garments which were not in the least like the chiton of Homer.

The alternative explanation is that Homer's men actually wore the fairly long smock which needed to be girdled up for active work; and that the word and the thing itself survived in the poems through an age when men in general wore the tight curt jerkin, or even the loin-cloth or bathing-drawers.

The chlaina of the Homeric men was a mantle, usually of wool, fastened with a golden fibula, like that of Odysseus. On the cover of the pin was represented to the life a hound catching a fawn.[116] This chlaina was red in colour and was double-folded. The great overgarment, the pharos, was usually of linen; and both these articles were unshaped and unsewn, mere pieces of material, also used for blankets in bed.

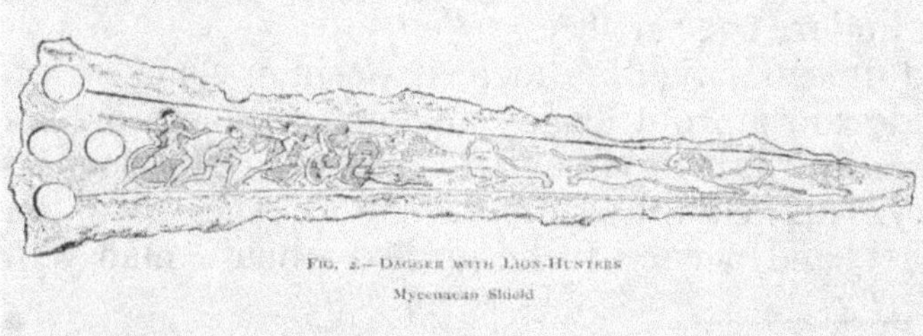

Fig. 2.—Dagger with Lion Hunters—Mycenaean Shield

However we account for it,

[116] Odyssey, cxix, 225 et seqq.

there was a long period in which Greek prehistoric and proto-historic dress was not the free-flowing costume which Homer describes, and which the appearance of safety pins, or fibulae, after 1400 B.C. attests. They are but rarely found in graves till the Dipylon age of Iron.

Now no critic has had the heart to say that the costume described by Homer, the loose chiton, was "written into" early epic lays (which originally knew it not), at the moment when it came into fashion in the sixth to fifth centuries. But criticism has taken a similar course in regard to Homeric armour. This armour, like Homeric male costume, is in essence, we shall show, that of the sixth to fifth centuries B.C. with the exception of the shield,—a huge body-covering shield in Homer (a shield probably of various shapes, circular, oblong, cylindrical or like a figure of 8),[117] suspended by a baldric (see fig. 2),—while in the seventh to fifth centuries we find a round or oval blazoned buckler worn on the left arm. While critics, following Reich el, attribute the Homeric body armour to Ionian interpolations of the seventh century, they have also followed him in not observing that Homeric body armour is not that of the seventh, but rather of the sixth to fifth centuries, as we shall prove.

We find, in art of the sixth to fifth centuries, or at least in the end of the sixth and the opening of the fifth centuries, such hauberks as Homer describes; they have variegated patterns of bronze scales; they are clasped down the front, and below are the bronze belt (zoster) and πτέρυγες, or mailed flaps.

On the other hand, the Ionic corslet of the seventh and earlier sixth century is made of plain plates of bronze, fastened at the sides—back-plate and breastplate—with a short projecting metallic rim to protect the hip-joints. There is no mailed kirtle, no decorated belt. The whole equipment, with the addition of mailed flaps to the plain corslet, is well rendered on a scaraboid gem.[118] In fact, this kind of plain corslet, with back-plate and breast-plate, fastened at the sides, is the regular Ionian or seventh to sixth century body armour, while the hauberk, of metal scales, or small plates, probably fixed on leather, begins to come in towards the end of the sixth century. Early in the fifth century, Polygnotus decorated the Lesche or lounge at Delphi with pictures of the Trojan affairs, mainly illustrating the Little Iliad, an Ionian cyclic poem attributed to Lesches. Among the pictures, says Pausanias, was represented an altar, and on it was a "bronze corslet, such as was worn of old, for now we seldom see them. It consisted of two pieces called guala, one

[117] See three sorts on the dagger from a tomb in the Mycenaean acropolis.
[118] Catalogue of British Museum Gems, 1888, No. 294.

to cover breast and belly, the other for the back, fastened by clasps." Unconsciously anticipating Reichel, Pausanias says that this piece of armour would be protection enough, "without a shield," as if a shield could simultaneously protect both back and front. "And so Homer represents Phorcys the Phrygian without a shield,"[119] "because he wore this kind of corslet."[120] Homer says that the spear of Aias burst the gualon of Phorcys, and the bronze let out the entrails.[121] The shield of Phorcys, if he wore one, must have been slung over his back or side at the moment. But in these two passages Homer seems to have in his mind a corslet of but two guala, back-plate and breast-plate fastened at the sides, like the eighth to sixth century corslet. If so, he knew both the corslet of two plates, fastened at the sides, and also the hauberk of scales or small plates of metal fastened in the centre of front and back. This is not impossible, for, as we shall prove, the corslet of metal plate was worn even in pre-Homeric Crete; while the hauberk is represented, if I am right, in art of the Dipylon, or pre-Dipylon period. Art in the late sixth century proves that both the corslet of back-plate and breast-plate, and the hauberk of small plates, fastening at back and in front, were worn.

Fig. 3.—Tirynthian Vase: Man in Hauberk

We have some red figure vases with the plain plate corslet, and some black figure vases with the decorated corslet or rather hauberk of scales, and mailed flaps; but the set of fashion is away from the plain plate corslet fastened at the sides, to the decorative hauberk of scale-mail, fastening in front,—Homer's type of corslet (at least in some cases), and the corslet of two very early Tirynthian vases.

As far as we can trust such crude art[122] (fig. 3), the Tirynthian body-covering was a jack or jaseran of rings or scales, probably fastened on leather, not the back-plate and breast-plate of the

---

[119] Iliad, xvii. 312-315.

[120] Pausanias, x. 26.

[121] So, too, Iliad, xiii. 507, 508.

[122] Schliemann, Tiryns, plate xvii. b.

eighth to early sixth centuries. Why, before the Persian war, Greek warriors adopted the hauberk of scale-armour in place of the back-plate and breast-plate, is unknown; probably it was borrowed from the late Assyrian hauberk of scales, of which many examples occur in Layard's Monuments. Judging from the later black figure vases, the process was gradual; some warriors wear the old back-plate, breast-plate, and jutting rim of metal; some the scaled hauberk, shoulder pieces, and plated πτέρυγες, or flaps, with or without the bronze girdle or zoster of Homer. A number of the scales, iron or bronze, of the hauberks have been found in the palace of the Egyptian king Apries, of the first part of the sixth century.

In archaic art, and in early sixth century black figure vases, the warrior wears the tight, un-Homeric, cypassis under his corslet. In later black figure vases, he wears the fluttering tails of his flowing Homeric chiton under his mailed kirtle. Thus the dress of men, in Homer, and the armour, in cases to be proved, are like those of the later sixth and early fifth centuries, rather than of the eighth to early sixth centuries.

Yet modern criticism, while it finds no fault with the sixth to fifth century costume of Homer's men, excises their sixth century hauberks, clasping down the middle, their zoster, or mailed girdle, their mitre, which served the purpose of the sixth to fifth century mailed flaps or mailed kirtle, and their greaves, as Ionian interpolations of the seventh century. We shall show that the back-plate and breast-plate of the seventh century are not the hauberk, clasping down the middle, of some passages in Homer; and that the jutting bronze rim of the seventh century is not the mitrê of Homer. Thus, if there were late interpolations of armour into Homer, they cannot have been made, as Reichel thought, in the seventh century, but very late, say 540-470 B.C., when armour shifted from bronze back-plate, breast-plate, and rim, to scaled hauberk, shoulder pieces, zoster, and metal plated flaps, equivalent in protective purpose to the mitrê.

The modern theory that Homeric armour is of the seventh century, which it demonstrably is not, starts from the late Dr. Reichel's essay on Homeric armour.[123] Reichel built on very slender and sandy foundations. He supposed that in the oldest parts of the Epics men fought in battle as six or seven men, in Aegean art, fight in chance encounters (that is, almost naked, or with shields which conceal the body, also taken for granted as naked). He did not know the proof of the existence of Aegean body armour, which we shall cite, and he really evolved things "out of his inner consciousness."

---

[123] Homerische Waffen, 2nd edition, Vienna, 1901.

Reichel, we must add, could not argue securely from the absence of actual corslets in grave-furniture of the Aegean age. Though hauberks occur constantly in the art, they are not found in the graves of the sixth to fifth centuries, in Greece; and even plate corslets are extremely rare. In Reichel's second edition, which he, unfortunately, left incomplete at his regretted death, "he contemplated an important change of ground.... He regards the thin gold plates found on the breasts of the skeletons at Mykene as possibly the funereal representatives of metal sewn on to the chiton, and thus forming a prae-Ionic corslet."[124]

Had he lived, he would have seen an undeniable "prae-Ionic corslet," no hauberk but a cuirass of plate, on the Minoan seal impressions of Haghia Triada.

But the evidence for the non-existence of prae-Ionic corslets based on their absence from tombs, even if it were absolute, which it is not, would have been of little avail. How many Ionic plate corslets are in actual existence, to our knowledge? Only fragments of one, as far as I am aware, and that one is not "Ionic," it was found at Olympia, and is "archaic." The fragments are of bronze plate, with decorations in the archaic style, figures of men and women in archaic costume.[125] Thus the non-existence of objects represented often in the art of remote ages cannot be demonstrated by our failure to discover specimens of them.

Reichel proceeds from the imaginary postulate that a man who has a body-covering shield dispenses with body armour. As a matter of historical fact he often does not.[126] Next, the Aegean shield, being heavy, made chariots necessary. (But chariots have been used in war by races with small shields, and the great shield is worn by Aias and Odysseus who had no chariots.) Next, says Reichel, parrying bucklers coming in as early as the archaic art (say 700-620 B.C.), big shields went out, and for protection the corslet, metal girdle, and mitrê, a mailed kirtle, were adopted about 700 B.C. As it was now ridiculous, says Reichel, to think of a man fighting only in his shirt, late poets introduced body armour into old portions of the Iliad, made when body armour was unknown.

Of course, by parity of reasoning, the new poets ought also to have got rid of chariots, bronze weapons, cairn-burial, the bride-price, Homeric chitons, and so forth, all of them obsolete or little used things in the age (700-600 B.C.) of corslets, greaves, and body

---

124 Leaf, Iliad, vol. ii. p. 629.

125 I have seen another archaic bronze plate corslet, with engraved designs, but do not know where it now is.

126 See Note to this chapter, "Shield and Body Armour."

armour. Their warriors should also have worn the contemporary tight fleshings, with the cypassis, and parameridia, cuisses, tight thigh pieces (the "taslets" of 1640 A.D.). That did not happen; Homer knows no thigh pieces or parameridia, so common in Greek armour of the sixth century; but, says Mr. Murray, "all the heroes were summarily provided with breast-plates, θώρηκες."[127] Mr. Leaf, on the other hand, denies this; "the corslet is given to some only, and that in the most capricious fashion."[128]

Mr. Leaf's contention (Mr. Murray's is an obiter dictum) rests on the postulate that, when the corslet is not explicitly named in connection with a hero, he has no corslet; he has only a shield. If so, why are his "pieces of armour" (τεύχεα), whether he is putting them on or off, whether he is being stripped of them or is stripping others, always called τεύχεα in the plural? Aias is not explicitly said to have a corslet, but the space of time occupied by his arming he asks the Achaeans to devote to prayer to Zeus. "So said they, while Aias arrayed him in flashing bronze. And when he had now clothed upon his flesh all his armour...."[129] The time required, and the phrase "all his armour" which "clothes his flesh," cannot possibly apply to slinging on or off a shield, and donning or doffing a helmet, the work of five seconds. The sword was always worn, in peace and in war.

This is so certain that we waste no more space over the matter. All the gentry wear τεύχεα, "pieces of armour," which they all take off and lay on the ground while they watch a duel, and which they always, when they can, strip from a fallen foe. Thus, before the duel between Paris and Menelaus, the men-at-arms dismount, take off their armour, and lay it on the ground.[130] They themselves "are leaning on their great shields," which are not their armour.[131] This use of τεύχεα is universal in Homer, and so, for men-at-arms, is the possession of body armour.[132]

---

[127] R. G. E. p. 143.

[128] Iliad, vol. i. p. 576.

[129] Ibid. vii. 206-209. Mr. Leaf's translation, 1906, p. 134.

[130] Iliad, iii. 114, 115.

[131] iii. 134, 135.

[132] Against this opinion may be cited Odyssey, xxii. 108-114, where the only protective armour used by the men of Odysseus is helmets and shields, yet the formulae of "doing on bronze over the flesh," and "donning the fair pieces of armour" are employed. To myself it may seem that these are epic formulae which arose in a period of corslets but are used where no corslets were being worn, in the fight with the Wooers. Mr. Murray, however, takes the absence of specific mention of corslets in the Odyssey generally as a proof of his theory that "the Odyssey has been altogether less worked over,

The difficulties which critics find in the details and mechanism of the armour cannot be impossibilities, for the "later poets" were familiar with corslets, and would not write nonsense about them. The opposing theory is that Ionian minstrels introduced the corslet of their own age, seventh century, (corslets not uniformly to be found in Homer), to satisfy the practical warriors who wore it. Yet, in doing so, the poets made incoherent nonsense. As Miss Stawell writes, "a warlike audience, versed in the use of the corslet, insisted on its introduction in the poems,—and yet never objected to the absurdities it introduced,—such a theory cannot bear thinking out."[133] When we came to discuss Homeric tactics, we found precisely the same objection to the German theories; they represent the poets as pleasing military experts by writing nonsense.

The body armour is thus an integral part of the poem. The word θωρήσσεσθαι, to put on the thorex or breast covering, is constantly employed in the general sense of arming, both in Iliad and Odyssey, though in the latter no corslet is specifically named. It would have been as easy to coin a verb for arming from ἀσπὶς, the shield, in an age when shields were the only armour. That θώρηξ should ever have been a term for the shield seems to me incredible.

The corslet has many epithets, expressing the elaborateness of its decoration, such as ποικίλος, παναίολος, πολυδαίδαλος; and no such words apply to the plain metal plates of corslets in archaic Greek art of the eighth to early sixth centuries, as shown in art. At most they were etched with designs of men and women, as in the example from Olympia, or have two volutes. The corslet was made of γύαλα whatever they may have precisely been, for sometimes the epithets applied to the Homeric corslet do not suit plate but mailed armour.

---

expurgated, and modernised than what books still persist in calling without qualification 'the older poem'" (R. G. E. pp. 145, 146). Here he has to discover why the Odyssey, according to critics, has (in his view) been "worked over and modernised" as regards the house and the bride-price, while in a few fighting passages the warriors are left in the supposed state of Aegean nakedness, save for the shield, which, unlike Mycenaean shields, has a bronze plating, as in the Iliad. Mr. Murray (R. G. E. p. 137, note 1) grants that armour of bronze "may have been, in some elements, a revival of something long forgotten...." but was still unaware that the seals of Haghia Triada

[133] Homer and the Iliad, p. 212.

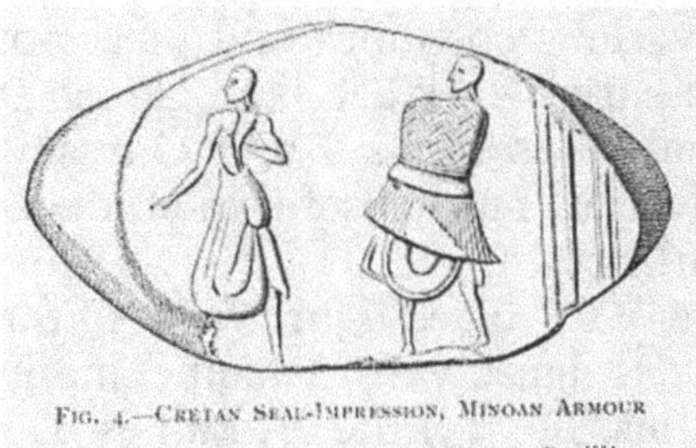
FIG. 4.—CRETAN SEAL-IMPRESSION, MINOAN ARMOUR
From the *Annual of the British School at Athens, No. XII.*
(*Macmillan & Co. Ltd.*)

Fig. 4.—Cretan Seal-impression, Minoan Armour.

Reichel argued from the absence of corslet, belt, greaves, and mailed kirtle in the few pieces of Aegean art known to him, that no such armour was used by Aegeans, and, again, that no such armour was known to the Achaeans. He was unacquainted with the scores of seal impressions which have been found at Haghia Triada in Crete.[134] The seals, it has been said, show a man in what Dr. Halbherr recognises as a heavy decorated plate corslet, with an obviously metallic belt, and below it a mailed kilt or apron, the Homeric mitrê. Dr. Mackenzie, too, recognises the armour.[135] It is unmistakable, and the corslet is so very wide, considering the wasp-like Mycenaean waist, that a spear could penetrate the side of it without wounding the wearer, a great puzzle of the critics when the fact occurs in Homer. (See fig. 4 A).

The armour is out of drawing, the man's head is given in profile, his armour is given full face. The same error is made by the painter of Menelaus fighting Hector on an archaic dish from Camirus. Euphorbus is lying on his back, but his corslet is given in full face, while his head is in profile (fig. 5). This is common in archaic Greek art. The arms of the man on the seal are not shown, just as the arms of women on some Laconian figurines are omitted.[136] There also occurs on the vase of Haghia Triada, a jovial figure in a very loose thick piece of armour, as some hold,[137] or "a Minoan cope," as others maintain. Beneath it is a short jutting ribbed kirtle, as in the seal. I am unable to decide between cope and cuirass in this instance,[138] but the bosses appear to be of hard material.

---

134 Monumenti Antichi, vol. xiii., 1903, pp. 42, 114.
135 B. S. A., vol. xii. p. opposite plate A.
136 Ibid.., vol. xiv., plate vii. A.
137 Savignoni, Mon. Ant., 1903, p. 114.
138 When disposing, in sixteen lines (R. G. E. 154, note I), of my Homer and his Age, Mr. Murray oddly represents me as maintaining that the body armour of Paris and Hector was "soft and very baggy like a Minoan cope." As at that time I had never consciously heard of this famous "Minoan cope," I never dreamed of such a thing as "soft and very baggy" armour in the Iliad, though I know the Protestant silk armour during "the Popish Plot." In fact, judging from the designs in Monumenti Antichi, the Minoan cope was of hard material.

An easy mode of comparing various costumes and pieces of armour as illustrated in archaic and early Greek art, is to glance at Engelmann and Anderson's Pictorial Atlas of Iliad and Odyssey, 1895. It is prior to the Cretan discoveries, but is useful to students remote from collections of Greek works of art.

We shall first take the evidence of the black figure vases of the sixth century, and then that of the red figure vases which came in near the end of that age. In one (Atlas, fig. 43) the armour is of a sort more common by far in red figure vases. The corslet of a warrior has broad shoulder pieces, and is decorated with three stars, like "the decorated starry corslet" of Achilles.[139] These stars appear on an Assyrian corslet in Layard's Monuments. There is a belt and a mailed kirtle or mailed flaps; below appears the tight cypassis, not the flowing chiton.

Next, in a Corinthian black figure vase (Atlas, fig. 45) the charioteer wears the plain corslet of two plates with projecting rim (no zoster and mitrê); the dress is a tight jerkin. The women wear large mantles over what appear to be long tight-fitting chitons. In "Carving Meat" the cook and his servant wear the tight cypassis (fig. 51). In three combats (figs. 63, 64, 65) the warriors wear the cypassis, or are naked (65), but (64) one has the plate corslet with projecting rim. In the well-known archaic pyxis from Camirus (see fig. 5), Menelaus, Hector, and Euphorbus wear, over the cypassis, plain corslets, with a hatched projecting rim.

In "Death of Antilochus" (Part II. fig. 15) the plain plate corslet is worn over the flowing chiton, there is no mailed kirtle and belt. In the "Death of Achilles" (fig. 14) we have the plain corslet over the cypassis. In "Departure of Amphiaraus" the hero wears the plain plate corslet, and no mailed kirtle (fig. 73).

So much for these black figure vases. The older they are, the more they favour the plain plate corslet fastened at the sides, and the cypassis; and the less they favour the decorated hauberk, mailed kirtle, and free flowing chiton. But the two styles overlap.

In the later red figure vases, the plain corslet sometimes occurs, but the vast majority show the flowing chiton, under the

---

Messrs. Hogarth and Bosanquet also report on "a very remarkable 'Mycenaean' bronze breast-plate" from Crete, which "shows four female draped figures, the two central are holding a wreath over a bird, below which is a sacred tree. The two outer figures are dancing. It is probably a ritual scene, and may help to elucidate the nature of early Aegean cults, in which female worshippers and sacred trees and birds are common." J. H. S., vol. xix., 1899, p. 322.

[139] Iliad, xvi. 134.

richly variegated hauberk of mail, clasping in front, and having broad shoulder plates coming over from behind and fastened in front; with the plated flaps, and below them the flowing chiton, as a general rule. It is this later style, or something very like it, that Homer usually describes.

Fig. 5.—Menelaus and Hector fighting over Euphorbus
Vase-Painting from Camirus, Rhodes, in British Museum

Fig. 5—Menelaus and Hector fighting over Euphorbus Vase-painting from Camirus, Rhodes

If the armour was written into the poem late, if in the earliest lays the men wore no armour but the shield, the change to hauberk, zoster, and plated flaps was made by late poets about the end of the sixth century or the beginning of the fifth, but the old huge shield with baldric was left unchanged. Meanwhile, as the tight cypassis scarcely reaching below the buttocks is the usual warrior's costume of the seventh to early or mid-sixth century, the loose chiton, like the variegated hauberk,—the chiton being "a loosely fitting garment, reaching apparently as low as the knees, but gathered up into the belt for active exertion,"[140]—must also have been interpolated into the poems about the middle of the sixth century, when the cypassis was beginning to go out of favour.

It is strange that these facts—the seventh century armour and costume are un-Homeric (though we cannot prove that Homer knew only the hauberk clasped in front), the sixth to fifth century armour and costume answer closely to Homeric descriptions—have not been observed either by Reichel or his English following. Nor do they notice that the thigh pieces of seventh to sixth century art never occur in Homer, as, on the Reichelian theory, they ought to do; practical warriors would expect to hear of them from the late minstrels. We now prove Homer's knowledge of the hauberk, clasped at front and back.

There is a passage in the Iliad (iv. 132-140) which vexes critics; we give it in Mr. Leaf's translation. To ruin the Trojans, Athene makes Pandarus break the oath of truce, and shoot at Menelaus. She then guides the arrow so that it may merely draw

140 Leaf, Iliad, vol. i. p. 580, citing Studniczka, p. 59.

blood. "Her own hand guided it where the golden buckles of the belt were clasped and the doubled breast-plate met them. So the bitter arrow lighted (ἔπεσε) upon the firm belt; through the inwrought (δαιδαλέοιο) belt it sped, and through the curiously wrought breast-plate it pressed on, and through the taslet"[141] (μίτρη, plated kirtle) "he wore to shield his flesh, a barrier against darts; and this best shielded him, yet it passed on even through this," and drew blood.

The arrow-head was of iron, not bronze, as was usual, and of a primitive pattern, inserted into the wood of the shaft, and "whipped" with sinew (νεῦρον, Iliad, iv. 151). When the arrow is extracted (line 216) the corslet is not mentioned, as I suppose because the arrow passed through the place where the corslet clasped in front. When the corslet was unclasped, the arrow had only to be pulled out of the belt and kirtle.

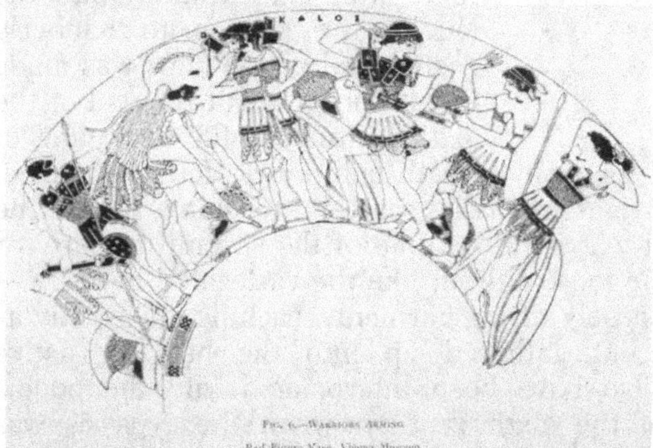

Fig. 6.—Warriors arming
Red Figure Vase, Vienna Museum

Now the whole passage is explained by a red figure vase in the Vienna Museum (Atlas, figs. 71 a, b, c) (fig. 6). Here we see first, a warrior in helmet and flowing chiton, putting on his greaves. Next him is a warrior clasping his variegated hauberk of scales, or small plates, in front, above his mailed kirtle, or flaps; below which floats the lower part of his chiton; the shoulder-plates of his corslet are still unclasped, and stand up behind his shoulders. For this arrangement see also Walters, History of Ancient Pottery, vol. ii. p. 176, fig. 137. In Iliad, xx. 413-417, Achilles sends his spear through the clasping plate of belt, buckle, and hauberk at the back.

In the third picture (fig. 7), a warrior, fully armed, has his hand in the richly adorned belt (zoster) which he is fixing over the juncture of corslet and mailed kirtle. If an arrow lights on the central clasp of this belt (1) it will pass through the meeting-place in front of his corslet, (2) and then will encounter, especially if it be a

---

[141] The "taslets" of Dugald Dalgetty (1645) were thigh pieces (cuisses), as in seventh to sixth century Greek art.

dropping arrow, (3) his mailed flaps or kirtle, exactly as in the case of Menelaus.[142] Nothing of this kind could occur with the plain plate corslets of the seventh to sixth centuries, which laced at the sides, and had no mailed kirtle or flaps, and no belt or zoster. Thus Homer's armour, in this passage, is precisely that of, say, 520-470 B.C. Meanwhile the arrow-head, whipped with sinew into the wooden shaft, is of a primitive pattern; and the accompanying reference to the art of Maeonian and Carian women, in staining ivory red, "a treasure for a king," shows no notion of the Ionians in Maeonia and Caria, or of the republics of 510-470 B.C.[143]

If, then, in the late sixth or early fifth century, a poet introduced the latest type of armour, he also preserved the primitive arrow, and the political and geographical conditions prior to the Ionian settlements in Asia. This combined innovation and conservatism are incredible.[144]

The general conclusion seems to be that there was, in men's dress and armour, a break of several centuries during which un-Homeric costume and armour existed, and that—about the time just preceding the Persian wars and later—Greece reverted to the Homeric types or men's dress and body armour, while the Homeric shield was never revived. It was invented as an umbrella against

---

[142] I had written this before the publication of Miss Stawell's Homer and the Iliad. In pp. 204-206, she has taken the word out of my mouth.

[143] Iliad, iv. 141-144.

[144] On the affair of Menelaus, see Leaf, vol. i. p. 581, and note I, where Mr. Leaf thinks the clasping of the corslet in front "an unreasonable arrangement." Mr. Murray (R. G. E. pp. 144, 145) also takes it that there was "a solid metal breast-plate." The term γύαλον (Iliad, v. 99), where an arrow hits "hard by Diomede's right shoulder the plate of his corslet," may refer to the broad plate over the shoulder-strap; some of the corslets of two metal plates have shoulder-straps in art. We really cannot expect to understand every detail with certainty, while we have no actual examples of the corslets and shields of many early centuries before our eyes. Mr. Ridgeway believes the body armour of the Achaeans to have been hauberks of bronze scales or small plates, not back-and breast-plates as in seventh and early sixth century art. He illustrates by many bronze studs found at Koracev and Ilijak in Bosnia, of the Glasinatz epoch (Early Age of Greece, vol. i. pp. 435, 436). Such a hauberk would well correspond to that worn by "the bronze-shirted Achaeans." The hauberk would be "a shirt of leather," with "small pieces of bronze, either in the form of studs, or scales, or rings, or by the addition of plates of larger size" (Ibid. p. 310). The hauberk made of metal studs on leather seems to be illustrated in Schliemann's copy of a man on a very old vase from Tiryns, of a style apparently earlier than the art of the Dipylon (Schliemann, Tiryns, plate xvii.).

arrows in far off days, when the bow, rather than the spear, was the chief weapon of attack, when arrow-heads were of stone; and it went out when glory was only to be won at close quarters.

Why the plain plate corslet tended to go out, about the time of the Persian war, while the flimsy but highly decorated mail hauberk came in, a mere jascran, it is not easy to conjecture; but probably the hauberk was adapted from Assyrian and Egyptian armour of the period. The jaseran went out again, and the plate corslets of our Museums came in again, in the fifth to fourth centuries.

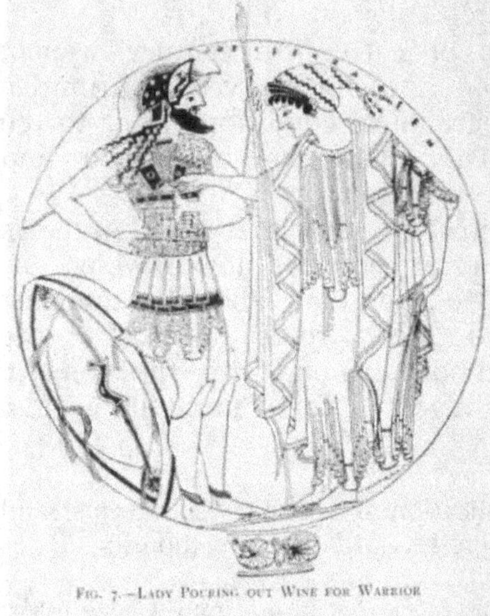

Fig. 7.—Lady Pouring out Wine for Warrior
R. F. Vase-Painting by Duris, in Vienna

It is manifestly open to critics to argue that Homeric armour never existed, in Greece, before the sixth to fifth centuries, and that it was then interpolated into the Epics. But if they say this, must they not apply the same argument to Homeric costume, loose and free flowing? Was that attire also interpolated into the poems at the date when it first appears in art? Or are we to say that the artists who represent it were "archaising," were making a guess at what the costume of the heroic age might have been?

This cannot be, for the dress is the historic Greek costume which they then wore. As Panathenaic vases maintained archaic costume long out of date, I have not appealed to their evidence as to costume and armour, but have relied on other vases,—on a vase from Sparta with warriors rendered in relief,[145] on a gem cited, on a remarkable bronze in the British Museum of a mounted man, and so forth.[146]

I cannot say that Homer always has hauberks, not corslets of back-plate and breast-plate in his mind. The two passages in which the front gualon is pierced over the belly, look as if Homer knew both corslet and hauberk. On the other hand, the epithets of the

---

145 Frontispiece.
146 B. S. A., vol. xii., plate A.

corslet commonly used, ποικίλος, παναίολος, πολυδαίδαλος, suit the hauberk, not the plain back-plate and breast-plate, as may be seen by looking at both kinds of armour as illustrated on countless vases, while the zoster and mitrê are common in Homer, and were never worn, as far as art shows, with the Ionian back-plate and breast-plate, though they both appear with the plate cuirass on the seal impressions of Haghia Triada.

NOTE

Body-covering shield with corslet.—Reichel's argument is that a man with a body-covering needs no corslet. I have shown (Homer and His Age, pp. 132-136) that warriors of the eleventh century A.D. and later employed the great shield reaching from neck to ankles, and also wore breast-plates. Again, Champlain (Les Voyages de M. de Champlain, Paris, 1620; Dix's Champlain, p. 113, New York, 1903; Laverdière's Champlain, vol. iv., 1870, opposite p. 85) shows Algonquins with shields cylindrical and covering the body from neck to feet, while both Champlain and modern authors, especially Mr. Hill-Tout, describe North American corslets of various materials, hide, wood, wicker-work, and copper, "the last armour was everywhere used," in addition to the great shields. For the eleventh to twelfth century of our era, see La Chancun de Willame, 716-726.

Reichel's argument against the combination of huge shield with corslet is thus historically valueless, though "the ancient Celts used no defensive armour but the long shield, and fought from chariots."[147]

If we only look at the Celts, Reichel seems justified, but we look also at the North Americans and at mediaeval Europe. Down to 1424, the fighting man in full body armour used large shields in attacking fortified positions se couvrant de sa targecte pour doubte des pierres. (D'Aulon, in Procès de Jeanne d'Arc, vol. iii. p. 216).

---

147 Leaf, Iliad, vol. i. p. 573, note I, citing M. d'Arbois de Jubainville, La Civilisation des Celtes et celle de l'Epopée Homerique, p. 349, Paris, 1899.

CHAPTER IX

WOMEN'S COSTUME

As to the evolution of feminine costume, I speak with the greatest diffidence. Homer's women wore the loose brooched peplos, with brooch, pin, clasp, and over it the pharos. Women of the later dark age and the Dipylon period apparently dressed otherwise. In the archaic period the brooched peplos, girdled at the waist, was worn; but I think that there was also a revival or survival of Aegean sewn and shaped bodices, jackets, and skirts. Lastly, historic Greece reverted to the Homeric peplos and chlaina.

The discussion is, inevitably, concerned with minutiae in details about which our actual information is far from being minute. We must therefore state here explicitly the conclusions to which we are led: namely, that neither the male nor female dress nor the armour described in the Epics was introduced, at any period, by the Ionians employed in any one of the four or five "recensions" which are postulated by certain critics, as in the "first Iliad" of Robert, and his "second, third, and fourth Iliads"[148] On the other hand, we contend that both the costume and the armour in Homer are of a single period, earlier than the Dipylon and barbaric Tirynthian age of art, while historic Greece from the middle of the sixth century began to revert to something like the Homeric type.

We must remember that hitherto no representations of Homer's people in the free art of the Aegeans have been discovered, and thence no light can be derived. When the crude art of Tiryns and, later (?) of the "Geometric" school of ornament comes into view (1000-800 B.C.?), the designs of men and women are childish. In painted vases which may represent the palsied decadence of the Aegean age, the human figures are simply absurd, still they are recognisably human; though in vases of what may be called the "dotted" style of outline, they have heads like birds, as on dotted bronzes of northern Italy in the Early Age of Iron. In the "Dipylon" style, again, as soon as human beings are represented, the heads of the men are like potatoes set on sticks; the torso is an inverted isosceles triangle, with the pointed waist for apex; and the naked legs are enormously thick in thighs and calves. The women's bodies also are often equilateral triangles; the parts below the waist are clothed in tight skirts, as a general rule; the breasts, when the bust

[148] Studien zur Ilias, von Carl Robert, Berlin, 1901.

is represented, are either bare, or clad in a very tight bodice, or are hidden by a hood which falls below the shoulders like a cape. In one Tirynthian fragment we see a stout lady in a "princess frock" tight, "of the Menzies tartan,"[149] and all of one piece; another design shows a waist no thicker than a broomstick[150] (figs. 8, 9). These costumes of women, in Tirynthian and Dipylon art, are un-Homeric and post-Homeric. I doubt if we find such female costumes as Homer apparently describes recognisably represented in Greek art till the sixth and fifth centuries.

Fig. 8—Princess Frock: Tiryns.

This seems to be stated with unnecessary force, because, it may well be said, the meaning of the sentence turns on the words "recognisably represented." How are we to "recognise," in art, costumes of which Homer gives us only brief verbal descriptions? Are we not deceived by the free and vivid style of Homer? All his human beings and gods come in such living forms before us, that we see the flowing, glistening garments of Nausicaa and Athene swaying with their motions. We can see nothing like this represented in Greek art till the late sixth century and onwards; because, it may be said, till that date Greek art is hard, prim, constrained, conventional,—in fact, archaic. It is therefore, we may be told, a kind of logical illusion which prevents us from recognising the costumes of Homer's women in Greek plastic art, till that art itself is beginning to attain Homeric freedom.

These considerations must be kept in mind. But another error is apt to be suggested when we read that the historic Hellenic costume, or that part of it styled "the Doric peplos," "is implied by the allusions of Homer," the view of the ingenious Studniczka.[151]

---

[149] The Menzies tartan is of white and pink checks, which the artist renders lovingly.

[150] Schliemann, Tiryns, plate xvii. Studniczka, Altgr. Tracht.

[151] Leaf, Iliad, vol. ii. p. 596.

The remark is illustrated by fig. 10, in which we see a lady in "a Doric peplos," though how Achaean women of Homer's time could wear the dress of the Dorians whom Homer ignores is not apparent. This graceful and breezy costume is, in fact, like what we suppose Homer to have had in his mind, and to have seen. But it is not in the least like the dress shown in the art which is immediately subsequent to his age, the art of Tiryns and of the Dipylon; and, as far as I can ascertain, it is not the costume displayed in the archaic art up to the middle of the sixth century. Archaic Greek female costume, however, has this much in common with Homeric and later Greek costume, that it essentially differs, often, from Aegean or Mycenaean dress.

In describing the contrast of styles between the pre-Homeric Aegean dress and the Homeric costume for women, Mr. Leaf says that the Mykenaean (Aegean) women wore "a close fitting bodice, sharply marked off from the full skirt..."; and though there were many changes of fashion in the Aegean world, this account holds good for its later periods. "The dress of Greek women in historic times is of a totally different kind. It is marked by simplicity and flowing vertical lines.... The peplos is, in fact, no more than a square woollen blanket ... taken up round the middle by a girdle and retained in its place on the shoulders by pins." The Aegean female dress, sewn and fitted, did not need pins or brooches, περόναι, ἐνεταί, πόρται.[152] On the other hand, "no pins or fibulae have been found among the remains of the Mykenaean prime," while they are common in the latter "lower city" below the acropolis of Mycenae.

Mr. Leaf therefore conceives that "during the prime of Mykene fashion was dominated by a non-Hellenic influence," perhaps Oriental. Bodices and separate flounced skirts were in, "but for some reason which we cannot expect to guess, fashion returned, at the end of the Mykenaean age, to the older and simpler dress" (the Homeric), "which held its ground till classical times."[153] The usual explanation is that the fibulae and the pinned peplos were brought in from the north by Achaean invaders; in the north the fibulae had long been common;[154] and that the style of costume persisted continuously into historic times, being the familiar classical Greek dress.

---

[152] Iliad, v. 425, xiv. 180, xviii. 401.

[153] Leaf, Iliad, vol. ii. pp. 595-598.

[154] Ridgeway, Early Age of Greece, vol. i. pp. 553-577.

Fig. 9—Costume of Women—Tirynthian Vase.

Now undoubtedly the fibula, and therefore the unsewn and unshaped female attire, did come in at the close of the Aegean or Mycenaean period in Greece; but, as far as I can interpret the art of very old Tirynthian and some Dipylon vases, there was an early post-Homeric period wherein women adopted the short hood-capes, the tight waists, the heavy skirts, and the princess frock.[155] This attire more resembles the Aegean than the Homeric and Hellenic. The "hood-cape" of Tirynthian art may conceivably be the κρήδεμνον, καλύπτρα or κάλυμμα of Homer; but if so, it reveals below it a waist of more than Aegean tightness, not the belted peplos. Such are the characteristics of Dipylon art, and of Tirynthian art which may have arisen before 900 B.C. It is hardly possible that if, in that age, women wore the loose Homeric peplos, the artists should have represented them with impossibly narrow waists, with the bosom fully displayed, and with heavy skirts. The women of this dark age, as far as art can enlighten us, had broken away from, or at all events are not wearing, the Homeric peplos.

This is, at least, my private interpretation of the Dipylon and the Tirynthian representation. But it is offered with diffidence, and is not shared by Mr. R. M. Dawkins, the Director of the British School of Athens. He "does not believe that the Dipylon women's dress is necessarily a tight one," and attributes the wasp waists to the limited skill of the early artist, thinking that if he had to draw a woman in a loose flowing dress he would still give her a tiny waist, because a small waist is one of the conspicuous points in the female figure. In the effort to give as much information as possible he would draw the small waist even if it were concealed by a loose dress. The primitive artist draws not from models, but from mental images.

There is much truth in this; for example, the ladies in a palaeolithic rock-painting[156] have very slim waists, clearly exaggerated, above skirts with a crescentine scoop at the bottom. But the primitive artist certainly draws under the domination of a

155 Tiryns, plate xvii.

156 In northern Aragon.

convention which differs in different places. The woman whose figure is repeated in the clay disk from Phaestus[157] has no more waist than the stout person in a princess frock from Tiryns. The Dipylon artists may be continuing the Aegean convention of the wasp waist; though the designer of the princess frock is as candid as the Phaestos artist. Thus the reader must interpret the Dipylon waist as he pleases.

We next reach the "archaic" art of, say, the seventh to sixth centuries. The chief article of female dress, as described by Homer, was the peplos, "a square or rectangular piece of material which," like the men's outer mantle, "could be used for various purposes." It was fastened by pins or brooches (περόναι, ἐνεταί), and the περόνη was sometimes a fibula or safety pin, the cover adorned by art, as in the case of the περόνη of Odysseus (Od. xix.). But when (Iliad, v. 425) Athene mockingly tells Zeus that the wounded Aphrodite must have scratched her hand, while caressing some Achaean woman, on her περόνη, the term "safety pin," or fibula, does not apply. We think rather of one of the long sharp stiletto-like pins found in Egyptian deposits of from about 1450 to 1200 B.C. and also at Enkomi in Cyprus, and at Sparta in the Orthia sanctuary from 900 to 500 B.C.[158] Fibulae of the same date also occur. These great pins had ribbed handles, and below the handle was a perforation or a metallic loop.[159] Now very long pins, also with ribbed handles, but without the aperture in the middle, fasten the peplos of one of the Fates on the Francis vase, which Mr. Evans dates in "the seventh century," but Mr. Walters—from the characters in the inscriptions on the vase—dates about 570-550 B.C.[160] The Spartan evidence for the pin and fibulae covers the later range of dates.

Much turns on the date of the François vase, for many critics, with Studniczka, consider that the costume of the female figures is like that which Homer's women wear, and is a "Doric peplos." Thus Miss Abrahams, in her Greek Dress (1908, pp. 29, 30) studies the arraying of Hera.[161] Of her dress Homer says, χρυσεῖης δ' ἐνετῇσι κατὰ στῆθος περονᾶτο: "And she fastened it over her breast with clasps of gold." "We gather from this passage," says Miss Abrahams, "that the garment was fastened on the shoulders by brooches or pins inserted κατὰ στῆθος, which Studniczka rightly interprets as

157 Scripta Minoa, vol. i. p. 282.

158 B. S. A., vol. xiii. pp. no, 113.

159 Journal of the Anthrop. Institute, vol. xxx., 1900, p. 203, fig. 2. Evans on "Mycenaean Cyprus."

160 Walters, History of Ancient Pottery, vol. ii. p. 270.

161 Iliad, xiv. 175 et seqq.

'down towards the breast,' a method of fastening which is represented on the François vase and elsewhere." "The material," Miss Abrahams goes on, "is drawn from the back, and wraps over that which covers the front, the pins are then inserted downwards, and hold the two thicknesses of material together...."

Fig. 10.—Metope of Athene, Olympia.

But (see fig. 11) the pins are inserted upwards; we observe the long ribbed head of the pin, of known form like that of the 1450-1200 B.C. pins of Egypt and Enkomi, stuck into the fabric above the right breast. It penetrates the fabric, and passes upwards into a large oval shoulder piece, perhaps the tail of the piece of cloth which covers the decorated collar over the shoulder-joint. The Homeric phrase "pins inserted down towards the breast" does not indicate this mode of fastening, which is upwards from the breast. "A method practically impossible—the pin would fall out," says Mr. Dawkins. "If so, blame the artist." Neither the "overfold" (ἀπόπτυγμα) nor the curious oval piece on the shoulder-joint (perhaps a portion of the fabric) is mentioned by Homer. Again, when we read,[162] "the dress is held into the figure by a girdle worn round the waist, over which any superfluous length of material could be drawn, forming a κόλπος or pouch," we must remember that in the dress on the François vase there is no superfluous material. The dress ends just above the heels, there is no "tunic-trailing"; as in Homer. A woman who drew her dress up to form a κόλπος or pouch, would show much more of her legs than was fashionable in the archaic period, and would destroy the collant fit over the breast. The costume fits tightly to the bust; and in art of 600-550 B.C. this is the rule. We see no women "with deep κόλπος or pouch," whereas the nurse of Eumaeus could conceal three cups in her pouch. Here, again, Mr. Dawkins thinks that the limitations of the artist cause the absence of the kolpos. "He made any dress look tight, because he could only draw his idea of the body and then indicate dress on the body. The artist has two mental images, one of

[162] Greek Dress, p. 30.

the natural body and the other of the dress, and he could only carry out his work by combining the two."

But I must reply that, in the François vase, we are far from the "primitive" artist. The artist knows very well what he is about. He draws short skirts and over the bust the dress is collant, because that is the fashion. The painter no longer draws impossible waists, they are in good proportion for girls. Moreover, artists of the same period when they design a woman in a mantle do so in the modern way. The bust is indicated; the mantle does not cover it, but covers the waist, and no attempt is made to show what the artist knows is there: he does not design what is not in sight. Even an Australian black fellow drew what he saw, not what he knew was there, in sketches of white ladies.[163] We must not explain the François vase by the limitations of "primitive art."

Fig. 11.—The Fates on the François Vase
From Miss Abraham's Greek Dress

My impression is that in the eighth to seventh centuries women still did, at least occasionally, wear a costume consisting, as in Aegean times, of separate bodices and skirts. Thus in an archaic Corinthian gold jewel we see an Ariadne naked from the belt upwards, beneath is a skirt falling to the instep. Skirts were therefore separate, and imply a separate bodice, if the upper body is to be covered[164] (fig. 12).

The pouch is Homeric, but in art of 600-550 B.C. no woman, as far as I have observed, has any "superfluous length of material," or, at least, almost none draws it up through the girdle to form such a pouch as we see on Miss Abrahams's fig. 10 (Metope from the temple of Zeus at Olympia). The wearer could hide the family plate in her pouch, not so the women of the Francois vase. Such a costume cannot be called, as a rule, τανυπέπλος, or ἑλκεσίπεπλος, "trailing robed," like Homer's women.

---

[163] Mrs. Langloh Parker, Australian Legendary Tales.

[164] See fig. 2 in Roscher's Lexikon, ii. 2. 3007.

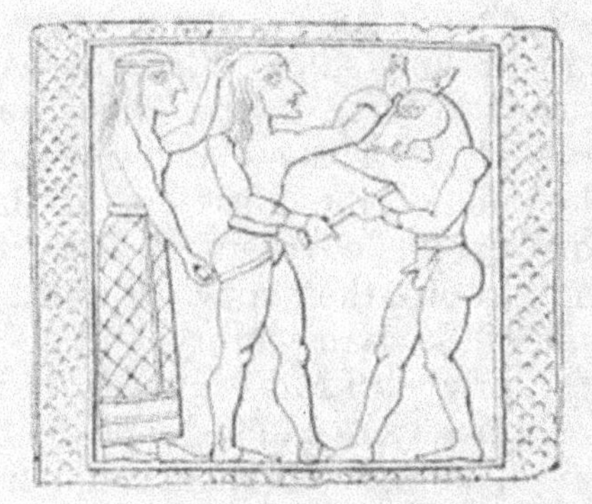
Fig. 12.—Ariadne, Theseus, and Minotaur
From a Corinthian Gold Ornament
From *Arch. Ztg.*, 1884

Fig. 12.—Ariadne, Theseus, and Minotaur
From a Corinthian Gold Ornament

Thus the Greek dress of the seventh to sixth century, when many artists drew what they saw under no "primitive" limitations, is not Homeric. Homeric female dress is loose and flowing, and trailing. Archaic Greek female dress is tight, not flowing, not trailing. Historic Hellenic female dress is loose, flowing, and trailing; it returns to the Homeric type. In holding these opinions we are not, then, deluded by the freedom of Homer's art; he insists on the kolpos, or loose fold which makes a pouch, and on the trailing loose peplos; nor, at least in my opinion, are we deluded by the stiffness of archaic art, which really represents the brevity and tightness of the prevailing fashion.

Thus we cannot cite the François vase "in illustration of the Homeric peplos."[165] The François dress is not trailing, nor is it pouched, nor is it Homeric. A thick, round, embroidered collar with no apparent breach in its continuity is either pinned or sewn over the François peplos, and the overlap is tight enough to indicate the bust very gracefully. Moreover, the costume of Athene[166] is not that of the François vase (fig. 13). Both, I think, cannot be "the closed Doric dress." Athene has a garment much more flowing than that of the François dress; and, unlike that costume, it has a pouch, though her dress falls rather lower than that of the François ladies; and she has no thick collar, and no long pins thrust up from the breast.[167] Athene's dress would be long and trailing, if it were not drawn up through the girdle. By the date of the Olympian figure of Athene, Greek female dress had moved back from the fashion of the François costume towards that which Homer knew and described.

We now reach the strange story which Herodotus tells to

---

[165] Greek Dress, p. 44.

[166] Ibid., fig. 10.

[167] Here, it must be said, Mr. Dawkins dissents, not seeing any difference in the two costumes. I think that is because he supposes the François artist not to be able to draw what he sees; for the dresses seem, in fact, to me different.

account for the alleged enforced change of Athenian women's costume from the peplos fastened with long stiletto-like pins, as in the François vase (an Athenian work of art), to the Ionic dress, which had no long pins. The women, he says, slew, with their long pins, a messenger who bore the tale of the massacre of their husbands; and the men therefore compelled them to wear the Ionian linen chiton, which does not require the περόνη, the stiletto pin.[168] The event was of the first half of the sixth century; 568 B.C. is the date conjectured, which tallies fairly with Mr. Walters's dating of the François vase made while long pins were still fashionable. But if the wearing of Ionic costume were, as Miss Abrahams supposes, one of the luxuries which Solon (594 B.C.) tried to check, then we must date the François vase in the seventh century. Yet the costume of the vase, with its expensive embroideries, is much more "luxurious" than the linen Ionian chiton or smock. In any case it is certain, from the dangerous long pins of, say, 1200 B.C. at Enkomi and in Greek deposits in Egypt, that women wore these stiletto pins five centuries before they did so at Athens, in, say, 620-560 B.C. So Homer had his mind, when Aphrodite scratched her hand with an Achaean woman's pin, on Achaean female dress, not on that of Athenians of the seventh or sixth century.

Fig. 13.—Historic Greek Costume From Leaf's Homer's Iliad vol. ii

In short, Homeric female dress was not introduced into the Epics by any "recension," by any interpolators of any post-Achaean date, as Pinza argues that it was.[169] He supposes the Ionian female costume to be a long linen smock with short sleeves.

Pinza argues that the costume of women in Homer "is wholly different from that of Spartan ladies of archaic and classical times; and, on the other hand, exhibits many analogies with the more antique linen chiton with short sleeves, certainly of Asiatico-Semitic origin, as is proved by the etymology of

[168] Herodotus, v. 87.

[169] Pinza, Hermes, 1909, p. 526.

the name" (chiton).[170] He supposes the Ionian costume of women, described as a long linen smock with short sleeves, to be derived, through Phoenicia, from the Syria of, say, 690 B.C., citing Hebrew female captives in Layard's Monuments of Nineveh (i. plates 61, 83, and others). In plate 61 we see a tall female captive, wearing a long garment, with a broad fringe over her head, and below it another long garment with short tight sewn sleeves, and a broad border which falls over the legs, leaving them bare from the calf. There are no pins or fibulae visible; the upper garment hides the girdle, if girdle there be. In plate 65 two figures of goddesses are carried, on chairs, in a procession. They wear long sewn smocks, with sewn sleeves ending above the elbows, and with very broad belts. The dresses end above the ankle bones. They are far from being loose or trailing; no pins or fibulae appear. The same costume, without any girdle, is worn by two women in a kitchen: they seem to have bodices and skirts (plate 30). The sleeves have no small round brooches like the Ionian chiton, which, like the Assyrian dresses, reached the feet (ποδήρης).

Miss Abrahams remarks that it is a mistake to suppose the Doric chiton to have been always fastened by pins or brooches, the Ionic always sewn on the shoulders (like those quoted from Assyrian monuments). In many Greek works of art, a chiton, clearly Ionic, is not sewn on the shoulders, but fastened down the upper arm by a series of small brooches.[171] The Assyrian dresses often answer to the Ionic chiton as thus described, but are without any brooches; and they are much shorter than the Ionic chiton, which, as thus described, is always longer than the height of the wearer; "the superfluous length is drawn up through the girdle to form a kolpos, which varies in depth according to the length of the chiton."[172] Not so in archaic Greek art! In any case, the Ionic dress as described is much longer than that of the Assyrian designs, has a kolpos, where they have none, and may either be sewn, like them, over the shoulder, or, unlike them, may be fastened over the upper arm with small brooches. Thus the Ionic, as described, is not the same as the Syrian, when the Ionic has brooches; nor is it, in my opinion the female costume of the Greek vases of the seventh and early sixth centuries.

In Layard's plate 67 A, from the Assyrian monuments, we see two of the captive women from Lachish kneeling and giving suck to their children. Their smocks are tight, girdled, and reach the heels.

---

170 Ibid. pp. 527, 528.
171 Greek Dress, p. 60.
172 Greek Costume, p. 60.

The dress of the upper woman has short sleeves on both arms, and the line where it crosses below the neck is perfectly well marked. How the infant, in these circumstances, reaches the natural source of nourishment is a deep mystery. In the figure of the lower woman certain faint lines appear to indicate that the dress has been opened at the centre of the neck and drawn aside over one breast. In neither case is there any trace of fibula, pin, button, or hook and eye, or loose hanging flap.

Pinza, however,[173] finds here an exact parallel to Hera's peplos in Iliad, xiv. 175, "fastened over her breast with clasps of gold," that is, "fastened on the shoulders by brooches or pins inserted down towards the breast"; and this, again, is said to be illustrated (as above) by the François vase. In answer, it may suffice to look at the two pictures, Layard 67 A and the Fates on the François vase. A simple button and button-hole, as Pinza remarks, in the dress below the centre of the neck, would, if withdrawn, do all that these Hebrew babies need. A man may illustrate this for himself by opening his shirt at the collar stud. The lower Hebrew woman might even be naked above the belt, like the kneeling woman just beneath her, were it not for the line of her dress across her neck. She has no sleeves. There is no sign of any openings at the shoulders or precisaménte come l' ἑανός della Epopea.

These Assyrian designs do not, it seems to me, encourage the opinion that Hebrew female costume of the date of Hezekiah, say, 690 B.C., was thrust into Homer about that period, at an Ionian "recension," and remained there unaltered by later "recensions."[174] The brooched costume of Homeric women is not the sewn costume of the Assyrian art. Other Hebrew ladies from Lachish wear the long piece of cloth over their heads, falling to the top of the ankle, and under that a tight smock of the same length. There is no girdle, the arms are bare, no fibulae are shown.[175] As the Syrian female costume never shows brooch, pin, or fibula, it certainly cannot be the origin of the Homeric or the Doric peplos, or of the brooched historical costume of Hellas.

Meanwhile a mere untutored man who looks at the Fates on the François vase thinks, I find, that the embroidered overlap is simply a short jacket worn over the peplos, This appears to be an error. But I had, as an amateur, come to the conclusion that the dress of the women in archaic Greek art often consists of sewn bodice and skirt, or of a tight jacket with a separate skirt, not of the

---

173 Pinza, Hermes, p. 538.

174 Ibid. p. 526.

175 Layard, Nineveh and Babylon, p. 152.

peplos. Mr. Myres had already expressed similar opinions as to the late survival (or revival?) of that Aegean costume.[176]

Moreover, Mr. Walters, judging from vase-paintings, says, "The Ionic costume is introduced about 500 B.C., but its vogue does not seem to have lasted long at Athens."[177]

Perdrizet thought that the archaic costume more resembled the Mycenaean (or Aegean) than the Doric style; while Mr. Wace (in the catalogue of the museum at Sparta), Mr. Leaf, Mr. Dawkins, and others hold that the archaic dress is merely a long chiton tied at the waist. This question of the late survival, or revival, of non-Homeric Aegean female costume is thus delicate and obscure, though I have little or no doubt that it did in many cases survive or was revived.

The woman in the archaic sepulchral monument from Etruria (British Museum) wears a short jacket, and a very brief skirt; and a woman in a leaden figurine of Sparta wears only a girdle and a kirtle. She is running, and has thrown off her jacket or bodice. An archaic Victory, a terra cotta in the British Museum, wears only a very short skirt.[178] The Ariadne of an archaic Corinthian jewel, in a belted skirt, with no bodice, has already been cited.

Thus the evidence of art, in the dark period of, say, 900-700 B.C., inclines me to believe that women sometimes wore shaped and sewn bodices and skirts, or jackets and skirts; sometimes a strait brooched and girdled peplos, not flowing, not trailing, not Homeric; that there was none of the Homeric uniformity of attire. Varieties of fashion are not discordant with feminine nature.

---

[176] Proceedings British School of Athens, vol. ix. p. 386, citing the difference of colour, and we may add of decorative design, on the part of the costume above, and the part below the girdle. This difference could not always occur in a dress all of one piece. For example, see the female figures incised on the fragments of a corslet of bronze plates at Olympia (Bronzen, plate lix.). But this question is sub judice; it is argued that the difference of pattern and colour in upper and lower parts of the dress is a decorative caprice of the artist, and corresponds to nothing that he saw in women's costume. It is impossible to deny that Ariadne in the archaic Corinthian piece of gold-work has come to see the Minotaur killed, wearing her skirt, and leaving her bodice in her bedroom (Roscher's Lexikon, ii. 2. 3007, fig. 2).

[177] History of Ancient Pottery, vol. ii. p. 200.

[178] Cf. B.S.A., vol. xii. p. 323, fig. K.

CHAPTER X

BRONZE AND IRON. WEAPONS AND TOOLS

The Aegean civilisation, till its last age of decadence in art, knew nothing about the use of iron for weapons or tools: at least no such relics have been discovered. Homer, on the other hand, is thoroughly familiar with iron as a commodity. A recurrent formula describes wealthy men as rich in gold, bronze, women, and iron.[179]

Iron, bronze, slaves, and hides were bartered for wine, at the siege of Troy, when a large trading fleet came in from Lemnos, sent by Euneos, son of Jason and Hypsipyle, a princess of that island.[180] Lemnos seems to have been rich in wine, which provoked the heroes to utter gabes (as in the Chansons de Geste) about their future triumphs in the war.[181]

Thus iron is abundant, but its uses are strangely restricted. All careful readers must perceive that Homer lives in an age of "overlap." Remains of such ages are common on European sites almost everywhere; the explorer finds in the overlap iron and bronze things together, iron comes gradually in: bronze, for weapons and tools, gradually disappears.

Thus at the great prehistoric cemetery of Hallstatt in the Austrian Alps, we find weapons of bronze fitted with iron edges, then swords with iron blades and hilts of bronze, then swords of iron, hilt and blade.[182]

In Crete was found a tholos tomb (a domed stone edifice) with a bronze spear-head, a set of iron tools including a double pick and an axe, and a sword of iron. This tomb was of the period when "geometric" ornament on vases had nearly supplanted the Aegean forms of decoration: in fact it was in the period to which we may assign Homer.[183] Other tholos tombs near the same site contained vessels Aegean in shape, with geometric ornament, and an iron dagger, and bronze fibulae and bracelets, objects for which iron was not used. In a tomb at Muliana in Crete,[184] were found bronze

---

179 Iliad, vi. 48, ix. 365, 366, x. 379, xi. 133; Odyssey, xiv. 324, xxi. 10.

180 Iliad, vii. 472 seqq.

181 Ibid. viii. 232.

182 Ridgeway, Early Age of Greece, vol. i. pp. 413-416.

183 J. H. S., 1907, p. 320.

184 Cf. "Burial and the Future Life."

weapons with human remains that had been buried beside iron weapons with cremated bones.[185] The vases were partly of Aegean, partly of Dipylon geometric style.

Now Homer describes this period of gradual overlap of iron and bronze. But he adds the strange peculiarity that the weapons, but for a single arrow-head[186] and an iron mace, mentioned as the peculiar fancy of a warrior when Nestor was young,[187] are always of bronze, while the tools and the masses of metal out of which they are forged are usually of iron. This fact has often been the subject of comment.[188] Of the critics mentioned in the note below, Helbig and Cauer think that the steady mention by Homer of bronze for weapons is a mere tradition of the epic, maintained by poets in the Iron Age. It would be interesting to find any such tradition in any other literature of the early Iron Age. But we do not find it. Moreover, the lays of the Bronze Age, when they mentioned tools, must have said that they were of bronze, as Homer occasionally does; but we are not told why later poets maintained the bronze tradition for weapons, but spoke of tools as iron. As in the case of the arrow-head it is called "the iron," so in the case of tools, and of knives (not used in battle); the wheelwright is said to fell a tree "with the iron," though Odysseus trims the wood of his bed "with the bronze." Achilles, it is feared, will cut his own throat "with the iron" (knife); the cattle struggle when slain "with the iron"—the butcher's knife; and Odysseus shoots "through the iron," through the holes in the axes. But no man, in battle, strikes with or dies under "the iron." This distinction could not have been uniformly maintained throughout several centuries by poets living in an age of iron weapons.

Naber and Bérard, unlike Cauer and Helbig, give the obvious explanation that when iron came in, but its manufacture and the sharpening of it were ill understood, men would make heavy axes and other rural implements of iron, but would not trust their lives to iron weapons which were brittle or which "doubled up." This is the view which occurred to myself before I had read the works of Naber and Bérard; but I then knew no proof that a stage of iron tools and bronze weapons had ever existed.

As Monsieur Bérard puts the case, "I might almost say that

---

185 Evans, Prehistoric Tombs of Cnossos, p. 134.

186 Iliad, iv. 123.

187 vii. 141 seqq.

188 Helbig, Homerische Epos, 1887, pp. 330, 331. Bérard, Les Phéniciens et l'Odyssée, 1902, vol. i. 435. Cauer, Grundfragen des Homer-kritik, pp. 183-189. Naber, Quaestiones Homericae, 1897, p. 60.

iron is the popular metal ... the shepherd and ploughman can extract and work it without going to the town."[189] It is probable that the princes who had lands remote from towns kept each his own smithy for rough work, like Highland chiefs in 1680-1745, who had the rough iron work done on the estate, but always imported their sword blades from the Continent. The hilts were made at home, basket hilts.[190]

Knives, never said to be used in war, agricultural and pastoral implements, and axes, though occasionally of bronze, are usually of iron in the Epics.[191] No graves opened in Greek soil have as yet yielded iron tools accompanied by bronze weapons alone. Mr. Arthur Evans, however, who accepts the view that Homer describes an actual period of bronze for weapons, iron for tools, writes, "This corresponds with a distinct phase of archaeological evidence. Thus in the Cypro-Minoan tomb at Enkomi the weapons were of bronze, but small iron knives also occurred (Murray, Excavations in Cyprus, p. 25)."[192] The Homeric state of affairs is illustrated by Mr. MacAllister's diggings in a certain stratum of the ancient city of Gezer in Palestine. All weapons are of bronze, all implements are of iron. Gezer was in touch with Aegean art; a bronze sword-blade of the Cnossian "horned" type (the hilt turning up like two horns) was found there.[193] Gaza also had "her Minoan traditions and the cult of the Cretan Zeus." Jewellery of late Aegean taste has been found at Gezer; and the Philistines are suspected of being settlers from Crete, whether Aegean or Achaean.

In the present state of knowledge we can say safely that Homer, with his bronze weapons and iron tools, has not invented a state of culture that never existed. The relative uses of excellent bronze for spears and swords, and of dubious iron for implements, were perfectly natural. Homer probably saw this stage in actual life; nobody could invent it; but no Homeric cairn with buried weapons

---

189 Iliad, xxiii. 826-835.

190 Napier, Life of Dundee, vol. iii. p. 724. Notices in the Stuart MSS., Windsor Castle.

191 Iliad, xviii. 34, xxiii. 30 (butchers' tools); Odyssey, ix. 391 ("great axes" and adzes); Iliad, xxiii. 850 (axes). The axes through which Odysseus shot the arrow (nine times in the Odyssey). Battle-axe; this is of bronze (Iliad, xiii. 611, ἀξίνη), axes as tools are πελέκεις. "Iron" as a synonym for wheelwrights' tools (Iliad, iv. 485). Iron butchers' axes (Iliad, xvii. 520; Odyssey, iii. 442-449).

192 Scripta Minoa, vol. i. p. 61, note 1.

193 Evans, Prehistoric Tombs of Cnossos, p. 107.

and tools has ever been discovered, and if any had been found, they would long ago have been plundered.

There are two lines, or rather one line is twice repeated in the Odyssey, which give the démenti to the uniform descriptions in both Epics. Odysseus bids Telemachus hide the weapons in the hall, and, if asked why he does it, reply that the Wooers in their cups may quarrel, and use the arms, and "shame the feast, and this wooing, for iron of himself draws a man to him."[194] This is a proverbial expression of the age when iron is, at least, the dominant if not the only metal for weapons. If, then, this line be as old as the rest of the Odyssey, in which weapons are always of bronze, its maker has let out that all the other makers have been saying what they do not mean; and in an age of iron, or overlap of bronze-and iron, have consistently maintained that all weapons are of bronze, while tools are of iron, as a rule.

Helbig and others[195] think the line a very late intrusion; it may be removed without altering the sense of the passage. Mr. Monro, on Odyssey, xix. 1-50, discusses the question fully. "Ancient and modern critics," he says, "are generally agreed that the first mention of 'iron' as synonymous with 'weapon'" (Od. xvi. 294), and the rest of the passage, "is an interpolation founded on xix. 1-50, and intended to lead up to it." But Kirchoff (Odyssey, p. 560) reverses the process, the second appearance of the passage is the earlier. Mr. Monro argues that both passages "are additions to the original context."

It is essential to the whole story that the Wooers, who, of course, wear swords, as was universally done in time of peace, should, when attacked by arrows, need shields and spears to throw. The interpolator, if interpolator there were, thought that, in ordinary circumstances, shields and spears would be hanging on the walls of the hall, as in the Ionian house of Alcaeus (Fragm. 15, Bergk.).

We do not know from other descriptions of Homeric halls that this was the custom in Homer's age; it is nowhere mentioned.

The war-gear in the palace of Cnossus was certainly stored apart in special chambers. Suppose, then, that a late poet, accustomed to see war-gear arranged on walls, had the opportunity to introduce the practice into the Odyssey, he would inevitably cause confusion; and the passage does cause great confusion, as Mr. Monro proves in his long note.

---

194 Odyssey, xvi. 294, xix. 13.
195 Homerische Epos, p. 331.

(1) The moment foreseen and prepared for by Odysseus never arrives, and that is quite contrary to "the Epic manner."

(2) It is a weaker argument, that the speech about arms tempting men to use them disregards the fact that the Wooers wear swords; what they need under the rain of arrows is shields and throwing spears. For these they send the Goatherd to the store-chamber, where, in fact, they were probably kept in a Homeric house, not, as in the case of Alcaeus, on the walls.

(3) The use of "iron" for "weapon" is, as Mr. Monro says, an anachronism.

(4) The vocabulary "has a post-Homeric stamp." Of this I am no judge; but I point out later what Mr. Monro omits to notice, that in the first passage, xvi. 296, the δοιὰ βοάγρια χερσιν ἑλέσθαι is archaeologically utterly un-Homeric (cf. p. 103); while the command to bring two βοάγρια and spears, as Mr. Monro says, is not repeated nor carried out in the second passage; again contrary to the manner of the Epic.

(5) In Odyssey, xxii. 23-25, when Odysseus has shot Antinous, the Wooers look at the wall to find spears vainly; but why? They do not expect a fight, they think (xxii. 31, 32) that Odysseus, aiming at some other mark, has shot Antinous by accident. In xxii. 5-7 he has said, enigmatically, that he will try, with Apollo's aid, to hit a mark that no man has struck before. The words about their looking to the walls for weapons "are an interpolation, and prove nothing about the removal of the arms."

(6) Mr. Monro renders the speech of Melanthius (xxii. 139-141) in this manner: "Go to, I will bring you gear to arm you from the store-chamber, for the arms are in their place (ἔνδον), I think, and Odysseus and his sons have not put them elsewhere." Melanthius merely means that the armour has not been moved by Odysseus and Telemachus from its natural place, the store-chamber; he will there find what is needed.

(7) The passage in Book xxiv. 164-166, where the ghost of Amphimedon tells the story of the removal of the arms to Agamemnon in Hades, is late, like all Book xxiv. It is possibly later than the passage about removing the arms from the hall.

Averse as I am to theories of interpolation, the whole passage in which "iron" is made a synonym for "weapon" is rich in the non-Epic manner as well as matter, and causes very un-Homeric confusions. Critics of all shades of opinion recognise this, and I do not object to the line about iron merely because it is as fatal to my theory as it is friendly to that of Mr. Ridgeway.[196]

---

196 Early Age of Greece, vol. i. pp. 295, 296. Mr. Ridgeway does not notice the many objections to the whole passage.

In this case the line contradicts the whole of both Epics, which in itself provokes suspicion; just as a single passage in which cavalry were introduced, or burials by humation were introduced, or armorial bearings on small bucklers appeared, would rightly be deemed a late interpolation.

This line apart, the two Epics seem uniform work of a peculiar stage, the Gezer stage, of the overlap of bronze and iron.

Hesiod knew all about the Bronze Age, and knew that his was the age of iron, whereas the ancients tooled with bronze, "and there was no black iron." Put Hesiod at 700 B.C., and we wonder why "late poets" about that date gave iron tools but bronze weapons to the Achaeans.[197]

The line in the Odyssey is found, one must add, in most suspicious circumstances, and in the worst of company. It first appears in Odyssey, xvi. 294, when Odysseus, at the house of Eumaeus, is prophesying to Telemachus about the misbehaviour of the Wooers. He bids his son, at his nod, to conceal the arms and the weapons in the hall, and if asked why he has done so, reply that they afford occasion for brawls, as "iron draws a man to him." The passage goes on, "but for us alone leave two swords, two spears, and two shields to grasp with our hands" Here the word for shields is βοάγρια, which occurs in no other line of Iliad or Odyssey except Iliad, xii. 22; while the following line (23), mentioning "demigods," "takes us at once away from the Homeric world, and opens an entirely new order of conceptions."[198] "The most careless critics," says Mr. Leaf, cannot pass this passage in the Iliad, nor can the most conservative critic defend it. As the dubious passage of the Odyssey concerning iron contains the same non-Homeric word for shields as the indubitably false passage of the Iliad, and as the poet of the Odyssey expects the shields to be held in the hand (an die Arme zu nehmen, Faesi) while Homer's shields are always suspended by baldrics, it is clear that the Odyssean passage with the mention of iron as synonymous with weapon is rather more than suspect.

The line recurs[199] in changed circumstances when Telemachus and Odysseus together remove the weapons, but do not leave two swords, two spears, and two shields (βοάγρια) for themselves. Everything falls out otherwise than Odysseus had practically prophesied in Book xvi., when we come to the slaying of the Wooers in Book xxii.

---

[197] Hesiod, Works and Days, 150, 151.

[198] Leaf, Iliad, vol. i. p. 524.

[199] Odyssey, xix. 13.

This would mean nothing in a modern novel; but, as Mr. Monro says, in Homer it is singular; it would be more in his manner to let events exactly fulfil the boding of Odysseus. I have proved that the whole passage not only contradicts the uniform tenor of the two Epics as to bronze weapons, but causes hopeless confusion, has the most suspicious associations, and contravenes the Homeric practice of suspending shields by baldrics. Even if we excised the line concerning iron, which can be omitted without injuring the sense, the whole passage in both of its appearances is decidedly suspicious.[200]

CHAPTER XI

BURIAL AND THE FUTURE LIFE

The most perplexing questions in Homer's picture of life are connected with the disposal of the dead. It is just here, where archaeology as a rule gives the surest evidence from the examination of graves, that archaeology so far seems to fail us. Yet Homer speaks with no uncertain voice. From the fifty-second line of the first book of the Iliad to the funeral of Hector in the twenty-fourth book, Homer always tells of cremation, "and ever the pyres of the dead burned in multitude." There may be slight variations in practice, as regards burning his armour with the dead warrior; and the funeral of Patroclus, in which the love and the rage of Achilles expended themselves, has features not usually recorded by

---

[200] Mr. Murray, R. G. E. p. 154, note 1, writes that when I regard the proverb that "iron of itself draws a man on" as an interpolation, "this seems like giving up most of the case." But it is no part of my case that not a single interpolation exists in either the Iliad or Odyssey. There is scarcely a critic, whatever his views, who does not suspect the passages which we have been discussing. If Mr. Murray does not see evidence of un-Homeric confusion in the passages, his view is peculiar; and if I am biassed, when I see those signs, by my ideas about iron, he may be also unconsciously biassed by his opposite ideas. If a critic desires to prove that iron was in common use for weapons during the evolution of the Odyssey, will he aver that—were no iron in question—he would see nothing suspicious in the passages?

Homer,—the circumstances being peculiar,—but there is always cremation, always the urn-burial of the bones, always the cairn piled above them with its pillar on the summit; yet no such Homeric cairn has yet been discovered.

Yet Homer certainly describes no invented rites: cremation, urn-burial, the linen wrapping of the urn (gold, bronze, or of pottery), and the cairn are familiar from remains of the Bronze and early Iron Age in northern and central Europe: the custom in our islands appears to have survived the dawn of Christianity, and is perfectly well remembered by the Christian author of the Anglo-Saxon epic, Beowulf. Contrasting pagan times with his own, he writes: "Woe is his who is destined, through savage hate, to thrust his soul into the fire's embrace, to hope for no comfort, in no wise to change."

"Weal is his who may after his death-day stand before the Lord, and claim a refuge in the Father's arms."[201]

This burial by fire, this want of hope, this changeless, helpless future, are what Achilles endured and deplored.[202] "Rather would I on earth be the hind of a landless man than king over all the dead." Thus the dying Beowulf asks to be buried: "Bid ye the warriors raise a far-seen cairn for me after the funeral fire on a head-land by the sea ... so that seafarers who drive their tall ships over the spray of ocean shall thereafter call it Beowulf's barrow."[203]

So, too, spoke the ghost of Elpenor on the limit of Oceanus to Odysseus: "Burn me with my armour, all that is mine, and pile for me a cairn by the shore of the grey sea, memorial of a luckless man, that men unborn may inquire of me."[204] The customs and ideas are identical, but no such cairns have we found in Homeric lands, whereas they are common in our islands.

Meanwhile the burial customs of the Aegean folk in Crete and in Greece were not those known to Homer. They used "shaft-graves," deeply sunk in earth, luckily for us, since in these were found the unsunned treasures of Mycenae. They also used "chamber-tombs," and "pit-graves," and stone-built tholos chambers, beehive shaped, not cairns of earth covering a small chamber of stone. They did not, in the Bronze Age, burn the dead, but buried him, often in a large larnax or coffer of pottery; and they deposited rich grave-goods, which Homer never mentions. In a chamber-tomb at Muliana in Crete were found unburned bones

[201] Beowulf, 184-188, Mr. Clark Hall's translation.
[202] Odyssey, xi. 489-491.
[203] Beowulf, 2803-2808.
[204] Odyssey, xi. 74-76.

with weapons of bronze, and an Aegean "false-necked vase"; while hard by in the same chamber were "cremated bones, in a cinerary geometric urn," and an iron sword and dagger.[205]

"Here," says Mr. Evans, "we have the interesting spectacle of the succession of corpse-burial by cremation, and of iron weapons by bronze, apparently without any break in the indigenous stock." The Aegean Bronze Age of burial passes into the Iron Age of cremation. About the change of custom without change of stock or race we cannot be quite certain, but cremation makes its appearance in association with iron weapons, which Homer's men do not use, while they do practise cremation and cairn-burial, which has left no known traces in the Bronze Age of Greece.

It is suggested by Mr. Murray, as by Helbig, that cremation was adopted, during the dark age of the Migrations, by men who wished to burn their dead "into their ultimate dust," that the dust might not be violated by hostile hands. The custom, Mr. Murray suggests, was a revival of what the Northerners had used "in the forest country from which they came." Possibly if wood were very scarce in Crete and Greece, the Northerners there might adopt the local method of burial, and revert to their own custom at Troy, where Ida furnished forests. But Homer supposes cremation and caim-burial to be universal in Greece; and his whole theory of the future life rests on cremation. The rite admits the dead to the House of Hades, ineffectual shadows, unfed, unfeared, unworshipped; and from the House of Hades they never return. By the eighth century, and so on continuously, ghosts can appear to men, and are fed, feared, and worshipped, as they had been in Aegean times. The belief of Homer is the belief of Israel, Hades is the Sheol of Samuel. The manners of ancient Israel are of interest as regards cremation. The Philistines treated the corpse of Saul as Hector meant to treat that of Patroclus, whose head he would have set on a spike above the wall of Troy. "They fastened Saul's body to the wall of Beth-shan." His sons' corpses were used in the same way, but were rescued by valiant Israelites, who burned the bones and buried them under a tree. This appears to have been done for the purpose of concealing the bones from further outrage. No cairn is mentioned.[206] But cremation, in the case of kings at least, appears to have persisted in Israel and Judah. Asa, king of Judah, when he died, was "laid in the bed which was filled with sweet odours and divers kinds of spices; and they made a very great burning for him."

---

[205] Burrows, Discoveries in Crete, p. 101. Evans, Prehistoric Tombs of Knossos, p. 134.

[206] 1 Sam. xxxi. 10-13.

His tomb he had caused to be digged for him; there his bones were laid.[207] Of Jehoram we read that "his people made no burning for him, like the burning of his forefathers."[208] Jeremiah prophesies for Zedekiah: "Thou shalt die in peace: and with the burnings of thy forefathers, the former kings which were before thee, so shall they burn odours for thee."[209] In Israel an unusual lack of interest in the future life accompanied cremation of kings, if cremated they were; but the commentators prefer to believe that they were not, and that only odorous substances and "furniture" were burned. Why burn furniture?[210] But Homer's faith is unique in Greece, Aegean or historic it represents a single age of culture—which has left no material proof of its existence.

Homer's burial rites cannot have arisen out of a practice adopted during the Migrations, for no people that wished to conceal the resting-place of their dead would raise above it a conspicuous cairn and pillar, for the very purpose of keeping the dead in perpetual memory. Such cairns would merely have invited desecration during the Migrations.[211]

I can only conclude that Homer describes what is certainly an actual and widely-diffused non-Aegean mode of burial, with the equally non-Aegean and non-historic belief about the future life. Why the practice has left no material traces, as of cairns, is an insoluble question at present.[212] The historical Hellenes, however,

---

[207] 2 Chron. xvi. 14.

[208] 2 Chron. xxi. 19.

[209] Jer. xxxiv. 5.

[210] Hastings' Dict. of Bible, art. "Cremation."

[211] R. G. E. pp. 72, 73. Mr. Murray supposes cremation, with secret burial. If so, the cairn was a later addition made in settled times, after the Migrations.

[212] Mr. Burrows remarks: "Neither Professor Ridgeway nor Mr. Lang is able to make the slightest use of the combinations suggested by the East Cretan graves," in which, for example, bronze weapons and inhumated bones are found side by side with burned bones, in urns, and iron weapons (Discoveries in Crete, p. 215). The facts are certainly of no use to any theory of mine: they are quite un-Homeric facts. I can only state the question thus: Homer uniformly describes a very well known mode of burial. Did he invent it? Did he receive it from tradition; and if so, from a tradition of what place and period? Is it possible that a poet of the age of overlapping of bronze and iron, of inhumation and cremation, in Greece, persists in reproducing, in great detail, a method of burial removed from his own experience by all the time that had passed since the Achaeans left their northern forests? If they retained the mode in Greece, where are the cairns?

knew many tombs, probably barrows or cairns, which they assigned to men and women of the Heroic Age. Pausanias often mentions such tombs, which he saw, but he does not usually describe them. In a few cases he speaks of barrows or cairns of earth, as at Epidaurus the grave of Phocus, slain by Peleus. It was a "mound of earth, and on it a rough stone." At Olympia was the tomb of Oenomaus, "a piled up mound, with stones" (vi. 21. 3). At Pergamus beyond Caicus, the grave of Auge, "a mound of earth with a stone wall round it" (viii. 4-9). The grave of Aepytus (mentioned in Iliad, ii. 604), "a pile of earth, not very high, surrounded by a coping of stone" (viii. 16. 3). The tomb of Homer's Areithous of the iron mace was near Mantinea in Arcadia; it is "a tomb with a stone base" (viii. 11). The attribution of the graves to known heroes may often have been fanciful; in many cases two or more have claimed one hero's grave. While the belief in heroes existed, barrows would not be robbed. Pausanias speaks, however, twice of cinerary urns containing heroic ashes of Ariadne at Argos (ii. 23. 8), and of Eurytus, son of Melaneus; but here a dream warned Pausanias to be silent about the urn of bronze (iv. 33).

Thus there were cairns enough, believed to be of heroic and pre-Homeric date.

It has been suggested that the elaborate enclosure of circles of stone, with a coping, round the shaft-graves of the acropolis of Mycenae, was originally meant to contain a barrow of earth. But several grave-stones were found in the earth; and it is unlikely that a barrow would be heaped over the grave-pillars, or that so many would be set up on the top of a barrow. The cairn seems to be Homeric, not "Mycenaean."

Historic Greece had no one orthodox belief as to the condition of departed souls. Homer has, on the other hand, an orthodoxy; the ghost of the man who does not receive due burning and burial is an outcast, perhaps a mischievous outcast from the company in the halls of Hades and in the meads of asphodel, while they are but shadows of themselves, unfed, unless some bold adventurer goes to them and sheds the blood of the black ram. That was another thing than pouring libations into the tomb.

Considering the fact that phantasms of the dead are probably as common in one age as in another, Homer is singularly free from superstition about them. Even Lucretius did not deny that such apparitions appear; he tried to explain their appearance as traces left, somehow, on something, we know not what or how, a theory lately revived. Homer denies ghosts; and his view, we may say, can never, in his own time, have been popular: it is the view of a class, not of a people.

But, as Mr. Leaf justly observes, there are vestiges in Homer of other rites than his own. The word ταρχύειν, to preserve, whether by embalment, or merely by drying or kippering, is used, in a general sense, for doing all the rites of the dead.[213] The word may survive from an age when mummification, not cremation, was the rule; honey may have been employed; and the pots of honey and of oil placed by Achilles against the bier of Patroclus may represent a faint vestige of survival.[214] The usage lasted at Athens, the pointed lekythoi were ranged round the bier. Why Achilles slew two dogs and four horses, and threw them on the pyre, he did not know himself; he thought that he slaughtered twelve Trojan prisoners merely in anger.[215] He had no conscious purpose to send horses, dogs, and thralls into Hades for the use of his friend; he did not burn the arms of his friend. In Iliad, xxiv. 595, he promises to Patroclus a share of the ransom of Hector's body; but all these things are spoken of only in connection with the passion of Achilles. Customs almost forgotten revive or are reinvented in the mind of the hero, extravagances of grief and anger.

There is a variation in the last book of the Odyssey; the souls of the unburied Wooers arrive among the dead in Hades, though their bodies are unburned. The passage is usually reckoned late, and these spirits are under the special guidance of Hermes.

Even in these shadowy matters, Homer presents a view' unusually consistent; and the view was not held either in Aegean times, or in "Dipylon" days, or in the eighth century by the Cyclic poets, or in historic Greece. In this, as in all things, the world of Homer stands apart. There is possibly one note of change in Homeric burial. The phrase κτέρεα κτερεΐξαι, as in Iliad, xxiv. 38, means the burning of some of a man's possessions on his funeral pyre. It occurs but once in the Iliad, in the case of the funeral of Hector; but frequently in the Odyssey, about the funeral rites of Odysseus, if he proves to have died abroad. The only possessions of Patroclus which are burned are dogs and horses; not his arms, as in the cases of Eetion and Elpenor. In these cases, perhaps, a slight variation in burial rites may be detected. It looks as though, in the cases where the arms of the dead are burned with them, they were expected to be of use to them in the future life, as to Melissa, wife of Periander, who was cold in Hades, because her wardrobe had not been burned.

---

[213] Iliad, vii. 85. The word is also found, Iliad, xvi. 456 = 674.

[214] xxiii. 170, 171.

[215] xxiii. 23.

CHAPTER XII

RELIGION IN GREECE: PRE-HISTORIC, HOMERIC, AND HISTORICAL

In religion, as in all things, the Homeric world at certain points stands apart from the worlds that preceded and followed it. The Aegeans probably did not give divine honours to the dead. Over Royal tombs in the acropolis of Mycenae was "a small round altar with a well-like opening in the middle, which had doubtless been used for sacrificing to the dead."[216] This is ghost-feeding, not ghost-divinising. We have also a Cretan picture of a ghost standing outside his tomb, while an ox is sacrificed to him, the blood falling into the vessel. But such traces of hero-worship are rare in Aegean art, and Cretan art shows no representations of sacrifice of animals to gods. There was, indeed, an ancient tradition that Minos abolished blood-sacrifices.[217] Certain sites, however, show bones of animals sacrificed in Minoan times.

On the other hand, worship of high gods is frequently represented on Aegean engraved rings and in pictures. While there is no representation of blood-sacrifice to gods, fruit of a sacred tree is often plucked, by attendants, for goddesses, standing or seated.[218]

In the acropolis of Mycenae (in 1886) was found an apparent representation of a god, on a table of lime-stone. "In the centre stands, on a blue ground, a man or an idol, covered with a large shield in the shape of two circles joined together." This is the usual Aegean figure-of-eight shield, which is found by itself in little objects of glass and other materials, called "palladia." "On either side of the idol stands a woman, apparently in an attitude of prayer. Between the idol and the woman on the right is an altar-like object, resembling the bases under the feet of the lions at the Lions' gate."[219]

On a scene of cult, on a large gold ring found at Mycenae, is, in mid-air "a small apparently descending image of a god," armed

---

216 Frazer, Pausanias, vol. iii. p. 105.

217 Helbig in Roscher, s.v. Minos, ii. 2. 3000. On this matter there is much controversy.

218 See several examples in Evans, "Mycenaean Tree and Pillar Worship." J. H. S., vol. xxi.

219 Ibid. p. 108.

and shielded.[220] He also appears on a ring of Cnossos, and is, in Mr. Evans's opinion, a sky- or sun-god. If so, the Greeks would identify him with their own Zeus, a sky-god in his earliest aspect as indicated by his name (also a god of everything, in cult).

This male deity is much less prominent in Mycenaean art than a great goddess. In the Mycenaean ring already cited she sits under a tree, probably sacred: a little female figure in a flounce skirt gathers fruit. The goddess, like Demeter in Theocritus (Idyll vii.), holds poppy heads in her hand; women bring her flowers. Above her is a ceremonial double axe, symbol of power, and overhead are sun and crescent moon.

Mr. Evans thinks that the ceremonial double axe, or rather pair of double axes, "may be an image of the conjunction of the divine pair, a solar and lunar deity."[221] The art indicates tree- and pillar-worship as prevalent, whether the deities were supposed to embody themselves in trees and pillars or not. A slab of offering, inscribed in Aegean characters, with three small basins for libations, was found in the Dictaean cave, and was appropriate to the offerings of honey, wine, and water to the infant Zeus of the Cretan birth-myth of Zeus, or to the Homeric three libations to the dead in Hades. There was also a sacrificial stratum, with bones of oxen, deer, and goats. It must be borne in mind that though the myth of the birth of Zeus in the Cretan cave is most famous, Pausanias says that it was hard to count the Greek cities which claimed to be the places of his nativity.[222] He gives four or five instances in Messenia and Arcadia.

A goddess between two lions,[223] or on a mountain top guarded by lions, an armed god standing by (in a gold ring), reminds us of Cybele, or of Rhea, mother of the Gods of Homer. A goddess holding in each hand a water fowl or other animal is common in Aegean art; and a god in the same attitude, is a gold figure of the Aegina treasure (circ. 850 B.C.), in the British Museum. In the contemporary and later finds in the temple of Artemis Orthia, at Sparta, such female figures are very common, and in the earliest Ionian temple at Ephesus. They persist into the sixth century B.C., and are representations of Artemis as a goddess of the wild things, Homer's Artemis Agrotera.[224]

---

220 Frazer, Pausanias, vol. iii. p. 121.

221 Evans, ut sup. p. 108.

222 Pausanias, iv. 33.

223 Evans, p. 164, fig. 44.

224 See "The Asiatic or Winged Artemis." by M. S. Thompson. J. H. S., vol. xxix. pt. ii. pp. 286-308.

Thus, undeniably, archaic and heroic Greece carried on Aegean representations of deities; even the Cretan goddess holding serpents has, in Greek art, an Artemis with snakes to represent her. But, so much earlier and nearer to Aegean times, in Homer, the goddess, as Artemis, shows her later and more truly Hellenic aspects, and is the chaste sister of Apollo. Indeed, the Homeric Olympians are already the beautiful beings which the best art of the Hellenic prime, in the fifth century, delighted to represent; while in art much earlier than Pheidias, but much later than Homer, the gods still appear in their old Aegean forms. This is the paradox of Homer. The poet lived while the Hellenes were but a small nation, occupying a narrow region in Thessaly; but his poems forestall the beauty which blossomed again, when art and religion were truly Hellenic. And in Homer the beauty bears none of the barbaric strains that deface the rites of Athens in her glory. "Homer's portrait of Artemis," says Mr. Farnell, "gives us not the first but the last point in the development of her character, and the conception of her in later Greek literature is not more advanced or more spiritual than his." But "Arcadian and Athenian rites and legends" (we may compare Boeotian and Spartan art of 800-700 B.C.) "provide us with testimony much earlier than Homer's."[225]

How are we to explain the facts? Homer is the poet of Achaeans, regarded as a stronger but less civilised race, invaders of a more civilised people. Yet this Achaean people, or their poet, is already on the highest Hellenic level in his conception of the Olympians, while the practical ritual and legends of Athens in her glorious prime retain many traces of barbarous and even savage conceptions at which Homer seldom glances, though even in his mythology there are hints of a truly barbarous cosmogony, the revolution by which Zeus overthrew more ancient divinities. Homer knew Hesiod's myth of Cronos,[226] which is precisely that of the Maoris. How then did his taste, and that of his audience, arrive at his beautiful portraits of the Olympians?

This is the great problem. The gods of Aegean art are strange if impressive beings, mixed up with tree- and pillar-worship. Their altars, in art, are not adapted for sacrifices for animals, but libations, fruits, and flowers are offered. The gods and goddesses of archaic Greek art are barbaric and unimpressive, and trees and stones, as sacred, endured through all Greek history. The Olympians of Homer are, on the other hand, the Olympians of Pheidias.

---

[225] Cults of the Greek States, vol. ii. p. 427.
[226] Iliad, xiv. p. 203.

Turning from Aegean religion before Homer, which shows infinitely more of the worship of high gods than of ghosts, we find, in early historic Greece, that the great Olympians are highly honoured, but that ghost-worship, ignored by Homer, is prevalent. From the seventh century onwards the possession of tombs of heroes, and of miracle-working relics of heroes, their bones, is essential to the well-being of cities. Finally, living men are freely divinised. Thus chthonic as distinct from Olympian worship, while it is ignored by Homer (whose theory of the state of the dead renders it impossible) gets practically the upper hand in historic Greece, though in the Aegean religion it is inconspicuous, and in Homer it is absent.

Thus Homer stands apart in religion from the world that preceded and the world that followed him.

The solitary passage in which the Iliad recognises sacrifice to a dead man, a hero, is in the description of the case of Erechtheus in Athens. In the temple of Athene "the Athenians worship him with bulls and rams as the years return in their courses."[227]

Owing, perhaps, to Homer's consistent avoidance of everything Ionian, he never speaks of the Mysteries of Eleusis, in Attica, celebrated in the Ionian Hymn to Demeter, or of the Attic Thesmophoria or the Brauronia, or, indeed, of any mysteries. These are now understood to have begun in savage and barbarous magical rites for the benefit of the objects of the food supply; or in initiatory ceremonies: both practices are still common among all the lower races; and agricultural magic still survives in European folklore, and we have the initiations of Freemasonry.

The rites of Eleusis, Athens, and of Artemis Orthia among the Dorians of Sparta are of immense antiquity in their origins. The magic may have been practised in Attica, in Homer's time, and, as folklore, may have existed in the rural classes among the Achaean states. If so, Homer has no interest in the matter, none in initiations. But both magic and initiations were sanctioned by the State in Attica and Dorian Sparta, in historic Hellas.

The two deities who chiefly presided over mysteries were Demeter and Dionysus. Demeter "has no real personality in Homer," says Mr. Leaf, "except in Odyssey, v. 125," where we merely hear that she lay with Iasion in a thrice ploughed fallow field, and that Zeus slew Iasion with a thunderbolt. Dionysus, again, to quote Mr. Leaf, is only mentioned in Iliad, xiv. 325, in the "Leporello Catalogue" of the amours of Zeus, and in doubtful passages of the Odyssey (xi. 325). He is the son of Semele, and a golden cup is a gift

[227] Iliad, ii. 550, 551.

of his. Finally, and most to the purpose, in Iliad, vi. 130-140, Diomede tells the story of Lycurgus, a Thracian king, who beat the nymphs, the nurses of Dionysus, with an ox-goad, and frightened Dionysus into the deeps of the sea. Zeus blinded Lycurgus, and he did not last long. This tale is regarded as a late and pious interpolation, because the whole scene is looked on as in crying contradiction with the events of Iliad, Book v. For proof that there is no inconsistency at all, see "The Great Discrepancies."

We must be very anxious to find "late" things in Homer, if we say that the passage about Dionysus in Iliad, vi., "dates from the very last part of the Epic period," namely, perhaps, from the seventh century B.C. It may be true that "the great religious movement" connected with Dionysus "spread over Greece apparently in the seventh century."[228] But it is more probable that the "movement" was especially taken up by literature, Orphic poetry, at that period, for I am unaware that we have any historical evidence, as in Herodotus, for the religious furies and homicidal ferocities of the women in the seventh century. These, all the stories of the sanguinary frenzy of the sex, their endeavours to "interview" kings, and tear them to tatters, are thrown back into legendary times. Nobody can tell how ancient the legends are, but it seems to be generally admitted that Dionysus and his rites are of "Indo-European" but not of Greek origin. His mother was Semele, and Kretschmer would connect Semele "with a Phrygian root, zemel," which occurs on Phrygian tombstones in curses directed against any one who should violate the tombs. The word Kretschmer interprets as meaning "earth." So Semele would be the earth goddess.[229]

Be it so, Phrygian Zemel, the earth, is Greek Semele, the earth-mother of the son of the sky, Zeus. But "Dionysus in Greek mythology is closely connected with Thrace," and Lycurgus, the enemy of Dionysus in Iliad, vi., is a Thracian king. Now "the result of recent philological inquiries is to show a close connection between the Thracian and Phrygian tongues, which are found to be both Aryan."[230] Again, Attica, if ever her legends deviate into truth, was closely connected with Thrace; and Homer himself treats the Thracian Chersonese as an ally of Troy,[231] and Rhesus brings in his levies.[232]

There is no reason in the world why so great a sennachie as

---

[228] Leaf, Iliad, vi. 130.
[229] Frazer, Pausanias, vol. iii.
[230] Ibid. ut supra.
[231] Catalogue, Book ii. 844-850.
[232] Iliad, x. 434-441.

Homer, who knew as many tales from all quarters as Widsith in the Anglo-Saxon poem, should not know a Thracian tale about Lycurgus and Dionysus and his mother, Earth.[233] Nothing prevented Homer from knowing a myth of a people whom he knew—the Thracians—very long before the seventh century.

Homer has not a good word for the cowardly Dionysus. Still, Zeus patronises him; he is a god, though he never appears among Homer's Olympians. To his mysteries, as to those of Eleusis (is it not in Attica?) Homer does not allude. He mentions no mysteries, no initiations, no hocus-pocus; these things were for Attica, and for historic Greece.

The ethical religion of Homer apart from his mythology is excellent, a good faith to live and die in. His gods, when religiously regarded, sanction all that is best in Achaean morals, and disapprove of all that is evil in human conduct, as a general rule. But Homeric mythology is manifestly another thing: in the stories told of the gods, they practise most of the sins which they punish in mankind. Mythology would cease to be mythology if it became consistent, but religion can never fail to be consistent while it expresses the highest and purest ethical ideas associated with a sense of their approval by a being or beings more than mortal. This note is again and again struck by Homer; and it can never fail to awaken a responsive thrill in all who feel, or have ever felt, the ethico-religious emotion.

Let me here give but one example. It is impossible for men to understand the mystery of an omnipotent and loving Being in a world of pain and ruin. Homer is as conscious of the insoluble problem as we are—and Zeus is conscious of it. In the great assembly of all gods, from Apollo and Athene to the nymphs of rivers, well-heads, and grassy water-meadows, at the moment when the final strife is set between Hector and Achilles, Zeus says, "Even in their perishing have I regard unto them."[234] The Father pities but he cannot save—there is some insuperable obstacle between his omnipotence and the end which he desires.

Such is the religious thought of Homer, while in his mythical thought Zeus is a humorous hot-tempered father of a family, who delights to tease, and finds as much diversion as Mr. Bennett did in the absurdities of his wife and children.

The Achaean mind, like the mind of any savage who recognises an All Father, has brooded over the sacred beings of religion in every mood, the most serious and the most frivolous;

---

233 Strabo, x. 3. 470; fragment 25. Miss Harrison, Prolegomena, p. 375.
234 Iliad, xx. 21.

every conceivable reflection of every age, early or later, has entered into a conglomerate of yearning desire for the gods, of fear of the gods' wrath, of absurd legends concerning the gods, of broadly humorous glances at them as members of a great whimsical family; and there are guesses at the enjoyments of divine people, so powerful, so irresponsible, and so far from spiritual; for the gods are not spirits, but beings compact of a subtler matter than our perishable flesh and blood and bone.

Thus the gods, in moments of human seriousness, are the guardians of Homer's highest ethical ideals; while for purposes of romance and diverting narrative they are examples of all the vices which he most detests and despises, and of a score of human foibles which he never illustrates in the persons of his heroic men and women. His mortal ladies never cuff and scold, like the village women whom he once glances at, shrieking forth their quarrel in the centre of the village street. But it is in public that Hera and Athene scold or cuff. The nearest approach to this treatment of sacred beings may perhaps be found in the broad waggeries of our late English mystery plays, like those of Cain and of the Shepherds of Bethlehem. An even better example is the ancient carol, The Bitter Withy, with the cruel cunning and crime attributed to Jesus Christ, and the story of His whipping by "Mary mild." Achaean humour is never so free as in its treatment of things which are also handled, in another mood, with the highest religious regard. Nobody, perhaps, has seriously credited Homer with "a purpose," the purpose of enforcing the serious things of ethics touched with religion, and, at the same time, of laughing popular mythology away. The notion seems far too modern and too subtle; yet if Homer had entertained that inconceivable purpose, he could hardly have written otherwise than he did write,—to the extreme perplexity of Greek and later "educationists."[235]

It is not necessary to discuss the chronique scandaleuse of Olympus; the stories of the amours of Zeus, the intrigues of Aphrodite, the jealousy of Hera, the domestic misfortunes of Hephaestus. Nor is this the place to show how this mythological

---

235 The distinction here made between "religion" and "mythology" is made merely for the sake of convenience. We may readily be told that the belief in a good God is as mythical as the tales about bad gods. But the belief in a just, wise, and loving heavenly Father, the source and sanction of ethics, represents one mood, and leads to one set of results in conduct; while the belief in wicked and buffooning gods represents another aspect of human thought, and leads to very different results, mainly to the bewilderment of late historic Greek thinkers.

element inevitably crystalised round a great figure like that of Zeus the father of men. But it seems well to point out that while, in playful moods, the Achaean genius wove a cycle of gross fabliaux around the Olympians, in serious moments men regarded them not sceptically but with perfect seriousness and devoutness. Though men or women conscious of a fault will say that Atê infatuated them, or that Aphrodite thrust them into temptation, nevertheless the gods work for righteousness. Men in the Epics have the strongest sense of dependence on them. They are the givers of good and evil. "Though thou be very strong, yet that, I ween, is a gift to thee of God," says Agamemnon to Achilles. The oath of truce, in Iliad, iii., which, when broken, seals the fate of Troy, is sanctioned by Zeus, the Sun, Rivers, Earth, and they that "in the underworld punish men dead, whosoever sweareth falsely."[236] In a later oath[237] "they" are the Erinnyes, who also punish sins within the family. We hear of no such posthumous punishments in Hades, when Odysseus goes thither in Odyssey, Book xi. The men whom he sees being punished, Tityus, Tantalus, and Sisyphus, have all offended the gods in person;[238] and manifestly to call gods as witnesses to an oath, and then to be forsworn, is to insult the gods, whether this be the explanation of the threatened posthumous punishment or not.[239] The promise of Zeus is an example to men, it can never be broken (Iliad, i. 526-527). "Father Zeus will be no helper of liars," and Achilles "hates a lie like the gates of Hades."

Penitence for wrongs done is recognised, "prayers of penitence are daughters of great Zeus, halting and wrinkled and of eyes askance, that have their task to go in the steps of Sin" (Atê). When the injured man will not listen to the penitence of him who did the wrong, the prayers of the penitent return to Zeus, and beseech him that the hard man "may fall, and pay the price."[240] It was because Achilles refused to accept the penitence of Agamemnon that he "paid the price," the death of Patroclus.

In the Odyssey the ethical aspect of the gods is perhaps more conspicuous, because their passions are no longer stirred by the great war. In the opening lines they discountenance adultery (Aegisthus and Clytaemnestra). They are equally offended by the

---

236 Iliad, iii. 279, 280.

237 xix. 259, 260.

238 Iliad, ix. 502-512.

239 For a variety of theories, see Leaf, Notes to Iliad, iii. 278, xix. 262. Quite possibly the formula of the oath is a survival from a stage of belief more archaic than the ordinary Homeric conception of Hades.

240 Odyssey, i. 263.

use of poisoned arrow-heads.[241] "All men yearn after the gods.". It is they who give happiness in married life.[242] It is Zeus who protects suppliants.[243] The just man is god-fearing.[244] The gods love righteousness and compassion.[245] Throughout the whole poem, notably in the case of the pious Eumaeus, a deep sense of dependence on the gods, and resignation to their will, is depicted. Yet Zeus permits Poseidon to wreak his grudge on Odysseus, and even on the Phaeacians who brought him home; while in the song of Demodocus, a divine adultery is matter of mirth to all Olympus.

Thus the religion of Homer is, ethically, a very good religion. Homeric religion is already national, that is, all Achaeans believe in the same Olympian consistory, with Zeus as the Over Lord. None the less many of the cities have each their favourite divine being, a special patron, just as cities had in the Middle Ages. All believed in the Deity, but Orleans had a special patron in St. Aignan; and "the guarded mount" in St. Michael. Athene was no less the patroness of Troy than of Athens. The Gods are all national, though they have their preferences. We may go further and say that, to Homer's mind, the Gods are universal.

To Homer, Zeus is anything but a "tribal" god: he is not even merely a national god; all peoples known to Homer acknowledge his supremacy. This was the tolerant view of historic Hellas: all nations had the same gods named by different names in different languages. There were not many Zeuses, but one Zeus, though various local names were given to the god, Dodonaean Zeus, Idaean Zeus, Pelasgian Zeus, or, again, Delian Apollo, Pythian Apollo, Smirithian Apollo, and so forth. The god is in no way restricted to a given place, Dodona, Ida, Delos, Delphi; these titles are his because he possesses a temple or Oracle in each district. Men may call to the gods or to a god wherever they find themselves, abroad or at home, on the sea or "in fairy lands forlorn," and everywhere they may sacrifice. To the devout mind, despite the local associations of the gods in mythology, the divine is omnipresent; can hear and help everywhere.[246] As for the local titles of gods, we know the same mediaeval usage in respect to the Saints. The Scot who, when at home, had a devotion to St. Catherine of Bothwell, in France sought

---

[241] iii. 48.

[242] vi. 180-185.

[243] vii. 165.

[244] xiii. 202.

[245] Odyssey, xiv. 82-84.

[246] Iliad, xvi. 516. Prayer of Glaucus to Apollo.

the aid of St. Catherine of Fierbois.[247] The gods, or at least Zeus and Apollo, are omniscient, yet they need, in myth, to be told about events remote or future, or need to make special observations from selected places, such as the crest of Ida. These are the inevitable and universal contradictions which beset all early and much late theological speculation.

When Ionia became speculative as to all things physical or divine, the mythological aspects of the gods in Homer were, what to the philosophers they remained, a stumbling-block. But philosophy could not cure Greece, or do away with her heritage of barbarism and savagery. Yet, in some incomprehensible way, the Achaeans, as represented by Homer, had an infinitely cleaner religion and ritual than the mother cities of the philosophers.

In the religion of historic Greece, from the Ionian age to the establishment of Christianity, the most active, and, so to say, practical element is, we repeat, that of hero-worship, worship of dead men. The great temples of the gods of Greece in general, especially of the oracular Apollo, and of Athene in Athens, Artemis in Ephesus, Artemis Orthia at Sparta, and so on, were maintained in splendour and enriched with treasures of gold-work, silver, and bronze. The god or goddess and the shrines were centres of pilgrimages, and pilgrimages were good for trade. By them were the cities nourished, as the maker of silver shrines at Ephesus declared. Miracles were wrought, the blind saw, the lame walked. The local deity was of as great economic service to a city of Greece as the bones of the Apostle were to St. Andrews, and the relics of St. Thomas to Canterbury.

But for practical purposes of securing supernormal aid in war or famine, the dead heroes were to each town or village what St. Aignan was to Orleans, a very present help in trouble. For near a thousand years St. Aignan routed the foes of the good city, and his image was adored and carried in processions in 1429. Thus "to Lycurgus, after he was dead, the Spartans erected a temple, and paid him great worship."[248] "So that, as might be supposed ... they straightway shot up and became prosperous." The Spartans, therefore, determined to annex Arcadia, but were defeated by the forces of Tegea. Later, in the sixth century, during the time of Croesus, the Spartans asked the Delphic Oracle to direct their choice of a patron god. They were bidden to bring home the bones of Orestes, son of Agamemnon, which were in hostile Tegea. In

[247] Cf. Miracles de Madame de Sainte Catherine de Fierbois, a chapel register of miracles in the Hundred Years' War.
[248] Hdt. i. 66.

Tegea, Lichas found the coffin which contained the bones, seven cubits long (half a cubit longer than Goliath), of Orestes, and carried them to Sparta. Thenceforth the Spartans were victorious. The bones were not in a cairn, for a blacksmith of Tegea first found the coffin when he was digging a well.[249] He would not dig for water in a tumulus or cairn.

We need not multiply examples of hero-worship and relic-snatching, and of such tricks of ghost-scaring as Cleisthenes played when, unable to cast the hero Adrastus bodily out of Sicyon, he drove him away by introducing the worship of the deadly foe of Adrastus, Melanippus.[250] Colonists carried the worship of Achilles into the coasts and isles of the Euxine, and even to Tarentum; while, according to Clemens Alexandrinus, the Spartans worshipped Zeus Agamemnon.[251] All this saint-worship and care for relics is, of course, absolutely un-Homeric.

The Odyssey[252] gives the perhaps Phoenician case of Ino, daughter of Cadmus, once a mortal, now a sea-goddess. But to Homer a dead man, be he Achilles or Aias, is merely a dead man. The cairn covers his bones; he has no chapel, no sacrifice; no men covet the possession of his relics; he can neither help nor harm; his spirit is in Hades, with the powerless peoples of the Dead. Trojans would leap and boast on the cairn of Menelaus if he fell at Troy (Iliad, iv. 174-182). Historic Greeks would have made offerings at the tomb. No such rites were in the belief of the society for which Homer sang. Had they been worshippers of the dead, the epic poet could not play the heresiarch, and tell them that their faith and hope were void and vain. No poet, no set of poets, who lived by pleasing could afford to horrify their hearers by such impiety. No poets could ignore the existence of normal rites that were familiar in practice to all. The most advanced modern novelist cannot ignore the Christian rites of marriage and burial, however much he may despise and detest them. It is, then, an historical fact that the society for which Homer sang did not adore and do sacrifice to dead men, did not make gods of them and do them sacrifice, did not scramble for their relics, as was the practice of proto-historic and historic Greece down to the time of Pausanias at least.

---

[249] i. 67.

[250] v. 67.

[251] See R. G. E. p. 128, note 3; and, for other instances, pp. 180-190.

[252] v. 333-335.

CHAPTER XIII

TEMPLES. ALTARS. RITUAL. PURIFICATION

Homeric religion is so advanced that we cannot expect to learn from it anything about the earliest origins, or to illustrate it from what we know of the most primitive forms of belief (it would be absurd to look in Homer for any trace of totemism or exogamy). Yet Homeric religion is so far naïf and fresh, in that it is not the work of a priestly caste; its services have not been elaborated by the mummeries of interested medicine-men. As for sacrifice itself, it were superfluous to quote passages in which sacrifice pleases the gods, and is counted to men for righteousness. But it appears that the Olympians valued sacrifice rather as a proof that men were mindful of them, and wished to stand well in their eyes, than for any good they got from the smoke and savour. They had their own nectar and ambrosia.

There were priests and there were prophets, but the State was decidedly "Erastian." The Commander-in-chief superintended sacrifices in the general interest, where the welfare of the host was concerned, and individuals sought the favour of the gods by sacrifices offered at their own expense. These were most elaborate after a theophany, or visit from a visible and friendly god, as when Athene sat at meat with Nestor in his house at Pylos. The rite is minutely described: the household of Nestor and the crew of Telemachus are summoned, the cow is driven up from the meadow; the goldsmith brings his tools: seats are set out, wood is collected, water for hand-washing is brought; Nestor provides gold to gild the horns of the victim, and make it seem splendid in the eyes of the goddess. The son of Nestor, Thrasymedes, holds the axe; Perseus has the vessel into which its blood fell,—whether to avoid making a mess, or because the ground must not be ceremonially polluted by the gore. But of ceremonial pollution of any kind, Homer is ignorant. He says nothing suggestive of a sacramental theory of the blood as apt "to pollute the earth or even cry for vengeance."[253]

Nestor, then, does the rite of hand-washing and scattering barley grain: Thrasymedes hamstrings the cow, which falls; and the

[253] Mr. Murray takes this view, R. G. E. p. 64; but there is no trace of such ideas in Homer.

women raise a cry, not a wail of sympathy as among the Todas in India. (It may be a cry of joyful vengeance. Odysseus forbids Eurycleia to raise this cry (ὀλυλύξαι) over the blood of the dead wooers.[254]) "The ὀλυλυγή was a joyful cry, uttered by women, especially at the moment of the consummation of a sacrifice."[255] Pisistratus then slaughters the victim; "the black blood flowed from it, and the life left the bones." The limbs are carved, fat is laid on them; the flesh is roasted, cut up, and put on spits; then follows the feast.[256] The same rites are practised on solemn occasions in time of war and in a hostile country, when a whole hecatomb is sent with Chryseis to Chryses, priest of Apollo.[257] We do not hear in this case of the gilding of the horns of the victims,—there were too many of them,—but Diomede promises a sacrifice of a heifer with gilded horns to Athene, before setting forth to slay the sleeping Thracians in the Trojan camp.[258] Sacrifice may be offered in a temple, or at an altar in the open air. Twelve kine are sacrificed in the Trojan temple of Athene,[259] but a temple could not accommodate a hecatomb.

An army in the field has no temples, and does sacrifice in the open air; indeed, even where temples exist there are abundant altars in the open air; for example, where Hector did sacrifice, "amid the crests of many-folded Ida," and at other times on the city height.[260]

Temples are not often mentioned in the Epics, where the host usually worships under the sky, and has no temples of its own; or Odysseus is wandering "in fairy lands forlorn." An army on the march or in the trenches would build no temples, nor would Odysseus find them among cannibals. But that fairy isle, Phaeacia, had its temples of the gods built by the first settler, Nausithous.[261]

---

254 Odyssey, xxii. 407-416.

255 Monro, Note to Odyssey, xxii. 408.

256 Odyssey, iii. 420-472.

257 Iliad, i. 447-468.

258 Iliad, x. 291-294. Mr. Murray compares Nestor's "timid, religious, almost tender sacrifice of the ox" with "the habitual sacrifices of the Iliad," which "seem like the massacres of a slaughter-house, followed by the gorging of pirates." In his opinion Nestor's cow was a kind of member of the family, "the common blood running in the veins of all," while the alien cattle at Troy are not the most distant relations of the invaders (R. G. E. pp. 59-65). Homer knows nothing of these ideas, as we see; all depends on the degree of solemnity and on the occasion of the sacrifice. If it be solemn, the same rites are used in Troyland during war as in Pylos during peace.

259 Iliad, vi. 308-310.

260 xxii. 170-172.

261 Odyssey, vi. 10.

Altars at the siege of Troy are set up in the field, as at Orleans during the two solemn masses on the day of the raising of the siege (May 8, 1429). The Gods have their groves, whether a temple was in each of them or not. Originally it is probable that caves, as at Delos, or the Dictaean cave of Crete, or gorges, as at Delphi, were the sacred places; but Homer knows the stone threshold of the temple of Apollo at Delphi, and the wealth of offerings within,[262] where Agamemnon consulted the Oracle.[263] The priest, Chryses, had "roofed a shrine" for Apollo.[264] Apollo, in Troy, had a temple, with a great adyton; and Athene's temple had a sacred seated image of the goddess.[265] Athene also in Athens[266] went to the temple of Erechtheus. Given the circumstances of the heroes in both Epics, an army in the field, a wanderer in unknown lands, the rare mention of temples is no proof that, when they appear, they mark "late" passages, while the altars in the open air mark "early" passages: moreover, hecatombs could not be slain in temples, nor could a large army be accommodated in the house of a god. When the Achaeans were sacrificing several hecatombs at once to Zeus, in Aulis, they naturally could not do so in a temple, but under a fair plane tree, by a clear running stream.[267]

In the symbolical sacrifices that sanctioned the taking of oaths, the rite was extremely simple. Agamemnon cuts the hair from the lambs' heads, utters the appeal to Zeus and all powers to bear witness, then cuts the throats of the victims, and libation of wine is made. Priam carries the dead lambs away in his chariot; but when a boar is the victim, in the oath of Agamemnon to Achilles, it is thrown into the sea.[268] We see no sacrifice within the temple of a city except that in association with which Theano, a married

---

[262] Iliad, ix. 404.

[263] Odyssey, viii. 79-81.

[264] Iliad, i. 39.

[265] Iliad, v. 445-448, vi. 297-310.

[266] Od. vii. 81.

[267] Ibid. ii. 305, 306. Mr. Murray supposes that the author of Iliad, i. 39, is later than the author of Iliad, i. 446 ff. The "earlier" poet of i. 446 makes Chryses sacrifice many oxen in the open air. The "later" author of i. 39 makes Chryses talk of roofing a temple. "The writer of that line did not observe that in his original there had been no temple, only an altar. To him an altar implied a temple, so he took the temple for granted" (R. G. E. p. 150). By such devices is the Iliad torn into tatters, later and earlier. Surely a god may have a temple, though the slaughter of hundreds of oxen is not carried on within its walls!

[268] Iliad, iii. 292-310, xix. 250-268.

priestess of a maiden goddess, lays a robe on the knees of Athene, while the attendant ladies raise the ὀλολυγή.[269]

In peace, as in war, Homer's people are free from the lower superstitions, if we except the belief in augury and the omens from the flight of birds. Hector's famous phrase, "one omen is best, to fight for our own country," would have shocked most of the Generals of Republican Rome. A phantasm of the dead, as we saw, may appear only in a dream or a "border-land case," to a man in bed, if the dead man has not been cremated. The boding visions of the second-sighted man in the Odyssey, the shroud of mist about the bodies of the doomed Wooers, may indicate a superstitious belief—to those who do not believe in second sight! The fairies of Homer, nymphs of mountain and well, wood and sea, are creatures of poetry, rather than of superstition; they are fair and frail, but their kisses, unlike those of their kindred from Argyll to the Pacific, are not fatal.

Homer knows nothing of taboos. That the Achaeans "let their hair grow long" is true enough, but does not suggest that they were under a vow not to cut it till they took Troy.[270] The representations of men in many works of Aegean art, such as the gold cups of Vaphio, show them wearing clustering love-locks that fall beneath the shoulder. We might as well accuse the Spartans and the Cavaliers as the Achaeans of wearing love-locks because of a vow. That the Achaeans were tabooed from love during the siege is a fact entirely unknown to their poet. "To every man a damsel or two" is his version, and the heroes couch with their fair captives; while Agamemnon takes a solemn oath that he has never done so with Briseis, and Thetis advises Achilles to rejoice in love. A goddess would not advise the breach of a religious vow of continence.[271]

To the folklorist it is almost annoying to find, in so ancient a poet, so little of the seamy side of folklore. But the later poets of Greece apply it very abundantly: it was rampant in their temple-rites and temple-legends. Homer speaks of no witches, of no incantations save the song for the staunching of the blood of Odysseus, when his thigh had been gored by the boar. The belief in such staunching is still common in Cumberland and in Ireland, as it was when Jeanne d'Arc refused to let the charm be sung over her arrow wound at Orleans.

Magic done for the good of the crops, as in the Eleusinian and

---

269 Ibid. vi. 297-301. Mr. Leaf remarks that "it is needless to seek for Athenian inspiration" in this passage.

270 R. G. E. p. 123, for another view.

271 See R. G. E. pp. 123, 124, for the religious vow of celibacy.

other mysteries, does not appear in the Epics. A good king has good luck, under him all things prosper; but the idea of sacrificing an unlucky king, or any other human being, would have surprised the poet. In all such matters he is on another plane than the authors of the Ionian epics, whose tales of constant human sacrifices are perhaps adapted from Märchen (where cannibalism is the horror) rather than inspired by veridical traditions. The great rite which Homer ignores, and which the pre-Achaean population probably, and certainly all post-Homeric Greece from the eighth century to the arrival of Christianity held in most regard, was the purification of manslayers by the blood of beasts. Achilles in the Cyclic poems is purified by Odysseus after the slaying of Thersites; Apollo is purified after the slaying of the dragon of Delphi.

But "the whole idea of pollution as a consequence of wrong-doing is foreign to Homer," says Mr. Monro.[272] When the house of Odysseus is cleansed of the blood of the slain Wooers, and when, on restoring Chryseis, Agamemnon "bade the folk purify themselves, so they purified themselves, and cast the defilements into the sea, and did sacrifice to Apollo,"[273] the pollution is mere physical filth of house and camp. There is no idea of magical riddance from either sin or danger at the hands of a pursuing ghost. Eustathius, bishop of Thessalonica, remarks, in his Homeric commentary, "on the cardinal difference between the religion of Homer and that of later (and earlier) Greece...."[274] It would have been safer to discriminate between Homeric religion on one hand, and Ionian, Attic, and historic Greek religion on the other.

The idea at the root of the purification of a man-slayer by a bath of blood is not, I think, that his sin is being removed by the "sympathetic magic" of new blood, but that the swine's blood poured over him throws the avenging ghost of his victim off his scent, confusing the trail; or that the angry ghost accepts the pig's blood washed from the slayer as atonement. Plato says that the myth held that the ghost of the victim communicates its own uneasy emotions to the slayer, telepathically.[275] Scores of savage and one or two Hellenic practices aim at actually disarming or mutilating the avenging ghost, by binding or dismembering the corpse which he tenanted. Homer believes that, a man once burned and buried, his ghost is confined, powerless, to Hades. Hence his Achaeans neither worship the dead nor practise purification to avoid avenging ghosts.

---

[272] Odyssey, vol. ii. p. 362.

[273] Iliad, i. 311-316.

[274] Miss Harrison, Proleg. Greek Rel. p. 29.

[275] Laws, ix. 865.

These rites are Ionic, Attic, and, in historic Greece, are Hellenic, also Asiatic. They make an insuperable barrier between Homeric and Ionian religion.

It is certain that among the Ionians of the seventh century B.C. a mystic purification from blood-guilt was the usual practice. Herodotus tells us that it was, in the sixth century, the practice of the Phrygians, Lydians, and, in his own day, of the Hellenes. "The manner of cleansing among the Lydians is the same, almost, as that which the Hellenes use."[276] 3 Aeschylus informs us that the blood of swine was employed in purification.[277] The purifier, in historic Greece, "washed off the blood from the suppliant who is being purified, and, having stirred up the washing, poured it into a trench to the west of the tomb."[278]

Possibly the Ionians had adopted, in Asia, the Oriental idea of pollution and the Oriental mode of cleansing. Homer not only ignores, but knows not these things. Nor, I think, do we find purification in early Celtic and Teutonic and Scandinavian "saga."

We have more light on the method of purification from works of art. On an Apulian vase, Apollo holds a little pig above the head of the polluted matricide, Orestes, with one hand, in the other he grasps a long bough of laurel, which in Roman lustrations had a purifying effect. Melampus, on a Greek cameo, purifies the daughter of Proetus in the same fashion.[279]

NOTE

There is a singular case in which later tradition introduced purification where Homer says nothing about it. In Odyssey, xxi. 1-41, the poet explains how Odysseus came to possess the Bow of Eurytus. When he was but a lad he was sent to recover certain sheep stolen by men of Messenia. He met Iphitus, son of Eurytus, of Oechalia, looking for his lost mares and mules, and Iphitus presented him with the Bow. Thence Iphitus went to the house of Heracles in Tiryns, and there was murdered by his host.

Now we know at first hand, from Nestor himself (Iliad, xi. 685-692), that Heracles, before Nestor's first feat of arms, had

---

[276] Hdt. i. 35.

[277] Eumenides, 273.

[278] Proleg. Greek Religion, 59, 60, quoting Athenaeus, ix. 78, 409 E, who cites two writers on Athenian rites, Kleidemus and Doritheus. Miss Harrison supposes that the ghost drinks the blood of the slain animal, washed off the body of the slayer, in place of the slayer's blood.

[279] Frazer, Pausanius, vol. iii pp. 278, 593.

attacked his family in Pylos, and that out of Nestor's twelve brothers he alone had escaped. "For the mighty Heracles had come and oppressed us, in former years, and all our best men were slain. For twelve sons were we of noble Neleus, whereof I alone was left, and all the others perished," but Neleus survived.

This feud of Heracles was a famous theme; the legend included the fairy story of Periclymenus, brother of Nestor. Poseidon had given him the gift of taking all sorts of shapes, but when he settled on the chariot of Heracles in the shape of a bee, Athene pointed out the bee to Heracles, who shot it. In Iliad, v. 393, we learn that Heracles once wounded Hades and Hera. The later Pylians conceived Nestor's wounding of Hades to have occurred at their town, when the hero attacked the household of Neleus. Nestor, in the passage quoted, says nothing about the help of Hades on this occasion, but Dione (v. 397) says that Heracles wounded Hades ἐν πύλῳ ἐν νεκύεσσι, "in Pylos among the dead." Aristarchus took this to mean in the gate, in the country of the dead. The incident would be part of the journey of Heracles to hell, to bring back "the dog" Cerberus. On this showing Homer is not saying that Hades fought vainly against Heracles in his raid on Nestor's town. But Homer never elsewhere uses pylos for "a gate."

The affair is confusing, but later legend associated Heracles's feud against Neleus with the rites of purification. Nestor does not tell us, but the Venetian scholiast on his speech does tell us that Neleus had refused to purify Heracles for the murder of Iphitus, his guest, under trust.

Was the Homeric poet of Nestor's speech (xi. 693) ignorant of this "cause of wrath," and is it a later invention after the custom of purification came in; or did Homer "expurgate" a rite which he found in pre-Achaean tradition?

The certain fact is that the society for which the Iliad and Odyssey was composed did not practise the sanguinary rite, and took no interest in it. In Mr. Ridgeway's theory, Heracles is not Achaean, he is Pelasgic. If, then, the poet, whether Achaean or, in Mr. Ridgeway's view, a Pelasgian minstrel of an Achaean lord, adopted Heracles from Pelasgian legend, and if that legend spoke of purification, the poet ignored it, as a thing not in the manners of his Achaean audience.

CHAPTER XIV

HOMER AND IONIA

Who were the Ionians?

While the ancients believed that the Homeric poems were composed in the Greek settlements on the Asian coast, and brought from Ionia to Hellas, modern critics often hold that the earliest lays were made in Greece, but that our Iliad and Odyssey contain a large percentage of much later Ionian work. In these circumstances it is natural to ask, Who were the Ionians? a point on which Homer throws no light. The Ionian name is not mentioned in the Catalogue any more than the Aeolian and Dorian names, and "the tunic-trailing Iaones" only appear in Iliad, xiii. 685, where they are very hard pressed in defending the part of the Achaean wall where it was lowest, near the ships of Aias and the dead Protesilaus. They are brigaded with Locrian light-armed archers, the Boeotians, Phthians, and Epeians of Elis, and "the picked men of the Athenians," whose leaders are Menestheus, king of Athens, as in the Catalogue, and three others. Thus the Ionians appear to be equivalent to the Athenians. The epithet "chiton-trailers" occurs but this once in Homer, and, of course, is inappropriate to the warlike occasion: the Ionians of the seventh century certainly wore the short tight cypassis, not the chiton, when actively engaged. In the Ionian hymn to Apollo the Ionians are "chiton-trailers," but the occasion is a public festival.

The whole passage, according to Mr. Leaf, is "very probably an Attic interpolation, with the object of giving respectable antiquity to the hegemony of Athens over the Ionian tribes"; but, as the Ionians of Asia were proud of their connection with Athens, and far from proud, says Herodotus, of the name Ionian, they are as likely as the Athenians to have added the lines. In short, the Ionian name, like the Dorian and the Aeolian names, never occurs in the Iliad; while the Athenian king, Menestheus, never draws sword or throws spear in the poem. It will be observed that, when he does mention Athenian leaders, Menestheus the king, Bias, Stichios, and Pheidas, Homer does not, as is his custom, assign to any one of them a divine ancestor, nor even name the father of any one of them, except Petoos, father of Menestheus. He tells no anecdote about any of them. In the Catalogue (ii. 546-551) the Athenians alone appear as worshippers of dead men, though in Mycenaean pre-Homeric

Greece this rite was certainly part of religion, as also in historic Greece, and in Attica it has an uninterrupted record. It is not inconceivable, though by no means certain, that the Athenians interpolated their own mention in the Catalogue, with the very few allusions to their king, Menestheus; but except for these, the epics almost ignore Attica, ignore the Ionians, and, to learn anything of their early history, we must turn to other sources.

By the time of Pausanias (post-Christian) and much earlier, for Euripides wrote a play against the myth, and it was current in the time of Herodotus, the Athenians and Ionians had arranged for themselves a fabulous genealogy. Their purpose was to connect themselves with the supposed most genuine prehistoric Hellenes, namely, those of Achilles's realm in Hellas, part of the kingdom of Peleus, in south-west Thessaly.

In precisely the same way the Scottish makers of fabulous genealogy connected the Stewart kings,—really Fitz Alans, with the Dalriadic Royal House of the Scoti from Ireland (descendants of the Scythian princess, Scota), who invaded Argyll about 500 A.D. The name of these Scoti of Ireland had finally been given to the whole country north of Tweed and Esk, and so its kings must be Eteoscoti, genuine Scots.

The Athenian and Ionian genealogists worked on the same principles. Their heroes are as apocryphal as Princess Scota of Scythia, and their genealogies vary with the motives of each genealogist. They believed that they were "Pelasgians," that they did not originally bear the name which was by their time prepotent, "Hellenes," and was applied to all Greeks; but, in the fable given by Pausanias they hitched themselves thus on to the Hellenes and Achaioi whom Achilles led from Thessaly. To the seacoast on the south of the Corinthian gulf, the Aigialos or "sea-board" (held by Agamemnon in the Catalogue) came Xuthus, son of Hellen, out of Thessaly; being expelled, after Hellen's death, by his brothers. He had first fled to Athens, which in all these fabrications represents herself as not originally Hellenic or Achaean, but as the constant asylum of all distressed Achaean princes; Theban, like Oedipous, or Eleian, like the descendants of Nestor, and Orestes, having here Homeric warrant (Odyssey, iii. 306). We have a parallel in the continuous efforts of Highland genealogists, at one period, to claim descent from Normans who came north out of England and married the heiresses of the Celtic chiefs; as the Campbells (Crooked-Mouths) claimed descent from a Norman "De Campo Bello," or Beauchamp.

On these lines, then, the Hellene from Thessaly, Xuthus, married at Athens the heiress of the king, the daughter of

Erechtheus; and had two sons, Achaeus and Ion. Thus the Achaeans of south-west Thessaly have a little of Athenian blood, for Achaeus went back to Thessaly and reigned there; and the Ionians of Athens are mixed up with the sons of Hellen in a more roundabout way. Ion, son of Xuthus, son of Hellen, was domiciled in the Aigialos, the south coast of the Corinthian gulf, because his father, Xuthus, had been driven thither from Athens, and reigned there. Ion succeeded to the throne of the Aigialos, but was buried in Attica, having died there while in command of an Athenian army. His seacoast subjects on the southern seaboard of the Corinthian gulf, originally "Pelasgians," but now called after him "Ionians," were thus in relations with Attica, and they migrated thither in a body, when they were driven from home by the Achaeans whom the Dorian invaders had expelled from their seats in the southern and western Peloponnese. The Ionians, so far, appear as a pre-Achaean people of the northern coast of Peloponnesus, Hellenic only through their Royal House, that of Ion; and later settled in Attica, among a people also pre-Hellenic in origin.

Attica later offered an asylum to the Neleidae, descendants of Nestor, who, like the Fitz Alan Stewarts in Scotland, obtained the throne of the country in which they settled. When a son of Codrus, the last of these Neleid kings of Athens, led a colony from Attica to the Asian coast, the most part of the Attic emigrants were Ionians settled in Attica, not Athenians, though some Athenians accompanied them; and the Royal contingent, starting from Athens, settled at Miletus.[280]

Thus, in this legend, the people of Attica, in the main, are not Hellenic, not Achaean in origin, but are connected with the Thessalian Hellenes and Achaioi by Royal marriages; while, though not in origin Ionians, they are intermingled, both in Attica and in the Asian settlements, with that seacoast people, themselves only Achaean through the grandson of Hellen, Ion, their king.

Historic Greek inquirers understood the matter in that way, and we must first examine their "Pelasgian" theories.

With theories ancient or modern, fantastic or scientific, or both scientific and fantastic, about "Pelasgians" and other "races" in the prehistoric south of Europe; with deductions from place-names in Greece, the isles, and the Asian coasts; with speculations about "Aryans" and "non-Aryans," long-headed and short-headed, dark-haired and light-haired peoples, I have nothing to do. We have not statistics of pigmentation in prehistoric or in historic Greece, or craniological statistics. We cannot translate certain fourth century

---

[280] Pausanias, vii. i. 11.

inscriptions from Crete, written in Greek characters, bat in a language which, though not improbably "Indo-European," must have been to Greeks as unintelligible as to ourselves. We cannot even read the characters of Minoan writing. The much manipulated legends of movements of peoples which reach us in Greek books vary enormously, as Pausanias says, from each other, and are no more historical than the Irish legends of the migrations of the Scots from Scythia to Scotland by way of Athens, Egypt, and Spain. My sole object is to make intelligible the version of their own origin which the Athenians and Ionians offered, and to show that they did, in some moods, draw a distinction between their own ancestors and Homer's Hellenes and Achaeans. There was a distinction, in tradition, religion, rites, and customs, but there may have been no great difference in blood and language.

One thing, then, is certain, the Athenians and Ionians admitted that they were Hellenic in race and speech merely through slight contact with Achaeans. Attica was never "Achaeanised" in religion, burial rites, and other ritual. Attica was never conquered by Achaeans, she stood apart. Now this claim to be a region apart, conquered neither by Achaeans nor Dorians, is certainly supported by the fact that the traditions and legends of Attica stand widely remote in all respects from the ancient Achaean legends in Homer, and in Theban and Minyan and Aetolian "saga," or bardic traditions.[281] The traditions of the Ionians in Asia, again, are connected with those of Attica rather than with the Achaean saga, although the Ionians of Asia were not, and were known not to be, by any means of solely Attic descent. This is confessed.

Returning to the Ionians of Asia, and their account of themselves given in the time of Herodotus, we find that it agrees with the fabulous genealogies already studied. The Ionians claimed to have in-habited twelve cities of what, in the time of Herodotus, was called "Achaia," the Aigialos in the northern Peloponnese;—that they were driven thence to Attica by Achaeans, fugitives from the Dorians in other parts of Peloponnese, is asserted by Herodotus. Ionians were also, of old, in Boeotia, neighbours of the "Cadmeians," and some of the Cadmeians were admitted, on conditions, to Athenian citizenship.[282]

---

[281] "Athenians and Achaean traditions."

[282] Hdt. v. 57, 58, 61. The Cadmeians, till very recently, were regarded as Phoenicians, Semites. Now the name "Phoenicians" ("red men") is understood to mean men of the old Aegean race, and no traces of Semitic import have been discovered in the soil of Boeotia. Thebes itself was "Minoan," not Semitic. Evans, Scripta Minoa, vol. i.

It thus appears that the people later called, in Asia, "Ionians," had been dwellers on the coasts of Boeotia and Attica, as well as on the northern Peloponnese. That they were then and there known as "Ionians" it would be difficult to prove. Homer has nothing to say of the Ionians as a peculiar people in the Peloponnesus or Boeotia. Of their twelve Peloponnesian cities, the Catalogue gives Orneai, Pellênê, Aigeira, and Helikê to Agamemnon.[283]

If Homer really knew any people called Ionians at all, they were Athenian. Meanwhile the people of the Ionian name in Asia were, according to Herodotus, "a mixed multitude," including members of the communities known to Homer as Abantes of Euboea, with forty ships, Phocians, even Arcadians, Cretans, and many others. All these could only be lumped together as "Ionians" after their settlement in Asia, and their alliance with the Ionian colonists from Attica.

If the so-called Ionian emigrants were thus mixed, and if some of them possessed Achaean lays or legends, and at first practised only the rites mentioned by Homer, such as cremation and cairn-burial, it would appear that the pre-Hellenic element among these settlers in Asia overpowered the other elements, or that the Cyclic poets of Ionia were mainly of pre-Hellenic origin. Their poems, at all events, are in harmony with Attic ideas and usages, not with Homer's statements: and, as we shall show, the Ionian poets cannot have tampered much with our Homer, for the two Epics never admit the Ionian manners which are copiously illustrated by the Ionian poets of the Trojan war, the Cyclics.

According to Thucydides as well as Herodotus, the so-called Ionian migration was a movement of mixed peoples. The leading men of various Achaean regions had found an asylum in Attica during the troubles caused by the Dorian incursions, and "so greatly increased the number of inhabitants that Attica became incapable of containing them, and was at last obliged to send colonies to Ionia."[284]

We are thus on almost historic ground when we believe that the settlers in Ionia, though their tendency was to claim Athenian connections, were "a mixed multitude" from many States, mainly of the seacoasts; and it is natural to suppose that they intermarried with Carians at Miletus, as Herodotus says that they also did with Lycians, and other Asiatic civilised peoples. Though alien religions might be accepted by the settlers, these beliefs would be Hellenised,

---

[283] Iliad, ii. 571, and Leaf's note, ii. 560. Hdt. i. 145.
[284] Thucydides, i. 2.

as usual; and the Olympian Poseidon, the Homeric sea-god, patronised the Ionian league of cities.

We really have no historical evidence for the earliest conditions of Ionian life in Asia. Mr. Murray supposes the early settlers to have lost all "tribal obligations," all "old laws," and even "household and family life." "It looks as if the ancestors of the Ionians had in the extreme stress of their migrations lost hold upon their Achaean traditions." But the Ionians had no Achaean traditions to lose! They built walls to their new cities, and inside the wall a man "could take breath. He could become for a time a man again, instead of a frightened beast." A terrible picture is drawn of the sufferings and ferocious cruelties of the invaders, who, however, remain orthodox in religion after all, and confident in "the manifest help of Zeus and Apollo."[285] This is not the condition of frightened beasts. In fact, they were not in that terror-stricken condition when they were able to build walls.

No doubt there was a great deal of rough work; though, as shall be shown, judging from the art of the Dipylon, the Attic colonists were highly civilised men, with large ships, and everything handsome about them, who could make well-organised short voyages, with abundance of stores. Nor, when they landed, were they, like the early Puritans of New England, in a country of naked savages. Lycians and Carians, in Homer, are as much civilised as the Achaeans: a Carian woman was not a bloodthirsty squaw.

It is not to late legends, but to archaeology, that we must look for information: "on archaeology fell, and falls, the burden of proof in this inquiry."[286]

First, as to the culture of the mainland which the colonists left; we do know through excavations at Sparta something about Dorian civilisation there as early as the ninth century B.C., and it is probable that the Ionians in Europe were rather in advance of than behind the contemporary Dorians in the arts of life. The precinct of Artemis Orthia at Sparta has been excavated, and yields "remains of a temple in crude brick with wooden frame-work ... this structure the discoverers" (members of the British School of Athens) "refer to the ninth century B.C." A similar temple "has appeared also in Hellenic Asia, at Neandria in the Aeolic Troad."

Near the Orthian temple was "a great Altar of Sacrifice, whose orientation was the same."[287]

Homer's men, we saw, usually sacrifice hecatombs outside of

---

[285] R, G. E. 50-57.

[286] Hogarth. Ionia and the East, p. 12.

[287] Hogarth, p. 34.

the temple, though twelve kine are sacrificed in the temple of the Trojan Athena.

The votive objects found in this Spartan precinct of the ninth century were pottery in the Geometric, post-Aegean style, with ivory plaques, at least as large as an ordinary playing card, covering the safety pin of the fibula. The earliest designs incised on these plaques of ivory "repeat in more than one case Aegean motives" (such as the goddess holding a bird in each hand); the style is touched with Mesopotamian influences, but more deeply by the art of the Bronze Age in the area of the Danube. The "double coil" or "pair of spectacles" shape of fibula-cover, familiar in the Danubian region, also occurs.[288]

Such being the art in the new home of the Dorian invaders, we expect to find art rather better than worse among the Ionians at Attica at the same period—the ninth century B.C., which is doubtless much later than the central period of the Ionian migration to Asia. The tombs of Spata in Attica, and the treasure from Aegina in the British Museum, are taken as relics of the late "Sub-Aegean" art of, say, the tenth to ninth centuries. The ivories of Sparta "suggest some art of West Asia": the Aegina objects in gold are partly "Aegean" survivals, partly show unmistakable Egyptian influence passed through an Oriental medium. The well-known gold cup of Aegina, with its rosette and four spirals, has a parallel from one of the rich royal tombs of the Mycenaean acropolis: there are also, as at Mycenae, many thin round plaques of gold, probably sewn originally on robes. The rings bear no signets: one is in the form of a buckler, like a reduced Mycenaean figure-of-eight shield, inlaid with blue glass paste. The figure of a man or god holding a water-fowl in each hand, and wearing a loin-cloth, is of a modified Egyptian character. The date of the objects is placed between the tenth and ninth centuries.[289]

Probably the Ionian emigrants from the mainland near Aegina left behind them some, and probably they took with them other craftsmen capable of executing such work in gold as we have described. But they also left in Attica the potters who, about the ninth to eighth centuries, B.C., covered the great vases, which did duty for headstones in the cemetery of the Dipylon, with geometric ornament and barbaric representations of life. It was no barbarian life that they knew, crudely as they designed it. The people of Athens, as the vases prove, had four-horse chariots; had large ships manned by many oarsmen, and furnished with a submerged sharp

---

[288] Ibid. pp. 34-36.

[289] Chipiez et Perrot, La Grèce de l'Epopée, pp. 235-246.

ram. The warriors in the chariots wore shields slung by baldrics: in form they were circular, in other cases they exaggerated, in much smaller dimensions, the features of the Aegean figure-of-eight shield, or were smaller forms of the Aegean oblong shield. Here and there a spearman holds in front of him an oval shield by the handle. The swords are straight short swords, worn at right angles to the waist, not heavy Homeric swords, slung by a baldric from the shoulder. In some cases, however, heavy leaf-shaped blades are used, both for cut and thrust.

The people had great spectacular funerals. The body of the dead lay on a bier in the house, while men, women, and children, mere skeleton figures, plucked out their hair with both hands. Then the body was borne in a chariot to the grave (it was seldom cremated), and a procession of charioteers followed.

The swords and spears were of iron, none had richly adorned hilts of ivory and gold.

The gold work of the period, chiefly stamped on thin bands, was not quite so crude as that of the potter with his triangle reversed for a body, the monstrous thighs and calves of his men, their bird-shaped inhuman faces,—all of them remote from the Aegean art, and apparently of northern origin. The artists in gold work were in advance of the vase-painters, whose horses usually have a thing like a fish for head, set on a neck like a serpent.

The Attic region, towards the end of the Ionian migration, thus presents the decay of Aegean and the bloom of geometric decoration, and of barbaric, probably northern design. None the less the life depicted so barbarously was no barbaric life. Bad as is the art, you see that the life is Hellenic.

At the same time the Dipylon life is wholly un-Homeric. The manner of burial, the huge vases in place of the cairn and pillar, the metal of the weapons, iron, their want of adornment, the size, shape, and mode of carrying the sword, the tearing out of their own hair by mourners, the size of the shields, and even the dress of the women who, in my opinion, wear skirts, not chitons, are all of a nature unknown to the Epics. Poets of the Dipylon age could never have preserved the uniform Homeric descriptions of details totally unlike what they saw in actual existence.

About the relics of the earliest Ionian settlements in Asia, archaeology now knows something. The excavations of Mr. Hogarth on the earliest site of the Ionian temple of Artemis at Ephesus (700 B.C.?), revealed thousands of votive offerings in gold, ivory, bone, paste, crystal, and other materials. These had been "carefully laid between the slabs for some hieratic purpose," probably under the central statue of the goddess. Mr. Hogarth dates the deposit at about 700 B.C., "some two centuries after the traditional landing of the colonists."

That date tells us little about the condition of the settlers at the time of landing (we can only guess as to whether they had almost ceased to be human at that moment), but many objects may be heirlooms of earlier date; "in any case the elaborate execution and design of the Ionian documents, notably the trinkets and jewels in electrum, imply a long previous evolution of skilled craft"; and there are indications "that this Primitive treasure was, in the main, made at Ephesus itself." This is proved by the presence of goldsmiths' refuse in the temple. The treasure has many analogies with that of Enkomi (Cyprus) in the British Museum, which is of the period of the re-occupation of the palace of Cnossos in Crete (dated about 1400), and is therefore of the close of the age of bronze. The Ephesian treasure has also many points of close analogy with the later Aegean remains at Mycenae and Sparta in Attica. There are the gold jewels meant to be sewn on to the robes; there are the clear crystals so common in the ancient graves of the Mycenaean acropolis; the familiar double axe of Crete is still a decorative motive; we find, as on the Lion Gate of Mycenae, two animals opposed in heraldic fashion, and fibulae decorated with Baltic amber, also the "spectacles" fibula-cover in ivory, common as far north as Bosnia.

The general result of the archaeological evidence for early Ionia is to show, in early Ionian work, the Aegean element stronger, and the Danubian or central European element less strong, than in contemporary Attica of the Dipylon period. In Attica of 1000-800 B.C. there was the mixture of new northern and of old Aegean blood and civilisation; but, says Mr. Hogarth, "the Aegean element was, I conceive, relatively very much more numerous and potent in the Ionian land,"—in Asia,—"although, to a very large extent, not indigenous there." The Ionians, as far as archaeology shows, were more Aegean than the people whom they left behind in Attica.

Thus the evidence, so far, is in favour of the mass of Ionian emigrants having been of the older people,—whether we call it "Pelasgian of the coast lands," or by any other name,—and of the older prae-Dipylon school of art. "The first departure," says Mr. Hogarth, "may have been due to the Achaean influx into Greece," though the later Dorian influx may have presented a more powerful motive; for, by the Greek story, the Achaeans driven from Argos and Laconia thrust the Ionians out of the Peloponnesus. The archaeological evidence does not go back far enough to enable us to estimate exactly the state of the Ionians when they first landed in Asia. We only know that, some two centuries later, their art was much more in the Aegean than in the Dipylon manner, and had been so for long. They must have rapidly recovered from their perfect oblivion of their ancient laws, rites, beliefs, and traditions.

Mr. Hogarth concludes: "Note that the date thus assigned" (for the Greek migration, a prolonged movement) "fits with the indications in Homer. The Epics, it has often been remarked, show not only no knowledge of a Hellenic Asia, but also none of a Dorian conquest of Peloponnesus. They were probably anterior in original composition to the establishment of both these states of things," of Greeks in Asia, Dorians in Peloponnesus.[290]

Now archaeology dates the Ephesian finds, which, in the main, are still "Aegean" in character, during the very age when, according to general opinion, the Ionian Cyclic Epics were composed. The early Cyclic poems are usually dated about 770-730 B.C., when the Ephesian treasure was being made.[291] Ionian art at Ephesus, and at that date, was much more Aegean than the contemporary art in Attica. There is thus a fair presumption that the Aegean element, Hellenised, was a strong element in the Ionian population; and we are to demonstrate that the Ionian Epics, though dealing with Achaean themes, abound in non-Achaean traits of life and religion; in the traits which Mr. Murray assigns to "the conquered races,"[292] apparently meaning the pre-Achaean Aegean inhabitants of Greece. These traits are undeniably non-Homeric, and the question must be faced, if the Ionian poets of the eighth and seventh centuries are profuse in such matter, in the Cyclics; and if they also added a great mass to the Iliad and the Odyssey at the same period, why did they keep their favourite themes out of the Iliad and Odyssey? This question we study in "The Ionian Cyclic Poems"; but first we must prove that, whether the people of Attica and the Ionians were apart in "race" from the Hellenes and Achaioi

---

[290] Hogarth, p. 104.

[291] Mr. Murray, however, writes: "We know that the great mass of the saga-poetry began to be left on one side and neglected from the eighth century on; and we find, to judge from our fragments" (of the Cyclic poems), "that it remained in its semi-savage state" (Anthropology in Greek Epic, 1908, p. 68). This knowledge is far from common. The Cyclic poems are in the highly developed Homeric hexameter; they are not, I venture to say, "semi-savage"; and, where they differ in beliefs, rites, and customs from Homer, they represent the usages of historic Hellas. They are generally believed to have been composed at the date when Mr. Murray says that they "began to be neglected." Far from being neglected, they certainly afforded much of the materials of the Athenian tragedians, and of the vase painters who choose many more subjects from the Cyclics than from our Homer.

[292] R. G. E. p. 134.

or not, they certainly stood originally apart from and out of the cycle of Achaean traditions. The Ionians and Attic tragedians were reduced to inventing new legends and new points of contact between themselves and the Achaeans.

NOTE

Language or Languages of Prehistoric Greece.—I have abjured all attempts to discern the truth about races and languages in prehistoric Greece. The two main theories appear to be that of the Greek speculators from the seventh century onwards, and that of Mr. Ridgeway.

According to the Greeks, who varied among themselves, the original population of prehistoric Greece was, at least mainly, "Pelasgian." Among the Pelasgians came a more cultivated people, the "Hellenes," in contact with whom the "Pelasgians" developed into "Hellenes" in language and culture. Granting an influx of Achaeans or Hellenes among the pre-existing population which enjoyed the Aegean civilisation, there is no doubt that this population, if spoken of by Greeks as "Pelasgian," was much more advanced in material culture than the Achaeans. This is proved absolutely by excavations in Crete, Greece, and the isles.

On this point, then, that the Achaeans and Hellenes were more civilised than the pre-existing "Pelasgians," the Greek thinkers were certainly in the wrong. But what about language? Was Herodotus right in holding that the "Pelasgians" spoke a "barbarous" language, and learned Greek from the Hellenes? He admits that he could not speak with any certainty about the language of the Pelasgians. But he infers from the speech of actually contemporary Pelasgians, for example, at Creston in Thrace, and at Placia and Scylace on the Hellespont, "and, in short, of any other of the cities which have dropped the name, but are in fact Pelasgian," that "the Pelasgians spoke a barbarous language" (Herodotus, i. 56-58).

If so, unconquered Attica and unconquered mountainous Arcadia must have spoken, in early times, "a barbarous language," and exchanged it for the Hellenic, though with the Hellenes they were, according to themselves, but slightly in contact. When we consider the pertinacity of parts of Wales, Ireland, and the western Highlands in clinging to Cymric and Gaelic, this theory of Herodotus seems highly improbable.

Mr. Ridgeway, on the other hand, holding that the Achaeans were "a Celtic tribe" who passed from Epirus into Thessaly, concludes that their language was what the Hellenes of history would have called "barbarous"; that they adopted the speech, Greek, of the Pelasgians among whom they settled, and that the Homeric poems descend from the lays of Pelasgian minstrels, who sang in Greek of the exploits of Achaeans who were Celtic, but became merged in a Greek-speaking Pelasgic population (Early Age of Greece, vol. i. p. 648). If so, the minstrels had entirely absorbed the non-Pelasgian customs and ideas, absence of ghosts, and hero-worship, of pollution, and ritual purification, and human sacrifice, and the professed Olympian religion of their Achaean lords.

To the objection that, if Homer's poetic Pelasgian predecessors had the good Greek, no Pelasgians known to Herodotus spoke it, Mr. Ridgeway can reply that "the Greeks considered Phrygians and Thracians to be barbarous, though both spoke languages akin to Greek; so that, although Herodotus thought the languages of Scylace and Placia" (and of all cities which were, in fact, Pelasgian) "barbarous, this does not prove that it was not closely cognate to Greek" (Early Age of Greece, vol. i. p. 146).

Yes, but why had the language of the Pelasgian minstrels of the Achaean lords, which was excellent Greek, become in the time of Herodotus the language which, to him, was barbarous? I understand Mr. Ridgeway to answer this question by saying that "there is no difficulty in supposing that certain Pelasgians long settled in Etruria, whither they had come from Thessaly, may have again emigrated" (out of Etruria) "from some external or internal cause, and settled in various spots around the Aegean, some of them going to Athens, and later to Lemnos." See Herodotus, ii. 50, 51, for Pelasgians who, when the Athenians "were just beginning to count as Hellenes," settled for a while in Attica. For this fact Herodotus cites Hecataeus. These new-come Pelasgians were unruly, and were banished to Lemnos (Hdt. vi. 137). They later came back to raid Brauron in Attica (Hdt. vi. 138). Let these much-wandering Pelasgians return to Thrace, or, at least, let the Pelasgians whom Herodotus knew in Thrace (and all Pelasgians wherever he knew them) have strolled from Thessaly to Etruria in Italy, and back again to the Aegean, and north to Thrace, and it is certain that their original language, Greek (like jour as derived from dies), must have been diablement changé en route, and quite unrecognisable as Greek by Herodotus (see Ridgeway, vol. i. pp. 144-146, and p. 244; also "Who were the Romans?" Proceedings of the British Academy, vol. iii.).

On the whole Pelasgian question, the most valuable analysis of the evidence, such as it is, appears to me to be that of Mr. Myres in the Journal of the Hellenic Society, vol. xxvii.

My only conclusion is that, whoever the Achaeans may have

been, and whatever their language, and whoever the pre-existing population may have been, and whatever their language, the Achaeans imported a new, lofty, and brief-lived set of ideas, customs, a new tone and taste. At the same time, Mr. Ridgeway's arguments in favour of his theory that the pre-Achaean population of Greece spoke Greek, have my assent for what it is worth, though I do not think that the evidence for the hypothesis of Dionysius of Halicarnassus that Thessalian Pelasgians went to Etruria, and that their descendants came back to the Aegean, has valid historical evidence.

CHAPTER XV

ATTIC versus ACHAEAN TRADITIONS

The mixed multitude of Ionian settlers in Asia must have had mixed traditions, not the legends of Athens alone, but those of the towns of the Calaurian amphictyony, and of many other regions, Cretan, Boeotian, Euboean, and so on. The dominant legends, however, in poetry, as known to us, were those of Athens, which are comparatively jejune, being often constructed, perhaps out of the competing variants of the Attic demes, to prove the legitimacy of one or another dynastic claim to the kingship of Athens. We are so familiar with the traditions as manipulated by the great tragedians, that we scarcely notice how absolutely Athens lies outside of the heroic myths of the rest of Greece.

Grote has justly observed that "neither the archaeology" (ancient traditions) "of Attica, nor that of its component fractions, was much dwelt upon by the ancient epic poets of Greece." He might have stated the case much more strongly, for he says, "Theseus is noticed both in the Iliad and Odyssey as having carried off from Crete, Ariadne, the daughter of Minos ... and the sons of Theseus take part in the Trojan war." But Demophon and Acamas, as sons of Theseus, appear, not in the Iliad, but only in the Ionian Cyclic poems; and if Theseus carries off Ariadne in the Odyssey,[293]

[293] xi. 321-325.

not in the Iliad, the passage is of the most dubious, and the myth is obscure.

"Homer is," says Mr. Leaf, "of course, ignorant of the Theseus myth in all its branches."[294] "There is no trace," says Mr. Monro, "in Homer of acquaintance with the group of legends to which the story of Aethra" (mother of Theseus) "belongs."[295] No acknowledged fact can more perfectly demonstrate the difference between Attic and Homeric or Achaean tradition than the circumstance that Homer, while he ignores Theseus, takes a view of Minos and of the Cretan empire directly opposed to Attic legend. This was perfectly plain to educated Athenians of Plato's age.

Thus in the Platonic or pseudo-Platonic dialogue, Minos, Socrates points out that to no other hero does Homer give the same praise as to Minos, as not only a son, but a pupil of Zeus (Od. xix. 178-180). Says Socrates, "Minos every ninth year conversed with Zeus, and went to be instructed by his wisdom,"—"this is marvellous praise." It is thus that Socrates understands the Homeric world. Μίνως ἐννέωρος βασίλευε Διὸς μεγάλου ὀαριστής: "Minos was king, who every nine years conversed with Zeus." "Every nine years Minos went to the cave of Zeus to be instructed," adds Socrates; but of the cave of Zeus, Homer says nothing.

The companion of Socrates then asks how Minos got such a bad name as "an uneducated ruffian"? "Because he made war on us of Athens," answered Socrates; "and we are strong in poets, especially in that delight of the populace, tragic poetry, which is very ancient with us; and on the stage we avenged ourselves on Minos."

In truth, while Homer presented Minos as a son and pupil of Zeus, as no god himself, but a mortal man, whose sceptred spirit administered justice to the souls in Hades, it was impossible for educated Athenians not to recognise that their own wild tales (how wild few knew), were partisan fabrications.

Not only Homer, but Hesiod took the favourable view of Minos, as against the hostile Attic legends; "and these two are more worthy of belief than all the tragic poets together," says Socrates (Minos, 318 d).

The Athenians heaped not only Minos, but his wife and his brother Rhadamanthus, under a pile of ordure. Helbig, who emphatically insists on the gulf between Attic and Homeric accounts of Minos, may be consulted for the abominable anti-Minoan stories.[296]

---

294 Leaf, Note to Iliad, iii. 144.
295 Monro, Odyssey, vol. ii. p. 370.
296 Roscher's Lexikon, under "Minos."

In Homer, Cretan Idomeneus (Iliad, xiii. 450) gives his genealogy as—

Zeus
|
Minos
|
Deucalion (Not he of the Deluge)
|
Idomeneus.

In the Odyssey, xi. 321-325, Minos is named as father of Ariadne, whose tale is alluded to in a puzzling way: the other heroines of the passage are Attic, Phaedra (wife of Theseus) and Procris. In xi. 568571, Minos, "splendid son of Zeus," is seen administering justice to the dead. In a false tale of Odysseus he calls himself a Cretan of the stock of Minos. In xix. 178, Minos is father of Deucalion, and in some way is "the nine years old," or is "at periods of nine years," the companion (ὀαριστής) of Zeus. There is in Homer nothing about the Attic fables of bulls, the Minotaur, or Minoan cruelty. Homeric tradition accepts and glories in the just king Minos: Athenian tradition, in which Attica suffers grievous things at the hands of Crete, heaps hatred and contumely on him, fixing on him the world-wide Märchen of the evil being whose fair daughter befriends the adventurous hero; and adding the Märchen of the black-sailed ship which should have borne white sails of good tidings to Aegeus.

It is not merely the Attic myths of Theseus of Crete, and of the character of Minos, that differ from the Homeric. Attic legends are quite un-Homeric in character.[297] Two Attic characteristics may be noted. "The story of the sacrifice of a maiden" (or of several maidens at once) "appears and reappears in Attic tradition.... We have it in Iphigeneia...."[298] But we have it not in Homer. Again, among the royal family of Athens, in Attic tradition, it was chronic to be metamorphosed into birds. The stories were meant, originally, to account for the colours and habits of birds; such tales are numberless in the legends of Australian and other savages, who have a whole mythology of primal fowls, which is restated in the parabasis of The Birds of Aristophanes. Homer tells but one such bird myth. In Odyssey, xix. 518, Penelope speaks of the daughter of Pandareus, the brown bright nightingale, lamenting "Itylus, whom

---

[297] See Miss Harrison's Mythology and Monuments of Ancient Athens, London, 1890.

[298] Ibid., p. 56, note. For human sacrifice see "The Cyclic Poems," later.

she slew with the sword unwittingly; Itylus, son of Zethus the prince." "The story has, as would be expected in a Homeric myth, nothing whatever to do with Athens."[299] The Attic story, much more horrible, is that of Philomela, Procne, and Tereus: it is as bad as Titus Andronicus. The Ionians transferred the scene to Miletus, Colophon, and Ephesus.[300] Homer wholly abstains from Attic myths, except for the mention of their heroines in a dubious passage of the eleventh book of the Odyssey.

Thus the Ionians, though they have adopted Homeric traditions, have counter-Homeric traditions, just as they have and retain the customs and rites of "the conquered race." These are demonstrable facts. On the other side, the Homeric poet ignores Ionian legends, and Ionians and Athenians have been unable to interweave Ionian tradition into the Iliad and Odyssey. There is no doubt about this matter; Homer has no Ionian, the Ionians had no Homeric traditions. This abstinence from Attic legends is not peculiar to Homer. The greatest Achaean tradition, after the Tale of Troy, was the Tale of Thebes. The Attic tragedians have so Atticised it, especially in the Oedipous Coloncus and the Suppliants of Euripides, that we think of the hapless Theban king as a patron saint of Athens; and of Theseus as his host and as the heroic friend of Thebes.

But the ancient epos of Thebes knew no more of Athens than did the ancient epos of Troy. The Athenians could not and did not pretend, like the Argives, Arcadians, and other Peloponnesians, to have taken part in the first great collective Achaean attack on Thebes, an attack led by Adrastus, Tydeus, father of Diomede, Polynices, and the rest.[301] Neither did they pretend, though Ionians dwelt near the Theban Cadmeians in Boeotia, to have aided Thebes in her peril. Athens did allege that the useful Theseus led her army to rescue the unburied body of Polynices, or the bodies of him and Eteocles; it was her favourite boast.[302]

But this tale, as Grote says, "seems to have had its origin in the patriotic pride of the Athenians," in their ceaseless efforts to attach themselves to the great traditions that steadily ignore them. Adrastus, chief of the army which failed at Thebes, came, said the Athenians, as a suppliant to the useful Theseus at Eleusis. Then Theseus, with an Athenian force, vanquished the Thebans, and gave due burial to the dead. Euripides and Isocrates boast of this Flower

---

299 Ibid. p. lxxxvi.

300 Ibid. p. lxxxvii.

301 Pausanias, from the Thebais, ii. 20. 4, ix. 9. 1.

302 Hdt. ix. 27.

of Chivalry, Theseus;[303] and Pausanias saw the tombs of Eteocles and Polynices—at Eleusis in Attica.[304] The Thebans denied the fable.

In the return match of the Epigonoi against Thebes, the Athenians did not pretend to have played a part. In the lists of heroes who take a share in the Argonautic expedition, and in the hunt of the Calydonian boar, the name of Theseus appears; but he did no more than Menestheus achieved at Troy. The Ionians in Asia made a desperate effort to connect themselves with the Trojan war by borrowing the descendants of Nestor, the Nelidae, who fled from the Dorians to Athens, obtained the throne, and led the Ionian migration into Asia.[305] The very fact that they had to borrow these refugees, in order to connect themselves with Achaean "saga," proves the Athenian lack of genuine mythical connection with the united efforts of the rest of Greece against Troy.

The burial of Oedipous at Colonus, the topic of the noble tragedy of Sophocles, is, poetry apart, mere body-snatching. The Iliad and Odyssey,[306] and even Hesiod,[307] know nothing of a sepulchral connection of Oedipous with Athens. Oedipous's funeral feast was held at Thebes. These sepulchral connections of Athens with the tale of Thebes are necessarily un-Homeric, for they are based on the very fanaticism of hero-worship, and fall into line with the craze of historic Greece for securing the relics of heroes, who will defend a city if duly propitiated.

Remote Aetolia is far more closely connected with the Tales of Thebes and of Troy than is Athens. For some reason, then, Athens, and with her the Ionians, is "not of the centre," is out of the central legends, and her efforts to attach herself to them are late, and are wholly un-Homeric. Naturally the really old Epic poets knew nothing of these Ionian pretensions, which are the work of Ionian Burkes tampering with the Homeric "Peerage." Athens wished to "have it both ways," to appear as a city that had always been held by the same race,[308] that stood apart, and had been the asylum of exiles from the rest of Greece; and also as a city that took a great part in the legendary history of the rest of Greece, whose traditions did not recognise her share.

Thus it seems probable that Attica was the seat of a people standing somewhat apart, and possessing an older stratum of

---

303 Suppliants, Isoc., Oral. Panegyr. p. 196. Auger.
304 Pausanias, i. 28. 7.
305 Hdt. v. 65.
306 Iliad, xxiii. 679; Odyssey, xi. 271-280.
307 Scholiast. Iliad, xxiii. 679.
308 Thucydides, i. 2.

inhabitants than the makers of Achaean saga. But Athens and the Ionians were not content with this respectable antiquity. The Ionians of Asia, first, in the Cyclic poems (750-600 B.C.) tried to prove that they and neighbouring and friendly peoples had their share in the Trojan war; and, next, the tragedians of Athens carried on this pseudo-tradition in regard to Thebes as well as to Troy. Their versions led the world captive for 2000 years. The oldest indications of the Ionian attempts to connect heroes of Athens and of her neighbours and friends with the Trojan affair are to be read in the fragments and summaries of the Cyclic poems.

Next, we find this cause taken up by the Athenian tragedians; and, lastly, we find in later sources the fables which the tragedians handled with poetic freedom; while, in the pseudo-Dictys of Crete, we have legends derived from the Cyclic poets, from other sources, and from the author's own fancy. The Roman poets, like Virgil, also reflect the Ionian and Athenian traditions, and their hostility to Agamemnon, Menelaus, Odysseus, and Diomede, with their partiality for Aias, claimed as a neighbour of Athens, and for the ill-used Philoctetes, and the martyr sage, Palamedes of Nauplia. Homer mentions neither him nor his city.[309]

CHAPTER XVI

HOMER AND "THE SAGA"

Every reader of the Iliad perceives that the poet knows an immense mass of legend and tradition. Thus, like Shakespeare, and our great masters of fiction, Fielding, Scott, Thackeray, and Dickens, he rarely introduces a minor character without marking the individuality in some memorable way. Often he does this by some line or two on the ancestry of the personage, and we are for a moment brought into touch with "old unhappy far-off things," or meet some notable trait of character. Thus Theano, daughter of Kisseus of Thrace, priestess of Athene in Troy, and wife of Antenor, is only introduced to utter the prayer of the women to the relentless goddess (Iliad, vi. 302-310). Yet we know her when we meet her, for

309 See "The Story of Palamedes."

(Iliad, v. 69-71) we have already heard of her goodness of heart. She reared Meges, a bastard of Antenor, "kindly, like her own children, to please her lord." Here we have probably no more than a touch of Homer's genial and discriminating art; it is not probable that the poet took this trait from any traditional "saga."

On the other hand, when in a digression he makes Nestor speak of old heroes, Epeians and Lapithae; or when Glaucus tells the tale of Bellerophon and the wife of Proetus; or Phoenix touches on the tragedy of fair-haired Meleager of Aetolia; or Agamemnon speaks of the birth of Heracles, or, in several other references to Theban wars, to the Amazons, and so forth, Homer is clearly drawing from the great legendary store of Achaeans or Pelasgians (to use that term for the earlier people).

All this matter is called "the saga" by the critics. As Homer comes at the crowning period of epic poetry, as his instrument, the hexameter, is delicately tempered by long processes, it seems probable that his mind was full of ancient lays on legendary themes as well, probably, as of Märchen and traditions told orally in prose. These things are to him what ballads and oral traditions were to Scott. Though he only once, in a suspected passage, touches on the Choice of Paris (Iliad, xxiv, 25-30), he must have known some tale which accounted for the enmity of Hera to Ilios, and the hatred of Athene to the Asian city of which she was patroness. Zeus himself (Iliad, iv. 31-33) seems puzzled by the fury of Hera against Troy. Quo numine laeso? The cause of wrath is, in fact, spretae injuria formae, the spite of neglected beauty. No other reason (setting aside the favour of Ganymede, to whom Homer only refers in the most casual way) has ever been given.

As to the Trojan affairs, Homer knows many things on which he only touches briefly. It is clear that he knew a great saga about Trojan legendary history; for example, about the wall built by the Trojans and Pallas Athene to shelter Heracles when he fought a monster that ravaged the land (Iliad, xx. 146). He also knows that Apollo was made thrall to Laomedon, and built the city wall of Troy, but was defrauded of his reward (xxi. 441-455). That Apollo and Poseidon therefore sent the monster to which Hesione, daughter of Laomedon, was exposed, Homer does not say; he commonly ignores the märchenhaft, the fairy-tale points in a legend, but he knows that Heracles was also defrauded, and avenged himself by sacking Ilios (v. 638641). Manifestly there was a rich growth of Märchen and legends clustered round Troy, and known to the Achaeans; Homer merely alludes to it, and to events posterior to the death of Hector.

He knows how Achilles fell in the Scaean gate, slain by Paris and Apollo; he knows the Sack of Troy, the wooden horse; the

Returns, prosperous, troubled, or fatal, of the heroes; he knows Memnon's part in the war, and the end of Aias; he knows that Philoctetes is to be needed, and that Eurypylus fought and fell, and so forth. Concerning some of these things he may have heard lays; others he may have learned merely through oral tradition in prose.

Now it is at this point, namely, Homer's peculiar treatment of the legendary material which reached him, whether in verse or in prose Märchen, that his art stands especially apart from the art of poets who followed him, whether the authors of the "Cyclic" Ionian Epics, or the Athenian tragedians, or the dim genealogisers in verse of the eighth and seventh centuries B.C. Homer deliberately selects from the "saga," or folk-tale, or bardic tradition, what is noble, heroic, possible, and human. He also, in the Iliad, deliberately rejects what is märchenhaft; the situations which belong to the datelessly old popular Märchen, or "fairy tale." Later poets put these things prominently forward; Homer ignores them. This is to be proved later in detail: meanwhile here is another mark of the aloofness of Homer, of his high aristocratic genius.

It seems certain that the Trojan legend, with the legends of the Theban wars and tragedies, of the voyage of Argo, and of the hunt of the Calydonian boar, existed in some consecutive form, and was supposed to be record of historical facts before our Homeric poems were composed. Actual history it was not, any more than the Chansons de Geste, the poem of Beowulf, the two Irish cycles of Cuchullin and of Fian, or the Volsunga Saga, or the romances of Arthur, are records of actual history.

In some of these cycles of western Europe we know that historical personages are involved,—about Charlemagne, of course, there is no doubt; and there really were wars of the Cymri of Strathclyde against the English invaders; and the romances appear to contain fanciful accounts of actual battles of Arthur fought in Cumberland, Lothian, Ettrick Forest, and the Lennox. But when King Loth of Lothian, whose house plays so great a part in the romances, appears, we see that he is only an "eponymous hero," his name being derived by legend from the name of his realm, Lothian. About any real characters whose fame may echo in the ancient Irish bardic traditions nothing can be known.

Homer's heroes are in the same case. There may have been a very early Achaean attempt against the northern Asiatic shore of the Aegean. There may have been wars of several States against Thebes. The voyage of the Argo, on the other hand, is nothing but a tissue of diverse Märchen, adroitly fitted into each other, as most formulae can glide into any other Märchen formula and be prolonged almost infinitely. The Argo saga, as currently told, begins apparently with the tale of the man who weds a fairy bride or a swan nymph, and later loses her, like the Eskimo Bird Bride, the Sanskrit Urvasi and Pururavas. In the saga the man is Athamas, king of the Minyae of Orchomenos, or of Halos in Thessalian Phthiotis, or of Phthia. The bride is Nephele the Cloud-maiden. The pair have two children, Phrixus and Helle. The king takes another wife, and has another child by her. We now have the stepmother formula. Ino ill-treats Phrixus and Helle. Nephele returns to the house disguised as an old nurse (East Lynne formula). She deceives Ino into slaying her own children in place of her step-children (Hop o' my thumb formula; but this is not the most current version). Ino roasts the seed corn; there is no harvest, she sends messengers to the Delphic oracle to bring back the false answer that Phrixus must be sacrificed. When Athamas is about to sacrifice him, or both him and Helle, Nephele produces as substitute the golden (or white, or purple) ram, a gift of Hermes. On his back Phrixus, or both Helle and Phrixus, escape.

This is merely the formula of the two children flying from cannibal parents by the aid of a friendly animal, often a sheep; in Samoyed a beaver which can speak.[310] In many variants of Cinderella the helpful sheep is the dead mother in that form. In Asterinos and Pulja, a tale from Epirus,[311] a dog is the helpful animal; but the boy is turned into a sheep, is slain by the girl's jealous mother-in-law, and from his bones grows a wonderful apple-tree. The girl is thrown into the deep water, but revives. In the Greek saga, Helle falls into the Hellespont off the ram's back: her name is eponymous, derived from the Hellespont. In some variants she does not escape on the ram. The later fortunes of Athamas and Ino are variously told.

But the Argo saga is continued by making the heroes of all Hellas join in "the classical Quest of the Grail," the search for the fleece of the Golden Ram. Where it was, Homer, we shall see, clearly did not know: the place was still in fairyland, unlocalised. Jason, as in a very common Märchen formula, collects companions with marvellous gifts, Keen Eye (Lynceus), the Strong Man (Heracles), the prophet (Orpheus), the winged men, sons of the North Wind, and so on. There is nothing historic here; even thus, in Celtic saga, the miraculously gifted heroes hunted the Twrch Trywyth, the boar. Even thus the miraculously gifted Finnish heroes seek for the mystic Sampo in the Kalewala. The Achaean heroes find the fleece in the hands of King Aietes, who represents the giant of fairy tale, and has a fair daughter (Medea) that aids the young adventurer, and enables

---

310 Castren, Ethnol. Vorlesungen, pp. 164-169.

311 Von Hahn, Griechische Märchen, 1.

him to plough the perilous field with the untamable bulls, like Ilmarinen in the Finnish Kalewala (Rune 19), like the hero of Kilwch and Olwen in the Welsh Mabinogion. She flees, as usual, with her lover from her father. Here this formula ends; the return voyage and the later adventures of the pair were fantastically told as geographical knowledge increased, after the home of Medea had been located at Aia in Colchis, at the east of the Euxine. Other formulae of Märchen were introduced, the venomed robe that burned up Glauce, the magic cauldron of youth that, in the wrong hands, is deadly. Medea is taken here and there, to Corinth, to Athens, mixed with the Theseus set of Märchen, made the eponymous heroine of the Medes.

The Hunt of the Calydonian Boar, again, is of the same character as the mythic boar hunt that ended in upper Ettrick; as the boar hunt of Diarmaid, in Irish; and the hunt of the Welsh Mabinogion, where Keen Eye and the rest reappear, in the Twrch Trywyth.

The growth of "Saga," or bardic tradition, is the same in all countries. First we have the Märchen, told in prose, as they still exist among European peasants and in many "non-Aryan" peoples, from the Samoyeds of the frozen north to the Red Indians, the Huarochiri of Southern America, the Samoans, the Bechuanas, the Kanekas of New Caledonia, the Santhals, and so forth. In the Märchen the characters are usually anonymous, a boy, a girl, a witch, a king, and the rest; real characters, as Charlemagne, may appear. The events are not localised. The situations are efforts of the primal romantic fancy; like the fragments of coloured glass in the kaleidoscope, they fall into any number of patterns.

As civilisation advances and a class of professional sennachies appears, they give names to the characters; the anonymous young adventurer becomes Jason or Theseus; the cunning man who plays tricks on Death becomes Sisyphus; the monster, giant or beast, who sets impossible tasks to the adventurer, becomes Minos or Aietes; his wife or fair daughter, who baffles him and helps the hero, becomes Ariadne or Medea. In place of the helpful old woman of fairy tale comes Hera, whom Jason carries across the ford; or it is Athene, who gives Bellerophon the golden bit that tames the magical horse; here he is Pegasus. The rescuer of the girl exposed to a ravening monster is now named Perseus or Heracles. The brother and sister who flee from cannibal parents, with the aid of a friendly animal, are named Phrixus and Helle. In place of throwing behind them combs or stones which baffle the pursuer by changing into forests or mountains, Medea and Jason leave the mangled limbs of Medea's brother Absyrtus.

The lad who effects wonders by knowing the language of beasts, is in Greece named Melampus; the giant, whose life-token is a lock of his hair, becomes Nisus of Megara; his daughter, who loves the adventurer, and cuts the giant's lock, purple or golden, so that he is defeated, becomes Scylla; and Minos, who answers to the giant of fairy tale in the Theseus Attic legend, in the Megarian fable is himself the adventurer aided by the giant's daughter.[312] He does not marry the treacherous daughter, but puts her to death; as Achilles, in the Lesbian story, does not marry Pisidice, who for love of him has betrayed her city, but has her slain. The man who, to fulfil a prophecy, unwittingly weds his mother (a favourite character in Märchen, as Comparetti has shown), becomes Oedipous: he is also the answerer of riddles, a character of Märchen found everywhere.[313]

Out of these originally anonymous and unlocalised personages and romantic situations of Märchen, the Greek States made the heroes and events of their legendary history. That history, as of Theseus, Heracles, Perseus, Jason, Sisyphus, even Odysseus, Pelops, Oenomaus, Athamas, Laomedon, is but a series of Märchen localised; while, in place of fairy godmothers, or anonymous benefactors, the old man or old woman of Märchen, the Olympian gods are introduced, with their fairy gifts, the cap of darkness, the winged shoon, the sword of sharpness (Perseus), the power of taking all animal disguises. Homer knows the attack of Heracles on the father and brothers of Nestor. Hesiod knew the cause of the feud, Neleus refused to purify Heracles who had slain his host under the hospitable roof. Hesiod knows that Poseidon had given to Periclymenus, brother of Nestor, the power to appear in any animal shape, eagle, ant, snake, or bee; and that while Periclymenus lived, Heracles failed in the fight, and could not take Pylos. But when Periclymenus, as a bee, settled on the chariot of Heracles, Athene shot that bee with an arrow (see fragment of the Eoiai 14 (33), with the scholia).[314] Other examples of the wildest absurdities of Märchen, retained and rejoiced in by the Ionic epic poets, are given later ("Homer and the Ionian Cyclic Poets"). But Homer, in the Iliad, takes his heroes forth from the prison of Märchen: whether the fairy tales had not yet become attached to Bellerophon, Achilles, and Meleager in his time, or whether his genius ignored such fanciful elements of tradition, Homer does not speak of the invulnerability of Achilles, save on his heel; or tell the wooing by his

---

312 Pausanias, i. 19, ii. 34.

313 Child, English and Scottish Ballads, vol. i., "Riddles wisely Answered."

314 Yen. A., Iliad, ii. 336. Rzach, Hesiod, p. 326.

father, Peleus, of Thetis as she takes a variety of bestial forms. Either these situations had not yet become attached to the story of Achilles, or Homer chooses to ignore them. Such things do not come into the natural objective world of the Iliad. In the digression of Bellerophon he recurs to the human natural side of Märchen, the story of the woman who, vainly attacking a man's virtue, accuses him falsely; the message or letter of death,[315] his three strange adventures to achieve, that of the Chimaera and others, and his winning of the king's daughter. This Märchen, localised, is in a digression; but Homer usually keeps his Märchen for the Odyssey, and the incidents occur beyond the bounds of the world he knows.

Now, even when Homer touches on the tale of Meleager, he says nothing of that fairy property the "soul-box" or "life-token," the brand snatched from the burning; or of the visit of the Spaewives, the Fates, and their prophecy. He actually does not seem to know that incident. Althaea, mother of Meleager, in Homer (Iliad, ix. 565-572), prays to the Erinnyes and they hear her. She has not her son's "soul-box" or "life-token" in her hands to burn it, and slay him. In Pausanias (x. 31. 3), Meleager is killed by Apollo, who is fighting for the Curetes against the Aetolians. Meleager died, like Achilles, by Apollo's hand, though Paris was an accomplice of the God in the case of Achilles. Pausanias follows the Hesiodic Eoiai, which Kuhnert supposes to have known the same story as Homer.[316]

As Kuhnert justly observes, the poetry of Homer is knightly. "An der Hofen wurden die homerische Gedichte versungen ... the hero must find his death at a divine hand in glorious warfare." The Athenian tragedians are our oldest source for the Moirae and the fatal life-token: a property very common in Märchen; but when the incident first attached itself to Meleager we cannot know. This avoidance of the folk-element, the Märchen, in the Iliad is one of the things that distinguishes Homer from the Ionian Cyclic poets, the Hesiodic school, and the Athenian tragedians.

Homer, again, in another way, stands apart from the genealogising poets of the eighth to seventh century (such as the school of "Hesiod," and "Eumelus" of Corinth) by his method of handling tradition or saga. These genealogising poets aimed at constructing history, and preluded to the "logographers" in prose of the sixth century. Both they and the logographers have the same simple method, that of the would-be historic early mediaeval writers on Scotland and Ireland. Their plan is to invent for each town or people an eponymous hero, whose name is simply the name

---

[315] For many cases in Märchen, see Mr. Crookes' Folk-Lore, vol. xix. p. 156.
[316] Roscher's Lexikon, vol ii. p. 2594.

of the city or people (as, in Scotland, Fib for Fife, Loth for Lothian, Scota for the Scoti). The hero, or heroine, founds the city, or is first ancestor of the people. Next follow the legends about heroic characters, as Perseus, Athamas, Pelops, Theseus, Aietes, Phrixus, which are mere Märchen of world-wide diffusion, localised, with named persons for the characters.

The region of legend expands with the expansion of geographical knowledge. Cities hasten, like Athens and Corinth, to attach themselves to sagas, as that of Argo, in which they had no original part. Hesiod extends the old saga, and carries descendants of the old characters, as of Odysseus, to Italy, to Latium and Etruria. "Eumelus" drags Corinth into the cycle of the Argonautic expedition: Athens, we have said, brings Medea to Athens, and into her Theseus fable. Later the logographers, in prose, continue the process and alter the genealogies to suit their historical theories.

From all these processes Homer stands apart. He has not any historical theory to prove. He seldom mentions an eponymous founder of a city, or ancestor of a people. Nausithous founds Phaeacia, his city is not called Nausithoa. Homer names Mykene (Odyssey, ii. 120), but does not say that she founded Mycenae, as "Eumelus" says that Ephyre founded the town of Ephyre (Corinth). You would not gather from Homer that the Achaeans were descendants of Achaeus, or the Danaans of Danaus.

All these things are obvious and undeniable. Homer is a poet: the genealogising writers in verse are aiming at constructing history (some history may be present), and at explaining the origins of peoples and cities.

But, according to some of the modern learned, our Homer contains borrowings from the Eumelian verses on Corinth. Thus Mr. Murray says that the Iliad and Odyssey "not only refer to other legends as already existing and treated by other poets; that every one admits; but they often in their digressions tell stories in a form which clearly suggests recapitulation or allusion. They imply the existence elsewhere of a completer poetical treatment of the same subject," as in the tale of Bellerophon, told to Diomede by Glaucus in Iliad, vi. "Is it not plain that the poet of Iliad, vi., is in the first place referring to an existing legend, and, secondly, one may almost say, quoting from an existing poem?"[317]

Certainly Homer is referring to an existing legend, and not improbably to a lay which in his time existed. But Mr. Murray goes on to suggest that the existing poem referred to is the Corinthiaca of "Eumelus," whom he takes to be a mythical name for the author of

---

[317] R. G. E. pp. 161, 162.

Corinthian traditional poetry; von Christ thinks Eumelus of the seventh century.

Mr. Murray's argument seems to be, Homer knew a legend, probably knew a poem, about Bellerophon, son of Glaucus, son of Sisyphus, who dwelt in Ephyre (Corinth). "Eumelus" wrote a poem about Corinthian affairs. Therefore the poet who introduced the tale told by Glaucus into Iliad, vi., took it (textually, it seems to be suggested) from "Eumelus."[318] In the same way the author of Iliad, v. 395-400, and Panyassis, the uncle of Herodotus, presumably adapt from the same source. Mr. Leaf, on the other hand, supposes the poet-uncle to give an "echo" from the passage in the fifth book of the Iliad. There may be an echo, in Homer on Heracles, from an older poem on Heracles, but that poem is likely to be long anterior to the end of the sixth century.[319]

In any case the "Eumelus" known to us in Greek literary tradition was a tendenz poet, a poet with a purpose, with a pseudo-historical theory to prove; he used the method of the genealogisers, who turned into heroes and heroines men and women who were constructed out of place-names; and he, in certain places, did not borrow from Homer, nor Homer from him, for he and Homer flatly contradict each other. If all this be not post-Homeric, what is?

Pausanias, in discussing Eumelus's peculiar version of the relations of Medea to Corinth, quotes a "History of Corinth," in prose, by Eumelus, "if he is really the author of it."[320] "Eumelus is also said to have been a poet," and Pausanias avers that the only poem recognised as genuine of Eumelus is a processional ode to Delian Apollo.[321] There was a prose version of his other work, and

---

318 Textually, for, in Iliad, vi. 200, 'Ἀλλ' ὅτε δὴ καὶ κεῖνος ἀπήχθετο πᾶσι θεοῖσιν (referring to Bellerophon), Mr. Murray renders, "But when he also was hated of all the gods," and asks, "Why the phrase, 'when he also'?" Homer is, "one may almost say, quoting from an existing poem." Now I understand Glaucus in this "he also" to refer to the remark of Diomede (vi. 140) on Lycurgus's being "hated of all the gods." He repeats the very words of Diomede. "Here is another man who, like Lycurgus in your story, was hated of all the gods." Consulting Mr. Leaf's note (vi. 200), I find that this is also the opinion of Ameis: Mr. Leaf thinks it "too far-fetched." The distance is sixty lines (vi. 140-200). In his translation of the passage in Leaf, Lang, and Myers, Mr. Leaf translates, with Monro, "even he," even Bellerophon, whom the gods had loved. Surely no textual quotations by Homer from the so-called "Eumelus" need be imagined.

319 R. G. E. pp. 164, 165.

320 Pausanias, I. I.

321 Ibid. iv. 4. 1.

Clemens Alexandrinus regarded Eumelus as a logographer like Acusilaus, who "turned the poems of Hesiod into prose."[322]

But, genuine or not, an "Eumelian" poem on a forged part of Corinthian legendary history did at some time exist, for the scholiast on Pindar (Ol. xiii.) cited eight lines of it; and these lines are manifestly complementary to the part of the prose history by "Eumelus" which Pausanias quotes. Taking the Eumelian verse and prose together, we find that "Eumelus" in his Corinthiaca appears in Greek literary tradition as a chronicler in verse, a genealogist, a maker of patriotic pseudo-history, and a narrator of a late version of the Argo story.

Now, as "Eumelus" began (as the Ram in the fairy story is requested to do) "at the beginning," at the founding of Ephyre, or Corinth; and as he told the Argonautic tale in full, including the aprocryphal adventures of Medea in what he chose to call her rightful kingdom in Corinth; and as the tale is a very long one, we may infer that this, and not the entire mass of Corinthian legend, was the topic of his book. If so, Bellerophon, though a Corinthian, was "out of the story"; for, by the Eumelian genealogies, he was four generations later than Medea's tenure of the Corinthian throne. She was succeeded by Sisyphus, whose exploits would fill a book; Sisyphus by Glaucus, and Glaucus by Bellerophon. But the aim of "Eumelus" was to glorify Corinth by attributing to her a share in the tale of Argo; its heroine, Medea, must therefore be of the Corinthian Royal House; and, after proving this, and telling the Argo saga, "Eumelus" must give her adventures, after Argo's return to Greece, in Corinth; and these were many and tragical.

Wishing, then, to attach Corinth to the Argonautic story, the genealogiser manages matters thus. Helios, the Sun, he says, had two sons by Antiope (daughter of the river god Asopus); the sons were Aloeus and Aietes. Homer does not borrow those facts from "Eumelus"; Homer tells a different story, but the historical effort of "Eumelus" constrains him to make his local nymph, Antiope, mother of Aietes. That is the basis of his forgery. Meanwhile Homer tells a contradictory story about this Antiope (Od. xi. 260). Her lover was not Helios, but Zeus. Her sons were not Aietes and Aloeus, but Amphion and Zethus. Homer is not borrowing from this genealogiser! The heroine Ephyre founded Ephyre. (She was daughter of Oceanus and Tethys, and wife of Epimetheus, or daughter of Epimetheus, an un-Homeric kind of person.) The river Asopus, father of Antiope (who was mother, says "Eumelus," by the Sun of Aloeus and Aietes), gave his name as "Asopia" to what was

[322] Frazer, Pausanias, vol. iii. p. 2, citing Clemens, Strom. i. 398, ed. Potter.

later Sicyon. The Sun gave to his son, Aloeus, "the land held by Asopus, to his son Aietes he gave Ephyre" (Corinth). Aietes goes to Colchis (a place necessarily unnamed by Homer, for it is at the extreme east of the Euxine); but previously had arranged that Bounos is to be regent of Ephyre till Aietes, or a descendant of his, returns and claims it.[323] Medea is to be that descendant.

So far we have Eumelian verse. How the story went on we learn from the prose version cited by Pausanias. Bounos died as king of Ephyre, and was succeeded by the nephew of Aietes (a son of his brother Aloeus), named Epopeus.[324] Epopeus was harsh to his son Marathon, and Marathon fled to Attica and founded the famous deme of Marathon. He had two sons, Sicyon, to whom, on the death of his own father, Epopeus, he gave Sicyon; while Ephyre he gave to his son Corinthus; hence Ephyre came to be called Corinth. When Corinthus died childless, the Corinthians sent to Colchis for Medea, in accordance with the entail made by Aietes (as "Eumelus" has told us in verse), when he left Ephyre for Colchis.[325] Nothing can be less Homeric.

The "Eumelus" of whom we have reports wrote pseudo-history in verse, for he has to make Medea survive Aietes, Bounos, Epopeus, Marathon, and Corinthus, and then, in the prime of beauty, succeed to the realm of Corinthus as Queen of Corinth. Leaving Corinth for Athens under a cloud, Medea gives Corinth to Sisyphus.[326]

"Eumelus," as Seeliger observes,[327] knows the Argo story in the common late expanded form, Colchis and all; but chooses to make Aietes, contrary to all other authorities, a king of Corinth. Attica, too, must needs attach herself to the story of Argo, by making Medea seduce King Aegeus, the father of Theseus, and try to poison Theseus himself: she also made Aegeus send him on the desperate adventure of fighting the Bull of Marathon.[328] This Bull of Marathon donne à penser. In one legend Aegeus, father of Theseus, sent Androgeos, son of Minos, to fight the bull, which killed him. It was therefore but tit-for-tat when Minos sent Athenian tributary boys and girls to fight his bull, the bullheaded Minotaur.[329]

"Eumelus," as far as our evidence goes, stands for the school

---

[323] Eumelus in Kinkel, p. 188.
[324] Pausanias, ii. 3. 10.
[325] Pausanias, ii. i. i.
[326] Ibid. ii. 3. 10, 11.
[327] "Medea," Reseller's Lexikon, ii. 2. 2492.
[328] Seeliger, Roscher's Lexikon, ii. 2. 2496.
[329] Roscher, Lexikon, vol. i. 342.

who, for every town, supposed an eponymous person as founder, for Ephyre (Corinth) he gives the nymphe Ephyre. Now Homer does not work on these lines. When "Eumelus" had got his pseudo-history and false genealogies to his taste, he must have told at full length the tale of Argo, for we have five lines of his describing the terror caused in Aietes and the Colchians by the throwing of the weight by Jason among the armed brood born of the plain, which Jason ploughed with fire-breathing bulls.

These things, then, are what Greek literary tradition reports about a pseudo-historical genealogist, and teller of the tale of Argo with a purpose. That he ever mentioned Bellerophon we have no proof: Pausanias does not cite Eumelus for Bellerophon. Homer, as usual, omits the Märchen of the winged horse Pegasus, whereby, in later poems, Bellerophon accomplishes his feats. Pindar is copious about Pegasus: that noble animal. The peculiarly gifted horse, hard to bridle, is common property of "fairy tales." Usually some friendly person tells the adventurous lad to use a peculiar bridle without which the steed is untamable. The boy can always sell the horse, but keep the bridle; the purchaser returns the nag, and the hero keeps the money. In Pindar's Fourth Pythian Ode, Athene is the benevolent person of the Märchen. Bellerophon, wanting to break in Pegasus, sleeps in her temple; she presents him with the magical golden bit and head-stall. Dropping Pegasus, magical bridle and all, Homer only says that the gods "gave Bellerophon friendly convoy to Lycia."[330] Mr. Murray asks, "What blameless guiding of the gods led Bellerophon to Lycia?" Clearly he flew thither through upper air on Pegasus, like Commodore Trunnion leaping a sunken way on the road to the hymeneal altar, "to the unspeakable terror and amazement" of a waggoner below, says Smollett. But Homer is not Smollett, and does not send Bellerophon flying through air on a horse. Pindar saw no objections to the incident.[331]

Here we must try to explain a point on which Mr. Murray remarks, "There has been an extraordinary reluctance among scholars to ... admit the possibility of 'Homer,' as the phrase is, borrowing from the supposed later author 'Eumelus,' or even from 'Hesiod.'" The reluctance is natural and justifiable; because when we say "Eumelus" or "Hesiod," we mean just what we have received from antiquity under the names of these men. Their work, as it reaches us, is un-Homeric, is later, we say, than the Iliad. But if

---

330 Iliad, vi. 171.

331 "Pegasus is omitted by Homer as a monster," Mr. Murray justly observes (R. G. E. p. 162, note I). No other poet omitted "monsters"; not Pindar for one, or Hesiod.

"Eumelus" be a mythical name for a supposed author of a body of Corinthian heroic poetry: if the Eumelian matter which we have received was not that, then we know nothing about that, and cannot say whether our Homer borrowed from some other Eumelian epê or not. Mr. Murray, as to Homer's debt to "Eumelus," writes: "If anything were needed to make it clearer still, it would be that the Verses of Eumelus are quoted as the earliest authority for the story of the Argo and Medea, and the composer of our Odyssey speaks of the Argo as a subject of which 'all minds are full'"[332] The reader naturally gathers that our Homer took his information about Argo from "Eumelus." We can only say, "not from the Eumelus known to us in Greek literary tradition." Thus Hesiod[333] tells of the birth of Circe and Aietes her brother (the father of Medea) in precisely the same terms as Homer does, and as Eumelus does not.[334] Both poets say that Helios, by Perses (Homer), or Perseis (Hesiod), a daughter of Oceanus, was the father of Circe and Aietes. Homer does not mention Medea, but Hesiod says that she was the daughter of Aietes. Now Eumelus, in what we have of him, says nothing of Circe, but makes Aietes the son of Helios and Antiope, not of Perses as in Homer. Manifestly, then, Homer did not take his version from this Eumelus; while, when Homer and Hesiod precisely agree, if either borrowed from the other, it were quite arbitrary to say that Homer borrowed from Hesiod, who knows Latium and Etruria.

Homer certainly did not borrow here from our Eumelus, for he differs from Eumelus; nor is Eumelus quoted, as far as I am aware, "as the earliest authority for" the story of Argo. The scholiast on Pindar, as I, for one, understand him, quotes Eumelus for something quite different, namely, for his peculiar account (adopted by Pindar when praising a Corinthian athlete) of Medea as rightful Queen of Corinth; a point on which no Greeks agreed with the patriotic chronicler, the Corinthian Eumelus, as Pausanias observes.

Homer knows about the ship Argo, and her escape from the clash of the Rocks Wandering, through the favour of Hera.[335] The dangers of these rocks are described by Circe to Odysseus, for he must pass by that perilous path of the sea; and Circe ought to know, for she is sister of King Aietes, from whose land Argo was sailing when she met the rocks. But where did Aietes dwell? On that point Homer says nothing and knew nothing.

It is manifest that Homer neither knows where Aiaie, the isle

---

332 R. G. E. p. 163.

333 Theogony, 956-962.

334 Odyssey, x. 137.

335 Odyssey, xii. 57-62.

of Circe, is, nor where the home of King Aietes is. To him Aiaie is "an unsubstantial fairy place." In the Odyssey (xii. 3, 4), Circe's isle is "near the home and dancing-places of the Dawn, and the land of sunrising." You cannot go farther east in a black ship. But in Hesiod,[336] Circe's Aia must be in the west, for her sons by Odysseus (unheard of by Homer) rule over Latins and Tyrsenians. Later poets placed the Aia of Circe's brother, Aietes, in the east, in Colchis, at the eastern limit of the Euxine; and Circe's Aia they located in the west, at the promontory of Circeei in Italy. Homer himself shows no knowledge of Italy, on one side, or of the extremity of the Euxine on the other.[337] Even Mimnermus places the city of Aietes vaguely "at the limit of Oceanus."[338] By way of finding reason where there is none, Apollonius Rhodius explains that Circe originally lived in the Aia of the east, as in the Odyssey, but was transported by Helios to the Aia in the west.[339] Homer being so vague, we do not say he is borrowing from our Eumelus, who locates Aietes in Colchis, under Caucasus, which Homer, if pre-Ionian, never knew. Had Homer, or any of the supposed late contributors to the Iliad and Odyssey, lived in the eighth to seventh centuries, and studied our Eumelus, or even our Hesiod, the Iliad and Odyssey would have had much more extensive geographical knowledge than they possess. No one will say that our Homer borrows from a genealogiser like our Eumelus, when Eumelus does not even agree with Homer about the mother of Aietes.

The Iliad does know that Jason, in the isle of Lemnos, had a son by Hypsipyle;[340] and the adventures of the Argonauts in Lemnos are part of the story of Argo. But Lemnos is well within Homer's geographical knowledge, while the homes of Aietes and Circe are far beyond its limits.

The confusion of early mythical geography is inextricable. In the Odyssey the ship Argo met the Rocks Wandering on her way home from Aietes. Odysseus meets the rocks on his way home from Circe. She dwells in the farthest east; so then, it seems, did Aietes. In Pindar,[341] Argo encounters the rocks on her outward and eastward way, before she enters the Euxine. Homer knows that Jason loved Hypsipyle in Lemnos, whether on his way to or his return from Aietes. Pindar says on his return westward to Greece,

---

336 Theogony, 1011-1015.

337 Roscher, Lexikon, vol. i. pp. 108, 109.

338 Mimnermus, Fragment 11. Bergk.

339 Argonautica, iii. 309 ff.

340 Iliad, vii. 468, 469, xxi. 41, xxiii. 747.

341 Pythian Odes, iv.

after he has visited Oceanus, the Red Sea, and Africa. The common story, as in Apollonius Rhodius, makes Jason love Hypsipyle in Lemnos as he sails eastwards and outward bound to Colchis. If he wooed her thus, on his way home, with Medea, as Pindar tells, one can only say that he was a brave man.

Let us next, before going deeper into the "Saga," examine the case of Thersites, the impudent demagogue of Iliad, ii., never again mentioned by Homer. Mr. Murray is rather surprised "to find that Thersites is really an independent saga-figure with a life of his own, and very distinguished relations. He was a son of Agrios, the savage Aetolian king, and first cousin once removed of the great Diomedes. His mother was Dia, a palpable goddess." He was killed by Achilles for jeering at his grief over the slain Amazon, Penthesilea. Achilles was purified by Odysseus, but Diomede took up his feud.[342]

In Pherecydes (fr. 82), Thersites is an Aetolian, thrown over a rock by Meleager for his cowardice in the boar hunt, but not killed.[343]

All this about Thersites is really "saga" stuff,—invented about the date of the Aethiopis. But Thersites was no hero of "saga" in the time of Homer. Had he been the son of a goddess (otherwise unknown) and of "a savage Aetolian king" (Homer's Aetolians are as civilised as his other peoples), the poet would have said so. He is most careful, we saw, to tell us who his heroes are (except the Athenians), even when they only appear for the purpose of being slain. But he says not a word about the genealogy and antecedents of Thersites, who is only a man of the λαός or host, food for bronze. "The savage king of the Aetolians," Agrios, has been picked out by some one suffering from la manie cyclique, who was anxious to tell "what became of them all," from Iliad, xiv. 114-125: "no doubt an interpolation," says Mr. Leaf, "like many others, of the genealogical school connected with the name of Hesiod."

Here, at all events, whether the genealogy be late and Hesiodic or not, Diomede gives to Agamemnon his genealogy, in Aetolia.

---

342 R. G. E. pp. 185, 186. All this comes from the Aethiopis, or Sack of Ilios, followed by Chairemon in his tragedy, Achilles Thersitoctonos, with scholia on the Philoctetes (445), Quintus Smyrnaeus (of the fourth century a.d.). Dictys Cretensis, the prose compiler of the second century a.d., does not mention Thersites.

343 do not enter into the theory of his relations (1) to the pharmakos, driven out of Athens as a human scape-goat, and whipped, perhaps sacrificed; or (2) with Theritas, a name of Ares in Laconia, according to Pausanias. Homer in his Achaean way never alludes to the cruel and lewd, or magical affair of the pharmakos.

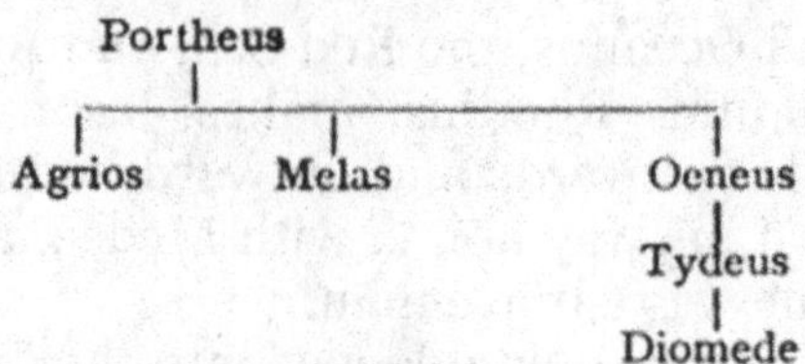

The manie cyclique inserted
Agrios
|
Thersites, for it was desired to tell what became of Thersites; and—not to lose sight of a person so notable as Thersites—the poet made Achilles kill him, a much older man than Achilles, for his mockery. Then Diomede (who does not remonstrate when Odysseus calls him the basest, socially, of the host, and beats him) takes up his feud when he is slain.[344]

Homer has plainly no idea that Thersites is of royal and divine lineage, all that is a later invention of "the cyclic mania," and is as old, at least, as the age of the Ionian cyclic poet of the Aethiopis.[345] The very scholiasts said that Homer marked the base birth of Thersites by saying nothing about his parentage and home.

In Homer, as in the earliest Chansons de Geste, there is the knightly poetic legend; and in the Cyclics, at least in the case of Thersites, there are the later expansions and continuations made under the influence of la manie cyclique. The dénouement of the Telegonia, the last of the Cyclics, is purely absurd. Telegonus marries his aged stepmother, Penelope, and Telemachus marries his father's mistress, Circe!

To explore the relations of Homer and of "saga" to Märchen,

---

344 Iliad, ii. 246-248. "I deem that no baser-born man (χερειότερον) came with Agamemnon." χερειότερον "virtually = χερείονα, see Iliad, i. 80" (Leaf), where a king is contrasted with ἀνδρὶ χέρηϊ, "a meaner man" (Leaf, in Leaf, Lang, Myers, The Iliad, p. 3).

345 The Cyclic story also demonstrates its un-Homeric origin by dragging in "the hocus-pocus of purification" (R. G. E. p. 134). But Usener, seeing, in Sir Walter Scott's words, "further into a millstone than the nature of the millstone permits," makes Thersites = Theritas = Enyalios (Hesychius), and suggests that two sacrifices by Spartan lads to Enyalius and Achilles, after a fight with fisticuffs, and ducking of the vanquished, may be "the ritual form of the old battle of Achilles and Thersites" =(?) "the common annual rites of the slaying of Winter by Summer, or of one vegetation god by another" (R. G. E. pp. 186, 187). There was not much of a "battle" between Thersites and Achilles! The millstone, really, has a hole through it. To Homer, Thersites is a nobody. His rank, relationships, and fate are due to the later "Cyclic mania," and to "poetic justice."

or popular tales, attached to real or fabulous heroes and heroines of the past, would require a volume.[346] Almost all Greek pseudo-historical tradition consists of a string of Märchen, known all over the world: any student of folk-lore who reads the Achaean legends in Grote can identify the masterless Märchen which have been attached to the heroic figures. In exactly the same way, Märchen are attached to Charlemagne in the Chansons de Geste; to Arthur in the romances; and we might as well look to them for political and personal history as to Homer. Naimes, Ganelon, Olivier, the expedition of Charlemagne to Constantinople, his wars with the Saracens, and other persons and events in the Chansons de Geste, yield no material to the historian; nor do Lancelot, Galahad, Palamedes, and Tristram, and Arthur's foreign conquests in the romances. What history there is rests obscure.

On the other hand, an attempt has recently been made to extract some grains of "tribal" history, before and after the Achaean migration to Asia, from the names of the heroes in the Iliad, and from the places where, in post-Homeric Greece, they received worship. This effort is made by Dr. Erich Bethe, in his Homer und die Heldensage, and Mr. Murray follows Bethe in The Rise of the Greek Epic. We may take a notable example of the method in the case of Hector. "Hector seems to belong to Boeotia." It may be worth while to examine the reasoning on which this most unexpected opinion is based. The idea was first propounded by Ferdinand Dümmler in a short Anhang to Studniczka's Cyrene. "Hector was worshipped as a hero in Boeotian Thebes," says Mr. Murray, quoting Dümmler, and Dümmler's source is apparently Pausanias.[347] If the Boeotians in the time of Pausanias regarded Hector as of Boeotian birth, the fact would be curious. But they did nothing of the kind. "The Thebans show the tomb of Hector near the Well of Oedipous. They say that Hector's remains were brought here from Ilium in accordance with the following oracle: "Ye Thebans, if you wish your country to be wealthy, bring to your city from Asia the bones of Hector the son of Priam, and respect the hero at the bidding of Zeus."[348]

This was a real or an imaginary case of the body-snatching of which Herodotus speaks frequently. The relics of St. Hector would be valuable to Thebes. The Thebans, in fact, may have wished to propitiate a hero who had slain, according to Homer, many Boeotians in battle, and who might still be hostile, and even fight

---

346 Will nobody write it?

347 R. G. E. p. 196.

348 Pausanias, ix. 18

against them in battle, as dead heroes were apt to do. Pausanias (ix. 4. 3, ix. 39. 3) mentions also the graves of certain Boeotian heroes, one of them wounded, the other slain by Hector, as still honoured in Boeotia. Hector slew, or wounded, or fought Homeric heroes from Phocis and from Boeotia; and Epeigeus, a suppliant of Peleus (Iliad, xvi. 570 et seqq.), and an Aetolian hero, an Athenian, a Mycenaean, an Elian, and so on. What follows? These names of heroes slain by Hector, Thessalians, Aetolians, Phocians, and Boeotians, are thought to suggest that, as Mr. Murray translates Dr. Bethe, "Hector, or rather the tribe which honoured Hector as their hero, migrated by this road,"—by the road on which these Aetolians, Thessalians, Phocians, and Boeotians—or the tribes which honoured them as heroes—used to live. "More accurately, the tribe gradually, in how many centuries none can tell, moved in a south-easterly direction, driven by a pressure which was no doubt exerted by the Aeolic tribe represented in the Epos by Achilles." "These are no pictures of phantasy that I let loose to play about here," says Dr. Bethe (p. 16).

What else but phantasies can we possibly call them? That Hector's tomb was shown in Thebes, does by no means prove that he, or a tribe which was the Hector tribe, once lived in Boeotia. Heroes, like saints, had tombs and chapels in many regions where they were not born, and which they never visited. The grave of St. James was shown—in Spain! Ariadne's ashes had been shown in Argos. Hector, in the Iliad, killed the men in his way. In addition to the victims chosen out by Dr. Bethe, he slew Stichios, an Athenian; Amphimachus, an Elian, and Periphetes of Mycenae.[349]

This does no more prove that Hector was a Boeotian than that he was an Athenian. He slew Schedios, a Phocian, yet he was no more a Phocian than an Athenian, he merely killed the men whom he met. If we are to argue, that he or the tribe which honoured him was driven out of Aetolia and Thessaly down to Boeotia, Phocis, and Attica, we must, by parity of reasoning, argue that the Hector tribe (in Gaelic, the MacEachans), were driven into Peloponnesus, to Mycenae and Elis, for Hector slew Periphetes of Mycenae, and Amphimachus, of Elis.[350] The Mycenaean, Elian, and Athenian are not mentioned by Dr. Bethe. Nor can Hector be converted into a Boeotian by the circumstance that he fought a kind of courteous duel with Aias, while Aias was really the Locrian Aias, we are told,

---

[349] Iliad, xiii. 185, xv. 329, 638.

[350] xv. 636-644.

and so a neighbour of the Boeotian Hector.[351] Hector's relations with Aias[352] are far from neighbourly and friendly.

This instance of Hector is one of many in which the names of heroes are taken to represent "tribes" which had a cult of these heroes, though Homer knows nothing about this cult as practised in heroic Greece, except in Athens. We learn nothing from Homer about "tribes" or clans with a sacred eponymous hero, or with any "hero" in the sense of the word as used in the Greece of history. We cannot assume that the Iliad introduces, in the combats of heroes, memories of tribal wars in Greece in the pre-Homeric age, and transfers them, in the shape of single combats, to the plain of Troy!

Heroic relationships were claimed long after Homer by peoples like the Dorians and Romans and English and many others, merely to connect themselves with the great legend of Troy; and the Greek cults of heroes, a religion unknown to Homer, were carried into regions with which Homer's men had no connection. We might as well look for Cymric tribal wars in the feuds and names of the knights in the Arthurian romances, or for Irish tribal feuds in the names of Ferdiad and Cuchullain, as for prehistoric migrations in the names of Hector, Leltus, Stichios of Attica, Periphetes of Mycenae, and Amphimachus of Elis.

"Hector," we are told, "was a great 'slayer of men,' and his victims in the Iliad make a sort of road from Thebes upward to the bounds of Achilles' region."[353] They also "make a sort of road" to Mycenae and Elis by way of Athens: that is the history of the tribe, preserved in the names of his victims,—names which, it appears, "are short" for defeated tribes. As for the evidence of a Helen tribe at Sparta, because Helen had a shrine and worship there, we have no evidence that the Achaeans had any heroic shrines or hero-worship,—the evidence is that they had none,—but the assumption is that Homer represents "another stream of history," and, apparently, that his people turned tribal names and tribal gods of an unknown past, into heroic men and women. The opposite theory is that the hero-worshipping people of historic Greece devoted themselves to such patron saints as they knew through Homer, as the Arabs have saints whom they know about through the Hebrew Scriptures.

I am not aware that in the bardic history, or "saga" of any people, tribes are spoken of under the names of their tribal heroes in such a way as to cause confusion. None is caused by Judah,

---

351 Bethe, p. 15.

352 Iliad, xiii. 801-832 and passim.

353 R. G. E. p. 197.

Benjamin, Ephraim, and so on in the Old Testament, but in other Biblical cases there may be trouble. Local tribes, as far as I am aware, are nowhere named by patronymics; certainly they are not in Australia, India, America, and Africa, except, among the Zulus, by the name of a man plus Ama, AmaFinn, and so forth. Thus the theory that Hector is the name of a prehistoric Boeotian local tribe seems to me fantastic. We might as well look for remnants of tribal history in Kay, Gawaine, Naimes, and Ganelon.

Surely it is an error in historical method to reason as if pre-Homeric Greeks were as addicted to divinising men, building their shrines, and sacrificing to them, as the post-Homeric Greeks were in the seventh and all later centuries. We might as well argue that the apostolic Christians practised mediaeval saint-worship, and adored and built innumerable chapels to dead Saints, because this was the custom of mediaeval Christianity.

To sum up, we have proved that our Homer, in his treatment of old tradition, is a noble poet, that he stands aloof from all the others of Greece in his refusal (save in the Odyssey, a romance) to introduce the wild elements of Märchen, the childish miracles; while he is equally remote from the methods of the pseudo-historians like Eumelus as known to us, and all the Hesiodic genealogisers and inventors of eponymous heroes; and from the manie cyclique of the Ionian Cyclic poets. Really no fact can be more certain; and this fact, even if it were not corroborated by all the others, would prove our Homer to be "alone, aloof, sublime."

CHAPTER XVII

THE STORY OF PALAMEDES

There is one hero of the Cyclic Ionian poems, at least of the Cypria, whose story illustrates the depth and width of the gulf which severs Ionia from the Iliad and Odyssey. The Cypria, like the Attic traditions used by Aeschylus, Sophocles, Euripides, and the Sophists, such as Gorgias, displays a strange hatred of Homer's favourite hero, the taker of the city, Odysseus. He, in most of the plays where he appears, is a peculiarly mean character: in the Iliad he is as noble and resolute as he is sagacious: in the Odyssey he is

ruse, because his desperate situation, alone in a throng of foes, requires cunning. Only Agamemnon once, in one of his tempers, accused Odysseus of "evil wiles" (Iliad, iv. 339). Professor Mahaffy has offered an explanation of "the degradation of Odysseus" (and of other Homeric heroes) "in Greek literature" very different from that which I shall venture to suggest.[354] Mr. Mahaffy thinks that "the Attic standard of morality, the standard of Aeschylus and Euripides ... was higher and not lower than that of the Ionic court poets, and that the degradation of the Homeric heroes was partly owing to a moral advance, and not a moral decay, in the Greek nation." But what has Homer to do with the morality of Ionic court poets, about whom we have no information, unless the Cyclic poets were court poets? In Mr. Mahaffy's opinion, the Sicilian Epicharmus began the attacks on "Odysseus the Knave." "At all epochs and among all Greeks, lying and dishonesty were prominent vices." Certainly they were in historic times. Traitors were too well known to historic Greece, but Homer seems never to have heard of treachery. Odysseus has his ruses in the Odyssey, and therefore, Mr. Mahaffy thinks, the Greeks, knowing their own weak point, falseness, attacked it through Odysseus. Epicharmus began the assault, Pindar followed Epicharmus, and, in the Nemean Odes, vii. viii., belittled Odysseus (all in the interests of honesty), while Sophocles in the Philoctetes carries on the crusade.

It did not occur to Mr. Mahaffy that the crusade began, long before Epicharmus and Pindar, in the Ionian Cypria. In the Nemean Odes, vii. viii., Pindar naturally belittled Odysseus, to whom were awarded the arms of Achilles, which the hero, Aias, desired to win. Athens always claimed Aias as a friend and ally, wherefore, and in pursuance, as we shall see, of the feud of Palamedes, Attic poets favoured Aias and maligned his successful rival. They also backed Philoctetes against these "tyrants," the Atridae; they had no grudge against Achilles, though they could not represent his chivalry. Mr. Mahaffy does not mention Palamedes at all, does not see that the Athenians take up the Ionian grudge, and is "somewhat impatient of all the fashionable enthusiasm about Homer's grace, and refinement, and delicacy of feeling."

It is to Ionia, and not, primarily, to the advanced morality of republican Athens, morality certainly not Homeric, that we must trace the degradation of Odysseus in the literature of later Greece and of Rome. Ionia followed the example of the base-born Thersites (Iliad, ii. 220). The true cause of this degradation is that Ionia possessed, in Palamedes, a hero infinitely wiser, braver, and more

---

[354] Hermathena, vol. i. p. 265 et seqq.

learned and inventive than Odysseus, and that the death of this very perfect knight, of whom Homer never says a word, is attributed to the jealousy and cruelty of the Ithacan, and of his chosen companion-in-arms, Diomede. All this appeared in the Cypria, and, later, Attic wits perhaps improved on the story, and implicated the Atridae and the whole Achaean host, as well as Odysseus, in the guilt of maligning, falsely accusing, condemning, and stoning Palamedes. It was to punish this collective guilt, we shall see, that Zeus, in the Cypria, detached Achilles from the Achaean cause.

Manifestly all this tale, known to us first in the Cypria, is un-Achaean and un-Homeric, and the question arises, did Homer know the story? If he did, and if he believed it, he deliberately chose to ignore it, and to represent Odysseus and Diomede in the most favourable light. But did Homer know about Palamedes; when Homer sang had Palamedes his place in the Trojan "saga"? I think not, for reasons to be given. To understand the subject, we must examine what remains of the tale of Palamedes as found in the fragments and epitome of the Cypria, and then consider the later expansions and additions.

The Cypria takes Menelaus to Crete before Helen's abduction; and in the legend as arranged in a late age in the prose of Dictys Cretensis (made in the first or second century A.D.), Agamemnon also is in Crete, with Palamedes, son of Clymene and Nauplius of Nauplia, on business connected with the inheritance of Atreus. How far Dictys follows the Cypria, how far he works here on other legends, and how far he invents, it is not easy to be certain. The Cypria certainly yielded the fact that, when Helen eloped, Menelaus was not at home, but in Crete. Probably the Cypria explained why he went thither.[355] The real hero of Dictys and, I suggest, of the Cypria is Palamedes, a character unknown to or ignored by Homer, but of high importance in post-Homeric Ionian and Athenian poetry. In all of these Palamedes is the best man in council and in the field, and is the victim of Odysseus (a very base scoundrel) and of the Atridae. It is clear that Palamedes occupied a prominent place in the Cypria, for a "part or rhapsody" in it "appears to have borne the special title of Palamedeia."[356]

This rhapsody must have contained much information which is not preserved in the summary of the Cypria. About Palamedes we learn no more from the brief epitome and scanty fragments of the Cypria than that (1) he detected and unmasked the feigned madness

---

355 Kinkel, p. 17.

356 Mure, History of Greek Literature, vol. ii. p. 281, citing Düntzer, p. 15. Welcker, Ep. Cycl., pt. i. p. 459.

of Odysseus, when he tried to shirk the summons to the Trojan war; (2) that Palamedes was treacherously drowned, when angling, by the Homeric companions-in-arms, Odysseus and Diomede. (3) According to the Cypria, the Achaean host, once landed in Asia, was perishing for lack of supplies, but Palamedes brought to the camp the three fairy daughters of the Delian priest of Apollo, who magically produced corn, wine, and oil.[357] This silly Märchen about the fairy gifts of the three girls could never have been introduced into an Epic by Homer, but it is quite in the manner of the Cyclics.

According to the account of Trojan matters in prose, by the Greek rhetorician, the pseudo-Dictys Cretensis, who rationalises everything, Palamedes was successful as head of the Commissariat, and obtained supplies when Odysseus failed. This is merely Dictys' way of narrating the Märchen of the girls with fairy gifts, and it was in jealousy of Palamedes' success that Odysseus, aided by Diomede, slew the hero, according to Dictys, treacherously, in the manner of the Märchen of Jean de l'Ours. According to Dictys, Odysseus and Diomede persuaded the guileless Palamedes that there was a hoard of gold at the bottom of a pit, induced him to descend thither, and then threw down stones and slew him. This is not, as we shall see, the Attic tradition, though in that, also, there is a fatal hoard of gold, and Palamedes is slain by stoning.

The Athenian tragedians either improved on the story in the Cypria, or found another legend, according to which Palamedes was treacherously accused of treachery, was tried, condemned, and stoned by the Achaean host: Odysseus being the contriver of the conspiracy. Thus Socrates, in the Apologia, is made by Plato to say that in the next world he hopes to meet Palamedes, and the Telamonian Aias, and others who died by an unjust judgment.[358]

Each of the three great Attic tragedians wrote a play on Palamedes; and Virgil makes Sinon speak of his unjust betrayal and death.[359] Aias, in Quintus Smyrnaeus, brands Odysseus with his guilt in the matter: "Thou didst destroy the divine Palamedes, far thy superior in strength and in counsel."[360] The current Athenian story was that Odysseus contrived to have an arrow, with a letter attached to it, shot towards Palamedes; that Odysseus got possession of the letter, forged by himself but purporting to be addressed by Priam, to Palamedes. Priam thanked him for his

---

357 Schol. ad Lycophr, 570 sqq.; cf. Sophocles's Palamedes, Fr. 438. N2. Cypria, Kinkel, pp. 20, 30.

358 Plato, Apologia, 41 B. Compare Scholion to Euripides, Orestes, 432.

359 Aeneid, ii. 81.

360 Post-Homerica, v. 198.

services as a spy, and promised a gift of gold. This gold was then hidden by Odysseus in the hut of Palamedes, and then discovered by him who hid it.[361] Agamemnon was implicated in the job.

In the Palamedes of Euripides the hero is not unavenged. His brother Oiax writes the shameful story of the Achaean treachery and cruelty, which ruined and destroyed Palamedes, on a number of pinakes, or tablets, like that which contained the fatal letter of Proetus in the Iliad. These tablets Oiax threw into the sea; some of them drifted to Nauplia, and the friends of Palamedes, by altering the guiding beacons on the Greek coast, caused the shipwreck and death of many Achaeans on their homeward way.[362]

Manifestly the whole scope of this Ionian and Attic favourite, the story of Palamedes, is non-Achaean, and was not likely to be known to Homer.

In Dictys, Palamedes is the true hero, and on every occasion takes the lead; while Odysseus, the scoundrel, is an inveterate forger of letters. By forged letters he induced Clytaemnestra to send Iphigeneia to marry Achilles at Aulis, his real purpose being to have her sacrificed to Artemis. In the Cypria, Iphigeneia is sent, on a false and foolish pretence of marriage, to Aulis; whether or not, in the Cypria, Odysseus managed the plot by forged letters, as in Dictys, we do not know.

Through Dictys and through Virgil the Palamedes legend reached the poets and romancers of the Middle Ages: there is even a Palamedes, a paynim knight, at Arthur's court. Thus in Roman times, and much more in the long mediaeval period of Homer's eclipse, Odysseus, Diomede, and the Atridae were under a cloud, Ionian in origin, and Athenian. The Ionians being "Pelasgians of the seacoast" (at least in the opinion of Herodotean Greece), and Palamedes being a man of Nauplia, on the sea, while the town was leagued with Athens, in the amphictyony of Calauria, he was naturally a favourite of Ionian and Athenian poets. In him they had a hero, the wisest and best, who perished from Achaean envy of his greatness.

Now, did Homer know anything of Nauplia and of Palamedes? Was this legend current in his time? If so, he ignored it, as Achaean poetry ignores all things Ionian. It was necessary for the Ionian poets to kill Palamedes just before the opening of the Iliad, for into that epic they could neither foist him nor anything that was theirs. In Shakespeare's Troilus and Cressida, Palamedes is fighting hard in what answers to the Iliadic battle of Book xi.

---

361 Servius on Aeneid, ii. 81. Hyginus fr. Fab. 105.

362 Scholiast, Aristoph. Thesmophor. 768.

I am inclined under correction to suppose that Palamedes was originally no warrior under Ilios, but a Culture Hero of the "Pelasgians of the seacoasts," the Culture Hero of a fairly advanced civilisation. He was credited with the discovery of written characters,[363] or, at least, of a syllabary; or he taught the Greeks to use Phoenician characters in the Ionian alphabet. He also discovered arithmetic, Weights and Measures; Astronomy; the reckoning of Time; military discipline,—with post-Homeric centurions;—sentinels, fire-signals; a number of games, such as draughts, and so forth. Homer knows nothing of such Culture Heroes in the Achaean camp, where they are manifestly out of place.

It has been suggested that Palamedes is Palamaon, an ancient understudy of Hephaestus; παλάμημα being τέχνη, art, or handicraft, and πάλαμις the Salaminian equivalent of τεχνίτης. Palamedes is properly "the Inventor." I suggest that, in the mixed multitude of Ionia, poets were found who simply inserted the old Culture Hero among the Achaean heroes, and asserted his supremacy in counsel and in war; while, as has been said, it was impossible to bring him into the Iliad, so he was made the martyr of the jealousy of Homer's bravest and wisest Achaeans at the moment just before the Iliad begins. In the opinion of Socrates, Aias, no less than Palamedes, was the victim of an unjust verdict, a belief which he never found in Homer. But Aias was claimed as an ally and neighbour of Athens; Palamedes was of a seacoast city allied with Athens; both heroes, therefore, were useful links between the Ionians and Attica and the Trojan affair, in which, as in the legendary affairs of Thebes and Calydon, the Ionians had no part, except what they invented for themselves.

They imposed their version on Rome and on the Middle Ages, but we repeat, they could not get a reference to Palamedes into the Iliad. Among all its alleged borrowings from the Cyclics, the Iliad never borrowed a hint of Palamedes.[364]

After thus examining what is known about Palamedes, we ask, is it more probable that the Cypria is older than the Iliad, and based on a totally different Achaean tradition about events and heroes; or is the Cypria later than the Iliad, and even intended as a kind of antidote to that epic? One thing is clear, the Cypria is Ionian, not Achaean, if human sacrifice is Ionian rather than Achaean. Students who think the Cypria the older poem might perhaps argue thus:

---

[363] Stesichorus, Fr. 4 B. Schol. Eurip., Orestes, 432. Euripides, Palamedes, Fr. 578, N.

[364] For the learning about Palamedes, see Roscher's Lexikon, s.v. Palamedes.

Many of the mixed peoples who made up the Ionians had ancestors at the Trojan war. Among these were Minyans, Boeotians, and Cretans. Their legends may have had an Achaean version of events which was not Homer's version, but was hostile to Odysseus, Diomede, and the Atridae. This version, Ionised, is given in the Cypria. Probably this version was continued (though we have no such continuation) from the resolve of Zeus to punish the host for the death of Palamedes: and the subsequent account, in this version of the war, would take no notice of the Wrath of Achilles about Briseis. Or, if that were assumed as the cause of the Wrath, Zeus embroiled Achilles and Agamemnon without any prayer from Thetis. Probably in this version, as in Dictys, Achilles was in love with Polyxena, and was treacherously slain while wooing her. This is the statement of the scholiast on Lycophron, and of Dictys, though it is contrary to the Cyclic Aethiopis, which follows the Iliad; Paris and Apollo slew Achilles, as Hector prophesied, in the Scaean gate. On this theory Polyxena was sacrificed to the dead Achilles precisely because they loved each other.

Thus the theory might go on, explaining that this Achaean version (wholly unknown to us), with Palamedes and all, was crushed by the supreme popularity of a later poem, the Iliad, but lived in an underground way till it revived, very late, in Lycophron, Dictys, and the rest. The details of ghosts, human sacrifices, hero-worship, and purification by blood (all un-Homeric), will be genuinely old Achaean, merely suppressed by some persons of taste who, later, "edited" the Iliad. In this case these details of religion were common to the Achaeans and the earlier populations, not peculiar to "the conquered races." They are Achaean, but were expurgated by the makers of our Homer, why, and when, and how, I do not conjecture.

I have here invented as coherent a hypothesis as I can imagine to account for Palamedes consistently with the theory that the Cypria is older than the Iliad. But the fact that Palamedes, "the inventor," is clearly, in origin, a Culture Hero, like Prometheus and Daedalus, does to me seem fatal to the hypothesis which I have sketched. If he had been, originally, just another such warrior as Achilles or Idomeneus, popular fancy would never have converted him into a being who won men from savagery and invented arts and sciences.

CHAPTER XVIII

HOMER AND THE CYCLIC POEMS

Few subjects are more recalcitrant to lucidity of treatment than the so-called "Cyclic poems." On the various meanings of the word "Cyclic" as applied to poetry by the ancients, very much has been written.[365] Into that question we need not enter, as we here call "Cyclic" all these old epics on the Trojan theme (outside of the Iliad and Odyssey) of which we have only fragments, in quotations by later Greek writers, and in fragmentary epitomes. Though these remains, including the prose of the Greek authors who cite and comment on them, occupy but forty-five pages of a book in small octavo,[366] the fragments suffice to prove that the lost epics are far apart as the poles from the Iliad and Odyssey in taste, tone, narrative art, descriptions of religious rites, customs, usages, and treatment of the heroic characters. This was plain to Greek commentators, and is even more obvious to modern criticism.

The questions, therefore, arise, were these Cyclic epics older in matter (as representing a more archaic tradition) than our Homer; are they older, or more recent, in composition, or are they and our Homer coeval? Mr. Monro expresses decisively the general opinion on these points. The Cyclic poems are by "the poets who carried on the traditions of Homeric art in the eighth and seventh centuries B.C."[367] He collects from them many incidents, beliefs, usages, and proofs of geographical knowledge "of a post-Homeric type."[368] Of these, from one poem, the Cypria, he selects five sets of examples. These represent (i) human sacrifice; (2) geographical

---

365 In English the best critical treatises are Homer and the Cyclic Poems, by the late Mr. Binning Monro in his Odyssey, Books xiii.-xxiv. pp. 340-384, with his "On the Fragment of Proclus's Abstract of the Epic Cycle," Journal of Hellenic Society, vol. iv. pp. 305-334. The discussion of the whole topic by Mr. T. W. Allen in The Classical Quarterly (1908) leaves no hint of ancient evidence unexplored, however remote and obscure its lurking place. Mr. Allen specially criticises the ingenious inferences of von Wilamowitz Moellendorff in his Homerische Untersuchungen, inferences which appear to be accepted by Mr. Murray in his Rise of the Greek Epic, and his lecture, "Anthropology in the Greek Epic Tradition outside of Homer," in Anthropology and the Classics, 1908.

366 Kinkel, Epicorum Graecorum Fragmenta, 1898.

367 J. H. S., vol. iv p. 305.

368 Odyssey, vol. ii pp. 352-354.

knowledge much beyond that exhibited in Iliad and Odyssey; (3) interest in magic, which is un-Homeric; (4) the introduction of a non-Homeric hero, Palamedes, of the first rank, of essential importance, and the "Cause of Wrath" of Zeus against the Achaeans; (5) hero-worship; (6) I add, introduction of a goddess unknown to Homer, but "a concrete figure of ancient Attic religion;"[369] (7) introduction of the puerile fairy element in Märchen or folk-tales. Of this trait, and of magical incidents, there are several examples. (8) loves of gods and goddesses, who take the forms of various animals. From other Cyclic poems he selects other instances of these non-Homeric types, and also un-Homeric apparitions of men who have been duly burned and buried; and cases of the purification of homicides by blood of pigs, wholly unknown to Homer.

All these traits of the Cyclic poems, with others, such as the invention of pseudo-historic genealogies, as of Thersites, are non-Homeric. Some, such as the genealogy of Thersites, due to the manie cyclique, with the extended geographical outlook, are post-Homeric. But the others, the religious and magical notions— hero-worship, the ghost belief, blood-purification,—though later in record than our Homer (we assume), are even earlier in development, and are beliefs and rites of the pre-Homeric population. (See "Who were the Ionians?" and Appendix, On "Expurgation.")

Now much confusion is caused by the term "old." The poems earlier in composition may represent Achaean ideas then new to Greece; the poems later in composition may, and do, contain ideas old in Greece, but alien to Homer's Achaeans. Meanwhile, Mr. Monro, as we saw, regards the actual Cyclic poems as works of poets of the eighth to seventh centuries B.C., who carried "on the traditions of Homeric art" in Ionia. This means that they take up Achaean themes and traditions and heroic characters, and use them in new poems "composed with direct reference to the Iliad."[370] They lead up to the Iliad by a long chronicle of previous events in the Cypria, and continue the Homeric narrative in their other epics. But they interlard the narrative with their own rites, beliefs, their own Attic goddess (Nemesis of Rhamnus), and their own non-Achaean heroes, such as the Attic sons of Theseus, and the great Nauplian, Palamedes. They also add silly elements of Märchen, and pseudo-

---

[369] Farnell, Cults of the Greek States, vol. ii pp. 488-493. Mr. Monro seems to have been unaware of these facts. Odyssey, vol. ii p. 354.
[370] Odyssey, vol. ii. p. 350.

historic genealogies. They carve and cook the great Achaean joint, and serve up with Attic and Ionian sauce and trimmings.

This is natural, for the Attic people, of the pre-Achaean population, had not, as far as I know, any epic tradition of their own. They knew that they were not engaged in any one of the alleged great collective efforts and expeditions with which the Achaeans credited themselves. Some legends were dynastic adaptations of Märchen, with kings and princesses changed into birds; or accounts of their relations with Thrace, or explanations of the origin of the Eleusinian mysteries. They had, too, the story of Theseus and the Minotaur, an adventure of an individual hero of Märchen; but that ran contrary to all Achaean and Cretan traditions, as we have seen. The Cyclic poets were mere imitators of the Achaean epic: epic tradition of their own, the people of Attica and their Ionian colonists (confessedly mixed with a mongrel multitude) had none.

Mr. Leaf takes the same view. He speaks of the Cyclic epics as "the imitative poems which dealt with the old Tale of Troy, and essayed to complete Homer."[371]

But a contradictory opinion seems to be held by von Wilamowitz-Moellendorff, and, as I understand, by Mr. Murray. The celebrated German scholar argued thus: Before criticism arose in Greece, almost all ancient Epic poetry, and the Hymns, were attributed to "Homer." As early as Herodotus, however, we find that historian regarding the Cypria (a chronicle of the whole events before the opening of the Iliad) as not by the author of the Iliad.

As time went on, and criticism advanced, the Iliad and Odyssey alone were assigned to Homer, while the Cyclic poems were attributed to various authors, such as Arctinus, Stasinus, and Lesches. The attributions are late, various, perhaps never "evidential"; but criticism came to recognise our Iliad and Odyssey as alone Homeric. The other epics, the Cyclics, were thought to be of a later age, and by inferior hands.

This view was evolved by Greek critics from Herodotus to Aristotle and Aristarchus.

On the other hand, according to Wilamowitz-Moellendorff, Homer and the Cyclic poems were all qualitatively equivalent, and more or less contemporaneous. A statement of this hypothesis, which deliberately rejects the views of Greek criticism, shall be quoted from von Wilamowitz-Moellendorff.[372]

---

371 Companion to the Iliad, p. 46.

372 Homerische Untersuchungen, pp. 374, 375. On Wilamowitz-Moellendorff's opinion that the Cyclics were lost before the time of

"The epos" (the whole mass of early epic poetry) "is by Homer," so says tradition. "The criticism of the subsequent centuries broke off from the mass of epos one portion after another: one after another must go, because it is inconsistent with the conception which has been framed of Homer. At last the Iliad alone abides. The only step that remained to be taken was to reject (athetiren) the Iliad also: this step the ancients refused to take, for fear of falling into the abyss. But the step has been taken long ago. The Iliad, as it stands, is not the work of one man, or of one century: it is not one work at all. The Iliad is nothing but a κυκλικὸν ποίημα. But we are in no abyss, no bottomless pit. On the other hand, we regain firm ground, which ancient criticism had in childish rashness abandoned. The Iliad is just as much and as little Homeric as the Cypria. There is no qualitative difference between ὁμηρικόν and κυκλικόν."

Now that careless child, Aristotle, was of a different opinion. He saw that the Iliad varies absolutely in nature from some of the Cyclics, and the fact is conspicuous. The Iliad also varies, as the scholiasts observed, from the Cyclics historically; varies in manners, rites, religion, taste, and geographical knowledge. All these facts are absolutely demonstrable. So great a critic as Aristotle, and, we may add, so unprejudiced a critic, for he lived long before Wolf, could not but remark the essential differences between the Iliad, on the one hand, and some of the Ionian Cyclic poems on the other, as far as quality is concerned. Into the differences which archaeology and anthropology detect, Aristotle did not enter, for he was writing on the Art of Poetry. Unity in a poem, he said, is not obtained merely by the selection of a single hero (the Cypria is so far like Vanity Fair that it is a chronicle "without a hero," unless the hero be Paris or Palamedes). Unity of action is, says Aristotle, essential to an Epic, and Homer observes this unity, grouping all the events round one motif, the Wrath of Achilles, or the Return of Odysseus. The Cypria has no such unity; it simply ends where the Iliad begins.

Unity, concentration, "with beginning, middle, and end," is as necessary, Aristotle holds, to epic as to dramatic poetry. The Trojan war, to be sure, has a beginning, a middle, and an end, but the whole could not be treated in an Epic under poetic conditions of space. One motif is therefore selected by Homer, with diversifying episodes. The author of the Cypria did not adopt the true method of epic: in the Iliad and Odyssey are subjects but for one or two

---

Pausanias, see Mr. Allen, Classical Quarterly, January, April, 1908. The Iliad, as it stands, appears to be regarded as later and more artistic than the rest.

tragedies; whereas the Cypria, extending over many years and dealing with many regions, yields subjects for many, and the Little Iliad for eight or more plays, which are enumerated.[373]

We would not now state the case precisely in the terms of Aristotle: and the Attic tragedians possibly chose so many topics from the Cyclics, so few from the Iliad, partly because the Athenians, as chiefs of the Ionian name, preferred Ionian versions of the legends; while, as Republicans, they used the Ionian term for Agamemnon and Menelaus as "tyrants"; and kept up the singular Ionian feud against Odysseus, preferring to him Aias, a neighbour of Athens; Philoctetes, oppressed by the "tyrants"; and Palamedes, the victim of the tyrants and of their minion Odysseus.

Such were the tastes of the Athenians; but we see that Aristotle observes the essential difference in poetic quality between the Iliad and Odyssey, which are Epics, while some of the Cyclic poems are mere metrical chronicles.

The difference between epic and versified chronicle is, I think, that which divides Barbour's The Brus and the Wallace of Blind Harry (poetical chronicles like the Heracleis, the late poem on the history of Heracles), from epics like the Chanson de Roland with its one motive, "The Wrath of Ganelon," its origins and consequences. Our Iliad, in Aristotle's opinion, then, is an epic; the Cypria, the Heracleis, and so on, are not epics, but rather are versified chronicles. In Mr. Murray's opinion, too, the Iliad is an epic, the Cypria is "an old chronicle poem." But this only proves, to his mind, that the Iliad is the further developed.[374] "They grew together side by side" or centuries; but the Iliad, as we have it, is, he thinks, of later and more accomplished art. Mr. Murray writes: "In its actual working up, however, our Iliad has reached a further stage of development than the ordinary run of poetic chronicles, if I may use the term."[375]

Now, as far as analogy serves our turn, the "poetic chronicle" is in a later stage of development than the epic. Thus Barbour's The Brus, or the Argonautic poem of the very late Apollonius, is in a much later stage of development than the old Germanic epics, or Beowulf, which selects two main events from the career of the hero. Again, versified chronicles in France are much later in development than the epic, the Chanson de Roland, "The Wrath of Ganelon."

However, as analogies are never satisfactory, let us be content to note that the Iliad confessedly differs in character from the

---

373 Aristotle, Poetics, ch. xxiv.

374 R. G. E. p. 165.

375 Ibid. p. 165.

Cypria, as the epic differs from the verse-chronicle. On this point von Wilamowitz Moellendorff appears to agree, as does Mr. Murray, who studies the subject in the spirit of the learned German. To repeat his statement, he writes, "These various books or masses of tradition in verse form were growing up side by side for centuries."[376]

Now, "masses of tradition" certainly grew up through many centuries, before and after Homer's time; but the Iliad is not merely "a mass of tradition." It is a splendid work of art, fashioned, in our view, by a great poet, out of masses of tradition, while what we know of the Cypria is a compilation, partly from hints in the Iliad and Odyssey, with popular tales or Märchen thrown in; and is animated by a distinct tendenz, a partisan desire to debase the favourite heroes of Homer, and to exalt a hero, Palamedes, who, to myself, seems intended to represent the Ionian share in the Trojan war, neglected as it is by Homer. To justify these criticisms as most probable on the evidence, it is necessary to offer an analysis of the Cypria, as far as its contents are known to us from fragments and epitomes.

The Cypria opened thus: Zeus takes counsel on the problem of over-population. He "resolves to relieve of her burden Earth that nourishes all, by raising the great strife of the Ilian war, that death may lighten the weight: the heroes were slain in Troyland, but the Will of Zeus was accomplished."[377]

The following account of the early part of the Cypria is given by the Scholiast in the famous "Venice A" manuscript of the Iliad. He enters here into more details than Proclus in his epitome of the work. "They say that Earth, burdened by the abundance of men, all impious as they were, prayed to Zeus to be relieved. Zeus then caused the Theban war, whereby he destroyed many. Later again he called Momus (Mockery) into council, 'the counsel of Zeus,' Homer styles it, though he might have destroyed the human race altogether by deluges and thunderbolts. But Momus prevented this, and suggested to Zeus the marriage of Thetis with a mortal, and the begetting of a beautiful daughter from these two causes arose war involving both Hellenes and barbarians, from which time Earth was lightened of her burden, so many men were slain. The narrative is by Stasinus, the author of the Cypria..."[378]

---

376 Ibid. p. 163.

377 The seven Greek verses to this effect are preserved by the Venice Scholiast on Iliad, i. 5, 6. The words Διὸς δ'ἐτελείετο βουλή are also in Iliad, i. 5, whether the author of the Cypria borrowed them, or whether they were an old epic formula.

378 Schol. Ven., Iliad, i, 5, 6.

In this version Themis is not mentioned as the adviser of Zeus; perhaps she suggested the Theban, and Momus the Trojan war.

In the epitome of Proclus, Eris (Strife) comes among the Gods at the bridal feast of Peleus and Thetis. Of this feast one detail remains in a fragment of the Cypria, which the Scholiast gives in prose. Cheiron the Centaur cut an ash-tree for a spear, as a wedding present to Peleus. Athene polished it, and Hephaestus forged the point. This spear, which Achilles alone could wield, is mentioned as the gift of Cheiron to Achilles in the Iliad (xvi. 143, 144, and xix. 389-90). If, then, we find in the Cypria decisive proof that there it is later than the Iliad, we may suppose the author to borrow here from our Homer, and to add the previous division of labour in the spear-making. As a bronze-smith Hephaestus only makes the metal point of the weapon. At the bridal feast, Eris rouses a dispute between Aphrodite, Athene, and Hera as to superiority in beauty.

To return to the Epitome of Proclus. The three contending goddesses are led by Hermes to Mount Ida, and Paris pronounces Aphrodite to be the most beautiful; he has been won by her promise of Helen as his wife. This is suggested by Iliad, xxiv. 29, 30, where the passage, according to some, suggests that all three goddesses wooed Paris, and that he preferred Aphrodite. But this is wholly out of keeping with the Greek conception of Hera and Athene; and the lines in Iliad, xxiv., must refer to the cause of the ferocity with which these two slighted goddesses persecute Troy, though Athene was its patron. No other cause has been adduced.

The counsel of Zeus could not have caused the Trojan war merely by making the goddesses quarrel. It was necessary to beget "the beautiful daughter," whom Aphrodite was to offer as a bride to Paris. According to the Cypria, this fairest of women, Helen, wife of Menelaus, was not the daughter of Zeus and Leda, but of Zeus and Nemesis; in Homer, Nemesis is little more than the emotion of virtuous indignation, she is not, as in the Cypria, a chaste and pretty nymph, "fair-tressed Nemesis." Her does Zeus pursue and, says the inept author of the Cypria, "the feelings of Nemesis were torn by shame and nemesis" (indignation). Mr. Murray devotes eight pages to the ethical meaning of Αἰδώς (shame) and of Νέμεσις (righteous indignation).[379] Surely we must recognise a great difference in manner between Homer, to whom nemesis means "righteous indignation," and the author of the Cypria, to whom Nemesis is a fair-tressed nymph? Homer, it is true, knows themis as customary

---

379 R. G. E. pp. 80-88.

law, and Themis, a goddess. But she is not a fair-tressed being who flees from her lover in a series of animal disguises.

Later Greeks, puzzled by the contending versions of our Homer and of the Cypria, declared that Nemesis was, indeed, the mother of Helen, but that Leda, wife of Tyndareus, was her foster-mother and brought her up.[380] Meanwhile Nemesis, in the Cypria, is not a mere personification of the sentiment of nemesis, or righteous indignation, but is, as we know, "a concrete figure of ancient Attic tradition," "a primitive goddess of Rhamnus," in Attica, associated with, or a local form of, "the wild Artemis" of pre-Achaean religion, "with deep roots in local worship." Nemesis had a famous statue at Rhamnus, attributed by Pausanias to Pheidias; a fragment of the face, in the British Museum, proves that it was at least of the school of Pheidias. She held in her hand a spray of the apple-tree, an attribute of Aphrodite, and the stag of Artemis was an ornament of her crown. She was also "a queen over death and the dead," a chthonic characteristic.[381] The Nemesis of Rhamnus was thus like the very primitive Artemis of Brauron in Attica. At Smyrna, where the population was very mixed, Pausanias mentions two Nemeses.[382]

We see that all this of Nemesis, in the Cypria, is at once apart as the poles from the Nemesis of Homer, virtuous indignation personified, and is also an Ionian celebration of an Attic goddess of the pre-Achaean faith.

In the Cypria, Aphrodite, mother of Aeneas (in Homer), sends him with Paris. Landing in Lacedaemon, Paris is welcomed by the brothers of Helen, and in Sparta by Menelaus, who then sails to Crete. (Different reasons for this voyage are given by later writers.) Paris then seduces Helen, who is brought to him by Aphrodite (as in Iliad, iii.); they take away property of Menelaus (as in Iliad, vii.). (The italics mark probable hints from the Iliad.)

The pair are wedded in Troy, where the story leaves them, and very needlessly goes back to Lacedaemon. Here are Helen's brothers, Castor and Polydeuces, who fall into a feud about cattle with Idas and Lynceus, the keen-eyed. Lynceus is merely the Keen-Eye, who can see through everything, a common personage in Märchen. The brothers of Helen hide themselves in a hollow tree, but Lynceus climbs to the crest of Mount Taygetus and "looks over all the isle of Pelops," that is, Peloponnesus. Homer never speaks of

---

380 Pausanias, i. 33.

381 Bekk. Anecdot. p. 282. 32. Pausanias, i. 33. 2.

382 Pausanias, vii. 5. 3. See Farnell, Cults of Greek States, vol. ii. pp. 487-495. 594. 595.

the country as a geographical unity, nor uses the word "Peloponnesus"; this is manifestly a post-Homeric term.[383] Idas slays Castor; Polydeuces slays both Lynceus and Idas, and Zeus assigns to Castor and Polydeuces immortality on alternate days. This is wholly unknown to the Iliad, both heroes are dead and buried in Iliad, iii. 243, 244. Their alternate immortality with their divine honours, mentioned in Odyssey, xi. 298-304, may be an interpolation (a kind of footnote in verse); it is, at all events, non-Iliadic. Homer knows the deaths of the two brothers, at home in Lacedaemon: we cannot tell whether he knew about the Keen-Eye of Märchen, Lynceus.

In the Cypria, Menelaus is now informed, in Crete, about the flight of Helen: he returns to the isle of Pelops and consults Agamemnon about collecting an army. Nestor, called to council, abounds in anecdotic digressions (whether the author borrows this trait from the Iliad or the Iliad from him, it is not hard to guess!). Among Nestor's themes—for he simply poured out stories—are Epopeus and his seduction of the daughter of Lycus; Oedipous; the madness of Heracles; and the tale of Theseus (whom Homer steadily avoids), and Ariadne. Theseus, as an Athenian, is dear to the Ionian poet: Homer ignores him.

The Atridae go through Greece collecting the heroes. Odysseus feigns madness with a view to shirking the war; he ploughs the sand, and Palamedes detects his sanity by placing the child Telemachus in the way of the plough. Here we have a hero, Palamedes, unknown to Homer, and an equally unknown Odysseus who is a coward, but is baffled by the superior wisdom of Palamedes. It is obvious that the poet of the Cypria is here introducing an un-Homeric character to serve his private ends: his methods are unveiled in Chapter XVII., "The Story of Palamedes."

The Cypria now relates the First gathering of the Greek forces at Aulis, with the story from the Iliad of the serpent and the sparrows, and the prophecy of Calchas. The ships, says the Iliad, "had been gathering but a day or two at Aulis," and the host was at a sacrifice, when a wonderful serpent came forth from the altar and killed eight nestlings of a sparrow, with their mother. Zeus then turned the serpent into a stone. Calchas prophesied, "we shall fight nine years there (αὖθι, at Troy), but take the city in the tenth year."[384]

Such was Homer's opinion, the Greeks were warring in Troyland against Ilios for nine years and more. But the author of the

---

383 Kinkel, Ep. Graec. Frag. p. 25 9.

384 Iliad, ii. 326-329.

Cypria desired to fill up the nine years before the Iliad opens in some way, and this is how he did it. (Italics mark possible hints from Homer.) Learning from the Odyssey (xi. 519-521) that Eurypylus, a Mysian chief, son of Telephus, came to the aid of Troy after the death of Achilles, he makes the Achaeans land in Teuthrania, and supposing the town to be Troy, they attack it. But Telephus comes to the rescue, and is wounded by Achilles. A storm falls on the fleet, and the ships are scattered. Achilles arrives in Scyros and weds Deidameia. The storm that sends Achilles to marry and beget a son in Scyros was an easy explanation of Achilles' own statement,[385] that he had a son at Scyros.[386]

In the Cypria, Achilles later returns from Scyros to Argos, apparently "Pelasgic Argos," that is, Phthia, to his home. The wounded Telephus, as advised by prophecy, follows Achilles thither, and Achilles' spear, or rust from the spear, in Dictys, heals the wound it had inflicted: by "sympathetic magic," unknown to Homer. Achilles did the healing, because it was prophesied that Telephus would pilot the fleet to Troy; whereas, in Homer, Calchas directs the voyage.

The author of the Cypria, who is filling up his nine imaginary years of the wanderings of the Greeks, now adopts the very stupid device of mustering the scattered fleet at Aulis for the second time. This enables him to please an Ionian audience by introducing their favourite incident, the sacrifice of a princess: Attic traditions harp eternally on this un-Homeric horror. Agamemnon shoots a stag, and boasts himself a better shot than Artemis. The angry goddess sends a tempest unceasing, the ships cannot sail, and Calchas (who dared not do such a thing, Iliad, i. 78, 79) says that a daughter of Agamemnon must be sacrificed, Iphigeneia. This name was, at least in later days, a name of the homicidal Artemis of Tauris, on the north shore of the Euxine. But Tauris, as Mr. Monro justly observes, was not known to Homer. In the Cypria, Artemis substitutes a fawn for Iphigeneia, and carries the maid "to the Tauroi," making her immortal. "This form of the story," the form in the Cypria, "is necessarily later than the Greek settlements on the northern coasts of the Euxine."[387] The connection between Iphigeneia and a Tauric Artemis is thus late, un-Homeric, and Ionian. Homer (Iliad, ix. 145)

---

385 xix. 326, 327.

386 The common tale that Achilles was sent to Scyros to avoid the war, in girl's dress; that he there begat Neoptolemus, and was then unmasked by Odysseus, was in contradiction with Iliad, xi. 766-785, where Nestor tells how he summoned Achilles at the house of Peleus, his father.

387 Monro, Odyssey, vol. ii. p. 352.

knows no Iphigeneia, but the daughters of Agamemnon are Chrysothemis, Laodice, and Iphianassa. Even so early a poet as Stesichorus could not account for Iphigeneia as a daughter of Agamemnon. He therefore, says Pausanias, made her a foster-child of Clytaemnestra, a child of Helen by Theseus (who, in Attic myth, captured her), and Helen hands her baby over to the wife of Agamemnon. Euphorion of Chalcis, Alexander of Pleuron, and the people of Argos generally, maintained this theory, and at Argos they showed a temple of Ilithyia, founded by Helen after her safe delivery![388] Tzetzes, the father of nonsense, makes Iphigeneia the daughter of Agamemnon and Chryseis; she is sacrificed, or threatened with sacrifice, during the return from Troy.

However, the Ionian author of the Cypria cannot deny himself an allusion to human sacrifice. Iphigeneia was brought to Aulis, he says, under the pretence that she was to wed Achilles. (See Euripides, Iphigeneia in Aulis. He may be following the Cypria.) She was tempted by letters forged by Odysseus, says Dictys Cretensis, who may be following the Cypria.

The Greeks, the storm abating, sail to Tenedos, where Philoctetes is bitten by a snake and carried away to howl in Lemnos. This might be taken from Iliad, ii. 718-725. At Troy on landing, the Greeks lose Protesilaus, slain by Hector. Here again the Iliad may supply the fact, not naming Hector. The author of the Cypria has now, we see, filled up his empty nine years by various expedients and delays. He next tells of the embassy to ask for the return of Helen and the stolen property; the embassy he could get from Iliad, iii. 204-207: a subsequent fight at the wall of Troy from Iliad, vi. 435-439, where it is described briefly by Andromache.

At what precise period the Greek commissariat took the form of three girls with fairy gifts, who produced corn, wine, and oil, is uncertain; but the incident was in the Cypria, on the authority of Pherecydes.[389]

The Cypria says that Aphrodite contrived an interview between Helen and Achilles, Thetis was chaperon, and that Achilles restrained the Greeks, who wished to go home. That Achilles sacked Lyrnessus and Pedasus, and sent Lykaon captive to Lemnos, was to be read in the Iliad (xx. 92, xxi. 55 ff.), where also the story of Briseis and Chryseis, given in the Cypria, was to be found. But not in the Iliad was Palamedes, with his murder by Odysseus and Diomede, whence, in the Cypria, came the will of Zeus to sunder Achilles from the Achaean host.[390]

---

[388] Pausanias, ii. 22.

[389] Kinkel, p. 29.

[390] See "The Story of Palamedes."

We now perceive how much of his material the Ionian author of the Cypria could obtain from out Homer. We note the marks of non-Achaeanism and lateness, and of Ionian geographical knowledge, in the reference to Tauris; in the Attic Nemesis; in the per-sonifications of moral qualities; in the intended human sacrifice; in the Märchen; in the telling of the tale of Theseus and Ariadne; in the hero-worship; and in the introduction of the Nauplian anti—Odyssean Palamedes. The lateness of the poem declares itself also in the naming of the Peloponnesus. The use of very childish Märchen is un-Homeric: Homer uses Märchen to better purpose. (See "Homer and the Saga.")

Perhaps few who have had the patience to read through this tedious analysis of the vast and wandering metrical pseudo-chronicle, the Cypria, with its marks of bad taste, Ionicism, and lateness, will maintain that, in character, it is on a level with our Homer, or is in age contemporary with his society.

Weary as is the task, we must in conscience expose the similar lateness and Ionic character of the other Cyclic poems on the Trojan affairs.

The authorship of the Aethiopis was attributed to Arctinus of Miletus. Tradition called him "Homer's pupil."[391] As condensed in the summary of Proclus, the Aethiopis was a mere doppelgänger of the Iliad. Taking up the tale after Hector's death, and under the shadow of Hector's prophecy of the doom of Achilles, "in the day when Paris and Phoebus Apollo slay thee in the Scaean gate,"[392] the Aethiopis fills out the story.

The Amazon, Penthesilea, comes to aid Troy, and is slain by Achilles, who is stirred by pity for the beauty of his victim. For this Thersites taunts him, and he slays the wretch: so he needs purification, in accordance with Ionian ideas.

The Aethiopis went on to mark the usual distinction between the Homeric and Ionian epic. Diomede took up the blood-feud for Thersites, and, in Homeric law, Achilles must have paid the blood-wyte, or gone into exile, or "tholed the feud." Even the Scholiast[393] knew that this was the Homeric (as it was the Icelandic) law. But the Ionian makes Achilles sail to Lesbos, to sacrifice to Apollo, Artemis, and Leto, and be purified (in pig's blood probably) by Odysseus.

Thus the Ionian makes us certain that he was of an un-Homeric state of society. He dates himself in similar fashion, when he makes Memnon (who, as in the Odyssey, slays Antilochus)

---

391 Welcker, Das Ep. Kyk., vol. i. pp. 211, 212.

392 Iliad, xx ii. 358-360.

393 Iliad, xi. 690.

receive after death the gift of immortality; and when he makes Thetis carry the body of Achilles (burned in the Odyssey) to be the worshipped hero of the isle of Leuke in the Euxine. There, when Ionian colonists reached the Euxine, Achilles became a ruling religious hero, recognised by Alcaeus (Fr. 49). "The Locrians in Italy," according to Pausanias, had a cult of Aias, whose armed ghost wounded Leonymus of Croton in battle. (In post-Homeric Greece the ghosts of heroes appeared in mortal wars, as St. James fought for Cortes against the Aztecs. Homer could conceive no such folly.) The Delphic oracle dispatched Leonymus to Leuke, where he found Achilles happily married to Helen, who sent by Leonymus a message to the poet Stesichorus, that had libelled her. Patroclus and Antilochus were with Achilles in Leukê, etc. etc.[394]

If the Aethiopis is earlier than these Ionian colonies, if Leuke in fable meant "the isle of light," then the colonists identified the Euxine isle with the isle of light, and so worshipped the dead Achilles of Leuke. The Ionian trading cities, of which Miletus was chief, had begun to adopt the new religious ideas that grew up, after the Homeric age, in honour of the national heroes.[395] It is more probable that the Ionians had never dropped the rites and religions of the conquered races, and merely added Achilles to Erechtheus. They had no spite against Achilles, who had never, like Agamemnon and Diomede, been their master.

For the rest, the story of the Aethiopis is conducted on the lines of the Iliad, as far as the events included in the poems, ending with the death of Achilles in the Scaean gate, permit imitation; and all concludes with a lament or regret, a funeral, and funeral games, as in the Iliad.

The Little Iliad contains several main incidents, of which seven were, or may have been, expansions of hints in the Odyssey and Iliad. The additions are the theft of the Palladium, a kind of fetich ignored by Homer; the magical power of the arrows of Philoctetes over the fate of Troy; the introduction of Sinon, as followed by Virgil in the Aeneid; and a long story about Aethra, mother of Theseus and slave of Helen in Troy, and about her grandsons, sons of Theseus, whose presence in the Achaean host is unknown to Homer. In Iliad, iii. 144, Helen has, in an interpolated line, an attendant, "Aethra, daughter of Pittheus." This was enough for the Ionian poets; for, as Aethra was the name of the mother of Theseus, "naturally the later poets took advantage of it in order to

---

394 Pausanias, iii. 19.

395 Monro, Odyssey, vol. ii. p. 361.

find a place for the Attic heroes in the main body of epic narrative."[396]

Mr. Leaf makes Iliad, iii. 144, "a clear case of an interpolation of a later myth," a myth introduced here to please the Athenians. Aethra and the rape of Helen by Theseus, to avenge which the brothers of Helen carried the mother of Theseus away, were depicted and described on the chest of Cypselus,[397] and painted by Polygnotus, following the Little Iliad of Lesches, on the Leschê at Delphi. But here Aethra was with the Homeric maids of Helen (Panthalis and Electra), but was being recognised by her un-Homeric grandson, son of Theseus, Demophon. According to the Little Iliad, Aethra escaped to the Greek camp: by permission of Helen, Agamemnon restores Aethra to her grandsons.[398]

Ionia could only drag fair Helen into the Athenian legend of Theseus by averring that he carried her off when she was a child, and that she was brought back to the house of Tyndareus her sire by her brothers, Castor and Polydeuces. They also seized Aethra, the mother of Theseus, who accompanied Paris and Helen to Troy, and was still in Helen's service after the ten years of the leaguer. Now as Theseus in his prime was contemporary with the youth of Nestor, and as Nestor was, say, seventy in the tenth year of the war, the mother of Theseus must have been more than a centenarian when she was the suivante of Helen, in Iliad, Book iii. But Ionians stuck at nothing in the effort to bring themselves into touch with the great Achaean enterprise; that is, stuck at nothing except at interpolating their fables into the Iliad. They could perhaps insert, as in Iliad, iii. 144, a mention or two of Theseus, and some lines on Attic heroines in Odyssey, xi.

There can be no more conclusive proof that Ionians did not possess the power of adding what they pleased to the Achaean epics.

The Ilion Persis, or Sack of Troy, was a poem attributed, like the Aethiopis, to Arctinus of Miletus. Herein occurs the affair of the Wooden Horse, familiar to readers of the Odyssey in the lay of Demodocus at the board of Alcinous.[399] Demodocus tells enough to serve Arctinus with a theme which only needs expansion. The story was given much as Virgil and Quintus Smyrnaeus render it; we have the portent of Laocoon and the serpents, which causes Aeneas and his men (not as in Virgil) to retire to Mount Ida. In the song of Demodocus, Odysseus gets most of the credit of success; the hero in

---

396 Monro, Odyssey, vol. ii. p. 370.

397 Pausanias, v. 19.

398 Pausanias, x. 25.

399 Odyssey, viii. 492-520.

Odyssey, xi. 504-537, gives the glory to Neoptolemus—and himself. In Arctinus, Odysseus murders the child of Hector, Astyanax (an un-Homeric cruelty); Odysseus is always degraded by the Ionians and usually by the Attic tragedians. Aias Oileus's son enrages Athene by dragging down her image while struggling with Cassandra; hence the sorrows of the Achaeans on their way home. The sons of Theseus carry to Athens their aged grandmother, Aethra. Could anything be more characteristic of the Athenians than the fact that the heroes looking out from the Horse, in a bronze group on the Acropolis, were Attic, the two apocryphal sons of Theseus, the Athenian Menestheus, and Teucer, "who expresses the Athenian claim to Salamis"?[400]

By a truly Ionian touch, Polyxena, daughter of Priam, is sacrificed at the tomb of Achilles. It seems probable that the Iliou Persis really took up the story with the suicide of Aias (from this part of the poem a fragment is quoted in the scholia to Iliad, xi. 515),[401] and that the poem contained the whole prowess of Neoptolemus at Troy, and the affair of the bringing back of Philoctetes from Lemnos. The prominence of Aeneas expands the hint in Iliad, xx. 307, 308, the prophecy of Poseidon that he and his children will long rule over the Trojans. Throughout the Iliad, Aeneas is protected by Aphrodite, and is looked on jealously by Priam, as a Stewart might look on a Hamilton; for, failing issue of Priam, Aeneas succeeds to the Trojan crown. The whole poem, wherever Aeneas appears, is affected by the tradition that he did continue the Trojan line.

The sacrifice of Polyxena at the tomb of Achilles appears to be peculiar to Arctinus. It would be interesting to know whether or not any Ionian poem was the source of the story of Polyxena as given by Dictys Cretensis. In Dictys, Patroclus moves Achilles to be reconciled to Agamemnon: the army goes into winter quarters, and Trojans and Achaeans meet on friendly terms in the grove of Thymbraean Apollo; Achilles sees Polyxena at a sacrifice, and falls in love with her. Hector offers her as the price of his treason to the Achaeans, which annoys Achilles. At Polyxena's request he later restores the body of Hector to Priam. At a subsequent meeting in Apollo's temple, Paris stabs Achilles to death. After the capture of Troy, Odysseus advises the sacrifice of Polyxena to the ghost of Achilles, but Euripides and later writers make the ghost or voice of Achilles demand her death. In other respects, as to the fate of the Trojan ladies, Dictys follows Arctinus.

---

400 Pausanias, 1. 23. 10.

401 Monro, Odyssey, vol. ii. pp. 372, 373.

All this tale deeply affected the mediaeval tale of Troy. Meanwhile, we do not know why in Arctinus, Polyxena was chosen as the γέρας, or honourable gift, of the dead Achilles. The idea may only have been that, while surviving leaders received each a damsel, the spirit of the great chief should not be deprived of its reward. No idea can be less Achaean, less Homeric, but it is congenial to the Ionian spirit.

The fact of the sacrifice would easily suggest, to still later writers, that in his life days Achilles loved Polyxena, and was loved by her; for Philostratus and Tzetzes aver that heart-broken by the murder of Achilles, she slew herself above his tomb.

Thus we see how, in the Ionian epics, and onwards through Stesichorus, the tragedians, the Roman poets, Dictys, and the mediaeval makers, the poetic consciousness played freely round the Homeric data, colouring them with the rainbow hues of changing beliefs and changing tastes. There is at least as wide a gulf between the tastes and ideas of Homer, on one side, and of the Ionians on the other, as between Arctinus, on one hand, and Benoit de Troyes and Boccaccio, on the other.

That the Ionian ideas, tastes, rites, and legends, as of Theseus and Palamedes, never were intruded into the Iliad and Odyssey, considering that for so long Homer was "taught, recited, imitated in Ionia,"[402] is an undeniable and amazing fact. How were Ionian hands restrained from touching the substance of the Achaean epics? This is, in the strict sense, a paradox, but the facts are undeniable: the epics were never Ionised. Homer was falsely claimed by Athens as an Ionian poet. Is there some basis of truth in the idea that the Aeolian Homeridae of Chios guarded their own?[403]

I have now given my view of the Cyclic poems as late, post-Homeric, and Ionian in (i) geographical knowledge; (2) in hero-worship; (3) in rites of human sacrifice and purification; (4) in the mania for inventing genealogies, as of Thersites, basest born of the host; (5) in partisan attacks on great Achaeans; (6) in silly Märchen; (7) in efforts to introduce representatives of Athens, the grandsons of Theseus, into the war; (8) the Attic goddess, Nemesis.

Of these eight proofs of lateness and Ionicism, Mr. Murray takes no notice: on the whole, he thinks our Homer later than some state of the lost Epics. He supposes parts of the Iliad to be borrowed from these Epics. "We happen to know that there was an old chronicle poem which both contained a catalogue of the ships and

---

[402] Monro, Odyssey, vol. ii. p. 476.

[403] Cf. Monro, Odyssey, vol. ii. pp. 398-402. He is sceptical, as is Mr. Leaf, Iliad, vol. i. pp. xviii, xix. But see Mr. Allen in Classical Quarterly, i. 135 ff.

also narrated at length the assembling of the fleet at Aulis—the so-called Cypria or Cyprian verses."[404] This piece of information may be correct, I know not; but no authority is cited for the statement that the Cypria contained a catalogue of the ships, and no such authority is known to me.[405] Von Wilamowitz—Moellendorff conjectures that the Cypria contained a catalogue of the Achaeans, but that is not evidence.

In support of his theory that our Iliad is "in a further state of development" than some poetic chronicles, Mr. Murray writes that passages in the Iliad "seem to be derived from the Cypria, the Little Iliad, and the Sack of Ilion, the so-called Acthiopis.... These, then, are all pieces of supposed history taken over from one traditional poem into another."[406]

This appears to mean that the poems named were complete before the Iliad was complete, though all of them "were growing side by side for centuries." Indeed, Mr. Murray might seem to change his ground in a later statement of his opinions. In The Rise of the Greek Epic we hear of borrowings by the Iliad from several Cyclic poems made in Asia, and from the "Eumelian" verses in Europe. (For "Eumelus," see "Homer and the Saga.") Of borrowings by the Cyclics and "Eumelus" from the Iliad we do not hear. On the other hand, in Anthropology and the Classics (lectures by various students), Mr. Murray writes, "the extant remains of the non-Homeric poems frequently show in their form, and sometimes even in their content, definite signs of presupposing the Iliad, just as the Iliad here and there shows signs of presupposing them...."[407] But, R. G. E. p. 160, meets the charge of changed views.

If the Cypria be earlier than the Iliad, yet presupposes the

---

[404] R. G. E. p. 164.

[405] Mr. Leaf writes (Iliad, vol. i. p. 86): "The conclusion is that the Catalogue" (of Iliad, ii.) "originally formed an introduction to the whole Cycle, and was composed for that part of it which, as worked up into a separate poem, was called the Kypria, and related the beginning of the Tale of Troy, and the mustering of the ships at Aulis." I do not quite know what Mr. Leaf means; but the evidence is that the Cypria contained "a Catalogue of the allies of the Trojans" (Kinkel, p. 20). Nothing is said of its containing a Catalogue of the Achaeans. Mr. Monro (Odyssey, vol. ii. p. 351) justly remarks that the Trojan Catalogue in the Cypria was intended to supplement the short Catalogue of the allies of Troy given in the Iliad: "Such an enlarged roll would be the natural fruit of increased acquaintance" (on the part of Greek settlers in Asia) "with the non-Hellenic races of Asia Minor."

[406] R. G. E. p. 165.

[407] Anthropology and the Classics, 1908, p. 67.

Iliad (about Palamedes it does not), I presume it may also borrow from the Iliad; whereas, previously, the Iliad was mainly credited with the borrowings from the Cyclics. Perhaps we are intended to understand that "had we seen these poems before they were made," we would find that they all borrowed from each other. My mind is not metaphysical enough to conceive what the poems were "before they were made." To me it seems that they must, before they were made, have been mere masses of materials, traditions, legends, lays of unknown extent, and Märchen that had no original connection with definite places and persons. There was no Cypria, no Iliad, no Little Iliad, no Aethiopis before these poems were made. We should not, I think, speak of any unmade poem in the making as borrowing matter from another poem which, by our theory, is also still unmade.

We can only speak of the poets as selecting, each for himself, from the same mass of materials. If we conceive one poem to have been made before another, then the author or authors of that other may borrow from the earlier work. Thus, when the Cypria or other Cyclic poems coincide in topic with the Iliad and Odyssey, that may be (1) because the authors work out hints given in these finished poems; or (2) the authors may have had recourse to the same "masses of tradition" as were open to the author of the Iliad. But the Cyclic poets do not often appear to know Achaean traditions, of the Trojan affair outside of our Homer. We have shown that Palamedes was not originally an Achaean of the Achaeans, but a culture hero. The legend of Telephus, with its sympathetic magic, is wholly un-Achaean; so is Iphigeneia; so are the sons of Theseus; so is the Attic Nemesis.

As we shall show in an Appendix, Mr. Murray accounts for the non-Achaean elements so conspicuous in the Cyclic poems, by the theory that they once also appeared in the lays whence our Iliad arose, but were expurgated by the clear Hellenic spirit of Greece in the sixth century, because these lays alone were recited at Panionian and Panathenaean festivals. Our own conclusion is that the Muses befriended Homer when they permitted the fragments of the Cyclic poems to escape the tooth of time. For these fragments suffice to prove that the Ionian poets could take up an Achaean theme, but in a score of ways, in their epics, betrayed themselves as non-Achaean.

Their poems are not sections cut out of an Achaean mass of lays, and our Homer is not a similar section, is not Cyclic. It has now been proved, I think, that in no point or trait of life, religion, legends, armour, tactics, rites, taste, poetic method, or anything else, is Homer affected by Ionian influences. The Iliad, and mainly the Odyssey, are entirely distinct in all their contents from Ionian work. They are much older, and are the fruit of the brief-lived flower of Achaean culture.[408]

CHAPTER XIX

THE GREAT DISCREPANCIES

The standing argument against the old belief in the unity of authorship of the Epics, has for several generations been based on the discrepancies and inconsistencies which are said to abound in these poems. "The only begetter" of the critical school which lacerates Homer was Wolf; but Wolf's suspicions were not originally roused by inconsistencies which shocked him in the poems. The poems, he said, had unus color, "one harmonious colouring." But if that be true, and it is true, how was this harmony preserved in a poem which, as Wolf decided from a priori considerations, cannot be the work of one man or one age? Now the work of many men in many ages inevitably must be a chaos, not a harmony, and so Wolf's followers have devoted their lives to the hunt for discrepancies and inaccuracies fit to support their preconceived opinion.

Meanwhile Wolf started, not from discrepancies which could only exist in a mosaic of the lays of several distinct ages, but from a priori reflections on the nature of the age and civilisation in which the epics began. Of that age and civilisation we have now some knowledge. Wolf had none. He reckoned that, granting the barbarism of the unknown age as he conceived it, and the abysm of time through which the poems passed before they reached the hands of competent grammarians,—the Alexandrians,—the texts of epics must necessarily have suffered terribly. If so, there necessarily must be many fatal discrepancies, —unless, indeed, the supposed Editorial Committee at Athens (600-530 B.C.) and the Alexandrian editors later harmonised the whole into the actual unus color. For the whole did seem harmonious to Wolf, with merely a few roughnesses, and passages suspected even by the ancient grammarians. But Wolf's successors, hypnotised by his original suggestion that, in the circumstances of the case, the poems must be

[408] See Appendix, "Homeric Epics, Lost Epics, and 'Traditional Books.'"

by many hands, have felt that, if so, they must contain many fatal discrepancies, have hunted for, and have, of course, found them. Thus an unscientific and illogical method has long prevailed.

Indeed, a method less scientific and less logical cannot be imagined. Critics already prepossessed by the suggestion of Wolf in favour of multiplex authorship, sedulously hunt, we repeat, through the poems for discrepancies in support of their case. They do what men have never done to any other long poetic work of imagination, they seek, with microscopic minuteness of inquiry, for inconsistencies in a fictitious narrative, composed not for analytic readers, but for a circle of listeners. When they find—or much more frequently imagine that they have found—such discrepancies, they proclaim them as proofs of multiplex authorship. Never have they as eagerly and carefully sought for such errors in long imaginative tales that are certainly known to be the work of one hand. Scientific method imperatively demands this investigation; but the critics do not listen. They have studied a work of pure literature with the desire to prove their own foregone conclusion, that the authorship of the Iliad is multiplex, and that it is the growth of several disparate ages.

When archaeological discoveries during the last forty years had thrown some light on the pre-Homeric age, then the material objects found were raked and sifted for proof of the foregone conclusion—the Epic is a mosaic of four or five centuries. We have examined the results of the archaeological inquisition into discrepancies in religion, custom, armour, tactics, and so forth. We try to prove that, in all such details, the epics are the work of a single moment of culture; and again, that no other work of the Greek genius, and no material relics of other moments of Greek culture, represent the religion, polity, armour, costume, morality, and taste of Homer. Not in these fields of ascertainable facts can the proof that the Epics are by many men in many ages be discovered.

Except in the general conclusion that the Iliad is a mosaic, produced (most of them think) by a long series of Ionian additions to an Achaean "kernel," there is no harmony among critics. For example, English savants usually, like Mr. Leaf, make no objections to the unity of the Odyssey. They do not read it in the same spirit, or torment it in the same style, as they rack and lacerate the Iliad. With Wolf, they recognise its unity, though it arose in the same dark age, and passed through the same adventures as the Iliad. Yet in Germany the Odyssey is even more and more variously lacerated than the Iliad.

Turning to the most recent English book on the subject, Homer and the Iliad, by Miss Stawell (1909), we find that while she rejects 6,000 out of 15,000 lines as non-original, she cannot believe in the critics' "original Menis" of only some 2500 lines. She, like the rest, believes (what Wolf did not believe) "that it is quite possible to disentangle the original core of the Iliad from the present mass." But of her Iliad, her "core" is by far the greater part, not a poor sixth. I am tempted to quote a long passage from Miss Stawell, because it seems to contain sound sense, and to be guided by fine literary appreciation.

"The reconstructions actually proposed seem open to serious criticisms. It appears to me that certain important considerations have been overlooked, and that in their light we should discover the original to be far more like the Iliad as we have it now than has usually been supposed.

In the first place, much of the traditional poem has scarcely had a fair chance at the hands of modern critics. Scenes where the drift and bearing are not obvious at once have been cut away without further thought. But a great dramatic poem does not give up all its secrets at once. There are subtle harmonies that can only be realised clearly after long and sympathetic study: the work on Shakespeare might suffice to prove this. And Homer, like Shakespeare, can put in very important points very quietly. We may miss them, and that is our loss. The poet will not over-emphasise them for our sakes. Therefore it is not enough to ask ourselves whether such and such a passage could be cut out and the story still hang together; we must ask, further, whether the omission really leaves the figures as solid, the story as enthralling, the background as grand, as before. I feel sure that the full consequences of their own excisions have not always been noticed by the critics who have made them. They cannot entirely strip away the memory of the "later accretions"; there are even instances of their praising the recovered "original" for effects which could not have been obtained without the "later interpolations."

Secondly, a theory of "accretions" that is formed to account for glaring discrepancies brings, or should bring, with it a clear presumption against a certain type of excision. To cut away not only individual scenes, but all allusions to such, however numerous, however far apart, however skilfully inwoven with their context, on the plea that they were added in order to harmonise old and new, is surely to prove too much. If the need for adjustment was felt to this extent, if the adjustment was done with this delicate care, how did it ever happen that the gross blots were allowed to enter or remain? That many scholars do overlook this difficulty will be shown in detail later—for instance, in the matter of Achilles' armour. The fact is that, on any theory, it must be admitted that the Iliad, as we have it, shows, again and again, the marks of carelessness at the joints. Whole scenes and passages which do not cohere with the rest have got into the poem somehow, and have been left there. This is perfectly intelligible on a theory of loose additions, afterwards piously preserved in one block without any attempt at elaborate harmonising between old and new; but a critical theory that assumes throughout the growth and the editing, a constant union of gross carelessness and minute care, is liable to just the same objection as the old theory of a great but negligent poet. It will not stand the test of thinking out in detail.

I have frequently insisted (in Homer and the Epic, 1893) on the points in the italicised passages. In the present book, which merely tries to prove that the poems are the work of a single pre-ionic age, I cannot again examine the numerous allegations of glaring discrepancies in the Iliad, such as no one sane poet could commit. As has been often proved, notably by Colonel Mure, the greatest fictitious narratives, known to be by a single hand in each case, contain discrepancies at least as remarkable as any that can be proved to occur in Homer. I have also argued that many of Homer's supposed faults exist only in the imagination of the learned. I cannot then, again, examine all, or even many of the imaginary inconsistencies: three of the most glaring must suffice. But I take advantage of a critique by a distinguished scholar, Mr. Verrall, to meet certain preliminary objections which he states. In The Quarterly Review,[409] Mr. Verrall writes concerning me:

"But when we turn to other parts, equally essential, of his argument for single authorship, our feeling always is that, in reality, he begs the question. He maintains, if we do not mistake, that there is no difficulty in supposing the Iliad, as we have it, to be the work of one poet; that the alleged dislocations, wanderings, inconsistencies of the story, so far as they exist at all, are nothing more than, from common experience, we might naturally expect in a single author. When he comes to establish this in detail, his procedure is to take the allegations separately, and to ask, in each case, whether it is inconceivable that the discrepancy (if allowed) is due to oversight on the part of the single composer. On these lines we may make short work. Hardly any error whatever of this sort is inconceivable, and hardly any, by itself, can be improbable. It would be nothing at all that, once in a way, Homer should forget that his Greek camp had a wall. We could scarcely call it inconceivable that, having himself described the 'Sending of

[409] July 1908, pp. 75, 76.

Patroclus' with one set of circumstances, he should make his Thetis relate it with a totally different set. If such flaws were few and miscellaneous, and if there were external testimony to the single authorship, we would pass them without a murmur. Mr. Lang always does argue on this head as if they were few, as if they had no apparent relation to one another, and, above all, as if single authorship were a datum. Any explanation will serve where none is necessary; and consequently Mr. Lang's explanations often seem to us hardly serious.

"We will give one specimen. In Book ix. the Greek camp has a wall (vv. 69-87). At the beginning of Book x., Agamemnon at night, looking from his tent on the plain, sees the 'many watch-fires' of the Trojans, who, on this particular night, are camping out before the city on the same plain. The wall is gone, as it does go and come throughout the fighting scenes of the Iliad. Nor is this a momentary inadvertence; for through the whole of Book x., though its story is such that the wall, if there, must be visible to the narrator (so to say) constantly, though the camp boundary is passed several times, never is there trace of anything but a ditch. We say that, for a composition meant to be continuous as it now stands, this is a most uncommon and surprising phenomenon; nor is it intelligible to us that any one so far should disagree. Mr. Lang, in a special chapter on Book x., disposes of the matter thus:

"'Agamemnon hears the music of the joyous Trojan pipes and flutes, and sees the reflected glow of their camp fires, we must suppose, for he could not see the fires themselves through the new wall of his own camp, as critics very wisely remark' (Homer and his Age, p. 260).

"'We must suppose.' But how can we suppose anything of the sort? 'Many fires' are not a glow. If the point were merely that the wall is ignored in this passage, let us say simply that the poet forgot it. But the point is, that the wall is ignored consistently throughout the Book, and that, all about the poem, similar traces of ignorance respecting this vitally important object are found from time to time. If that is a phenomenon commonly observed in narratives known to be from one hand, or otherwise designed for continuity, let some of these narratives be produced for comparison."

Mr. Verrall argues, we see, that I ask, in each case, "is this discrepancy too bad for a single author?" but neglect the cumulative weight of all the discrepancies. That is not, consciously, my method; that fallacy I seek to avoid. I try to prove that most of the discrepancies which I examine are not really discrepancies at all—

have no weight,—and a mass of such imponderable objections has no cumulative ponderosity. I do argue that the actual inconsistencies are comparatively few, not more or worse than the similar inconsistencies in the Aeneid, or Don Quixote.

But Mr. Verrall thinks that my explanations, or defences, of the alleged discrepancies "often seem hardly serious." He gives one example of my deplorable flippancy from Iliad, Book x. Now I readily grant to Mr. Verrall that I had no right to explain Agamemnon's view, from bed, in his hut, of the Trojan camp-fires beyond the wall of the Greek camp as merely the glow in the sky caused by these fires.[410] As Mr. Leaf puts it, "the poet does not seem to have a very vivid picture of the situation." In bed, in a hut (x. 11-14), Agamemnon could only see the Trojan fires on the rising ground beyond the wall, and the Greek ships, "in his mind's eye."

But Mr. Verrall proceeds to give a fine example of what I call "an imaginary discrepancy." "The wall is gone.... Nor is this a momentary inadvertence; for through the whole of Book x., though its story is such that the wall, if there, must be visible to the narrator (so to say) constantly, though the camp boundary is passed several times, never is there trace of anything but a ditch."

This is merely an inadvertent misstatement of fact. Not only the new fosse round the Greek camp, but the gates of the new wall are mentioned. No wall, no gates!

Let us examine the history of wall, gates, and ditch. "In Book ix. 69-87 the Greek camp has a wall." The nature of the wall is explained by Nestor in Book vii. 337-343. The wall-making is similarly described in 437-441. The wall has (1) towers, (2) gates (or one gate), "that through them (or it) may be a way for chariot-driving," and (3) there is "a deep foss hard by to be about it," with a palisade, to "hinder the horses and footmen" of the Trojans.[411]

Now, even if only the fosse were mentioned in Book x., that fosse is part of the fortification first made and mentioned in Books vii. viii. and ix. 87, 88, where the advanced guard takes position "between the fosse and the wall." Precisely there, Agamemnon, in Book x. 126, 127, expects to find the advanced guard. The poet, in Book x., has certainly not forgotten the fortification of Books vii. viii. ix., for he does not merely, as Mr. Verrall declares, mention the fosse, though why does he do so, if he forgets the wall which was made at the same time? By a negative hallucination Mr. Verrall has failed to see that he also mentions the gate. "We will find the advanced guard before the gate," says Agamemnon (x. 126).

---

[410] Homer and his Age, p. 250.

[411] Mr. Leaf's version, Lang, Leaf, and Myers.

Now no mortal can assert that when a poet mentions the gate, he mentions nothing but the fosse! Both fosse and gates are new: the gates are a necessary part of the wall; and only a critic on the search for a discrepancy could overlook the fact that the poet of Book x. knows all about the fortification of Books vii. viii. ix. The poet has no occasion to say "the gates in the wall"; the gates could be nowhere else. Had there been a wall with no gates, which is absurd, the poet would have had to make the princes scale the wall; and, had he known nothing about the new fortification, he could not have mentioned the new gates and the new fosse.

I repeat, in ix. 65, 88, Nestor bids the advanced post take position; and they do so, "betwixt fosse and wall"; and there, "before the gate" (x. 126, 127), Agamemnon expects to find them. The "discrepancy" is due to Mr. Verrall's imagination.

Before accusing Homer of extraordinary discrepancies, we ought to read him with ordinary care.

Knowing the new fosse, and the new gate, both of them unheard of before Book vii., the poet is beyond doubt acquainted with the whole of the new fortification. "The analytic reader," for whom Homer did not sing, catches him at another place. How did Dolon expect to creep among the host, when there was a wall? How was he to enter? We can only reply that if he found the advanced post drowsy, he must enter in the darkness, by climbing up "where the wall was built lowest." The host was suspected to be meditating flight, and, in their confusion, keeping no guard, so Hector fancied (x. 310-312).

Mr. Verrall says that in Book x. "the wall is gone, as it does go and come throughout the fighting scenes of the Iliad." I have carefully re-read Books xi.-xv., in which the wall is of importance, and find no moment in which the wall is absent when, if present, it ought to be mentioned. It is true that Mr. Leaf infers that it was absent in a portion of the poem earlier than our present Iliad, but that is merely a conjecture of his own. He also says (Introduction to Book xiii.) that the Aristeia of Idomeneus (xiii. 29-518) "altogether ignores the wall." The whole passage is occupied with fighting within the wall, which the Trojans have entered en masse. The reader or listener knows that, and the poet has no sort of reason for mentioning the wall. But he remembers that the Trojan chariots, except that of Asius, stopped and were arrayed at the ditch, so (xiii. 535, 536), the wounded Deiphobus, like the stricken Hector later, is carried out of the fight "to the swift horses that waited for him behind the battle, with the charioteer and chariot," and is conveyed to Troy. The wall is never forgotten, though the description of simultaneous confused fighting at several points is not a model of lucid military history. So much for "the heavy and the weary weight of all this unintelligible" wall. The alleged discrepancy in Book x., insisted on by Mr. Verrall, is an imaginary discrepancy; a thousand such would, collectively, be imponderable.

We now turn to what Mr. Leaf calls "a crying contradiction, a contradiction perhaps the most patent in the Iliad, which can in no way be palliated." Mr. Leaf's point is that "the words (and acts) of Diomedes in vi. 123-143" are "in crying contradiction" with "the words of Athene in v. 124-132, and the subsequent victories of Diomedes over the gods."[412] In fact, Diomedes, in Iliad, vi. 123-129, doubts whether Glaucus, whom he has not encountered before, be a man or a god, and says that he will not, if the stranger be a god, fight against him. He then adds (130-143) the story of the punishment of Lycurgus by Zeus, when Lycurgus had beaten the Maenads, and driven Dionysus to seek refuge with Thetis. The whole passage is easily detachable, and may, Mr. Leaf says, be the work of "some pious revivalist; the Bacchic worship was unknown to the Achaean heroes." We cannot be certain that they did not know the Thracian myth which Diomedes tells: this they might know, though they did not worship Dionysus, who, like Demeter, is scarcely alluded to in the Iliad[413]

But the point is, are the words of Diomedes to Glaucus in crying contradiction with the words of Athene in v. 124-132, and with Diomedes' "subsequent victories over the gods?" First, he had but one such victory; encouraged by Athene, he wounded—the harmless Aphrodite! We quote the words of Athene to Diomedes: "Moreover, I have taken from thine eyes the mist that erst was on them, that thou mayest well discern both god and man. Therefore, if any god come hither to make trial of thee, fight not thou face to face with any of the immortal gods; save only if Aphrodite, daughter of Zeus, enter into the battle, her smite thou with the keen bronze."

The subsequent events are (Iliad, v. 330-340), Diomede scratched the hand of Aphrodite with his spear-point. Much encouraged, he tries to spear Aeneas, over whom Apollo has spread his arms. Apollo threatens and terrifies him (434-442). Diomedes has now had enough of braving the gods. He gives way; and bids his men give way when he sees Ares with Hector (601-606). But Hera and Athene have the command of Zeus to stop the fighting of Ares (765, 766), and Athene bids Diomedes attack the god. He refuses, "You bade me fight no god but Aphrodite" (819-824). Athene

---

[412] Iliad, vol. i. p. 256.

[413] See chapter on "Homeric Religion."

thrusts away Diomedes' charioteer, drives his chariot against Ares, grasps and turns the spear of that god, and herself drives the spear of Diomedes into the belly of the god, and withdraws the spear (825-859).

This is no victory of Diomedes', and he knows it. It is, says Homer, Athene who has stopped Ares in his manslayings (see 909). Athene and Hera now leave the field; Ares has fled, no god is any longer present. It is after the retiral of all the gods, notably of her who had given him, "for this occasion only," the gift of knowing god from man, that Diomedes doubts whether Glaucus, whom he has not encountered before, be divine or human. Having been terrified by Apollo, and remembering Athene's command to fight no god but Aphrodite, Diomedes is naturally cautious, in view of a splendid unknown antagonist, and asks, "Who of mortals, sir, art thou, for never have I seen thee before? thou alone darest to meet my deadly spear. If thou art an immortal, then I will not fight with the gods of heaven."[414]

The gift of Athene, the discerning of gods from men, has lapsed when it ceased to serve her turn, now that her task is ended. She has fulfilled the command of Zeus, has stopped Ares, and has retired to Olympus; while no god is left in the field to be discerned. To this is reduced, when we look at the facts, "a contradiction perhaps the most patent in the Iliad, and one which can in no way be palliated." The audience of Homer would understand, naturally, but "the analytic reader," in hot search of discrepancies, credits Diomedes with "victories over gods" which he did not gain, and overlooks his caution, and his obedience to the command of Athene. What must the other contradictions be when this is "perhaps the most patent"?

A yet more scandalous discrepancy in the Iliad remains to be noticed. "It is a contradiction," says Mr. Leaf with manly indignation, "at the very root of the story, as flagrant as if Shakespeare had forgotten in the Fifth Act of Macbeth that Duncan had been murdered in the second."[415] If Shakespeare had made that error, and, like Fielding, had told his manager that the public would never notice it; like Fielding, when he heard the hisses and catcalls, he would probably have murmured, "Damn them, they have found it out!" But though Homer's error was as flagrant as the suggested resuscitation of the gracious Duncan, for three thousand years nobody "found it out." It was discovered by Mr. Grote, an excellent banker, but no great poetical critic; and by a German who, in search

---

414 Iliad, vi. 123-129.

415 Iliad, vol. ii. p. 153.

of discrepancies, had been "nosing the body" of Homer "with passionate attention."

Now an error cannot be blazingly flagrant, nor vociferously crying, if it escapes a hundred generations of hearers, readers, Pisistratean "recensors," and Alexandrian and modern Editors. Moreover, if the Greek recensors laboured to harmonise old and new by skilfully interwoven cross-references (and the critics tell us that they did), "how," as Miss Stawell asks, "did it ever happen that the gross blots were allowed to enter or remain?" That this blunder was allowed to remain, unnoted and unrebuked, till about 1840 A.D., proves beyond contradiction that, at least, it is not "flagrant"; does not resemble the appearance of Duncan in Act V. of Macbeth, when "after life's fitful fever he sleeps well," in Act III. Mr. Leaf only shows us how far a passion for discovering discrepancies, if not early checked, may hurry the learned.

Again, if Homer's blunder were as glaring as the forgetfulness by the author of Macbeth that Duncan had been murdered, it is unlikely that, by "Bergk, Hentze, Monro, and Lang," to quote Mr. Leaf, Homer would be pronounced innocent.[416]

We have "weakened some of the chief arguments stated by Grote," that is admitted, "yet their general force is unshaken." How this can possibly be, if Grote's chief arguments are sensibly weakened, does not appear; for the general force must be shaken when some of the chief arguments which make up that force are impaired.

Grote's chief argument is that the poet who composed Books xi.-xvi. "could not have had present to his mind the main event of the ninth Book,—the out-pouring of profound humiliation by the Greeks, and from Agamemnon specially, before Achilles, coupled with formal offers to restore Briseis, and pay the amplest compensation for past wrong. The words of Achilles (not less than those of Patroclus and Nestor), in the eleventh and the following Books, plainly imply that the humiliation of the Greeks before him, for which he thirsts, is as yet future and contingent."[417]

Here Grote and his followers appear to forget that, from the very first, in Book i., the heart of Achilles was set on revenge, and on one definitely stated form of revenge, and not on atonement. On this point Grote had not Book i. present in his mind: he says that Achilles asks no more from Thetis, nor Thetis anything more from Zeus, than that "the Greeks may be brought to know the wrong they have done, and be humbled in the dust in expiation of it." This is an

---

416 Iliad, vol. i. p. 370.

417 Grote, History of Greece, vol. ii., 1869, pp. 179-183.

egregiously absurd misstatement! It seems that the great historian forgot to verify his reference, with the usual result, a misstatement of fact as the basis of a charge of discrepancy. What Achilles bids Thetis ask from Zeus is, "hem the Achaeans among their ships' sterns about the bay, that they may make trial of their king...."[418] Achilles does desire the humiliation of Agamemnon, but that humiliation must arise from a massacre of the Greeks among their ships' sterns; and from their prospect of annihilation.

Already, to Agamemnon, during the quarrel in Book i., Achilles had said that his day will come "when multitudes fall dying before manslaying Hector."[419] In the state of affairs in Book ix. no great multitudes have fallen before Hector. Zeus again, in Book viii., promises to fulfil the desire of Achilles to the letter. "Headlong Hector shall not refrain from battle till that Peleus' son shall have arisen beside the ships, on that day when these shall fight amid the sterns in most grievous stress around Patroclus fallen. Such is the doom of heaven."[420] Achilles cannot be reconciled and take arms till the doom is fulfilled.

Not only does Homer keep the prayer of Achilles in Book i. constantly in view till it is accomplished in Book xv., but after its accomplishment he returns to and insists on the fulfilment by Zeus of this rash prayer. The whole burden of the Iliad rests on this prayer of Book i., and in its disastrous consequences not only to the host, but to Achilles. In Book xvi. 97-100, a part of the genuine kernel, Homer makes the last words that Achilles ever spoke to Patroclus express a fury of revenge which Nemesis could not pardon.

"Would, O Father Zeus, and Athene, and Apollo, would that not one of all the Trojans might escape death, nor one of the Argives, but that we twain might avoid destruction, that alone we might undo the sacred coronal of Troy."

This is the very extreme of pride and passion, an extreme which Greek thought regarded as entailing its own inevitable punishment. Achilles, when the news of the death of Patroclus reaches him, recognises this. Thetis says, "My child, why weepest thou?... One thing at least hath been accomplished of Zeus according to the prayer thou madest ... that the sons of the Achaeans should all be pent in at the ships, through lack of thee, and should suffer hateful things."

Achilles answers, "My mother, that prayer hath the Olympian

---

[418] Iliad, i. 409, 410.

[419] i. 240 ff.

[420] Iliad, viii. 473-475.

accomplished for me. But what delight have I therein, since Patroclus is dead?"[421] Observe that the critics, and even Miss Stawell, think Achilles too sweet to refuse atonement in Book ix. There is not much sweetness of soul in his furious desire for the complete destruction of the Greeks in his very last words to his friend in Book xvi.

Thus, from first to last, Achilles asks nothing less than what Zeus, in Book viii., just prior to the impeached Book ix., declares that he shall receive,—the massacre of the Achaeans among the sterns of their ships. Grote has misstated the facts of the case. He represents that the Embassy of Book ix. offered Achilles all his heart's desire. This they did not and could not do, they had not been slain among the ships; they had not been put in deadly stress; and Achilles would be inconsistent if he accepted atonement before he got revenge, before instant ruin was upon the Achaeans. "Agamemnon," says Achilles in Book ix., "shall not persuade me" (by gifts richer than he offers), "till he have paid me back all the bitter despite."[422] A payment in gold and lands and women Achilles disdains: he will not take it till he has a payment in revenge. This he has insisted on in Book i., this Zeus has promised in Book viii., and this inexorableness is the sin and stumbling-block of Achilles. Customary law and public opinion acknowledged his right to apology and atonement, but condemned his insistence, after these had been duly offered, on a bloody revenge. All the world recognised the facts before Grote went hunting for discrepancies, and bagged the greatest of all,—which is no discrepancy!

The whole story, including Book ix., is absolutely consistent. Grote argued that Agamemnon, by his offers, had done all that was necessary. He had, according to customary law; but Achilles had set his heart, in Book i. as in Book ix., on much more, on "a contented revenge." In Book ix. he had not enjoyed his revenge, and he said as much. Had he yielded in Book ix., the prophecy of Zeus in Book viii. would have been falsified;[423] the doom of Zeus would have been frustrated; the bitter word of Achilles would have been broken; he would have deserved no heart-breaking disaster. Grote sees nothing of all this, nor do his followers.

When Agamemnon sent his embassy with apologies and offers of atonement to Achilles, in Book ix., the Achaeans had not been

---

[421] xviii. 73-80.

[422] Iliad, ix. 380-387.

[423] The words of Zeus in Book viii. will be explained as a late insertion, to harmonise old and new. If so, why did the harmoniser leave the flagrant discrepancy uncorrected?

punished as Achilles, from the first, expressed his desire to see them smitten. Diomedes had shore in the day of his valour, his aristeia; Hector had the worse in his passage-of-arms with Aias; Hera and Athene had abetted the Trojans; and though they camped in the plain, they had not smitten the foe "by the prows of the ships"; nor were they even likely to do so, for the Achaeans had built the wall and dug the trench around the ships. Therefore the demand of Achilles was not yet granted; and though Agamemnon abjectly implored forgiveness and offered the customary atonement, that was not what Achilles wanted. He spurns the gifts, and repeats the whole long story of his wrongs.[424] Agamemnon, he says, has a ceaseless grudge against him: the king's submission is merely hypocritical, and Achilles declines to be deceived. "Let him not tempt me, who know him too well; he will not persuade me"[425] "His gifts are hateful to me"; not for ten times these gifts will Achilles be reconciled, till he has glutted his revenge.

The long speech of Phoenix[426] partly mollifies him, and, in place of persisting in his intention to sail homewards at once, he tells Aias that he will not fight till Hector comes, slaying the Argives, even to the ships of the Myrmidons.[427] This is an advance even on his demand in Book i. In short, Achilles abides by his determination as announced to his mother in the first Book of the Iliad, and goes further. He is consistent.

To this resolve, and to his plighted word (for he "hated a liar as the gates of Hades"), Achilles is as constant as the fond of his character—an unexampled tenderness—permitted him to be. This tenderness of the fierce hero who, in grief, cries to his mother like a child; who, in the height of his passion, compares his own labours for the Achaeans to those of "the hen-bird that brings to her unfledged chickens whatsoever morsel she may find, and it goes hard with herself";[428] who likens the suppliant Patroclus to "the little girl that, running beside her mother, and catching at her skirts, cries to be taken up in her arms"; and who gives quarter to fallen foes, distinguishes Achilles. The contrast between this emotion and his pride and later ferocity makes his character; and his chivalry shines out most clearly in his reception of Priam, which is declared to be un-Homeric! The triumph of his fierce pride over his tenderness, when he refuses the gifts in Book ix., is the ἁμάρτημα,

---

[424] Iliad, ix. 315-343.
[425] ix. 434 ff.
[426] ix. 345, 375. 376.
[427] ix. 6502.
[428] Iliad, ix. 323.

the sin or blot on a noble character, which is the keynote, or pivot, of Greek tragedy (as in the Oedipous Tyrannos), and of the Iliad.

Remove Book ix., and Achilles is no longer himself, there is no motived tragedy, and the supposed primal kernel, the fancied Achilleid (wherein atonement is not offered or refused), is a poem without a motive. The heart of Achilles is to be broken by the loss of Patroclus, though, according to the ideas of the age, he has committed no wrong; he has renounced his allegiance when he had a right to renounce it till he had received atonement for an intolerable injustice.

Grote did not think himself back into the legal and ethical atmosphere of Homeric life; he and his followers have failed to understand the moral centre of the tragedy, the ἁμάρτημα, the sin of Achilles. In place of doing that they have found the great discrepancy, exactly where they should have found the central situation and turning point of the epic. It has, in Aristotelian phrase, "a beginning, a middle, and an end." Book ix. is the middle. The critics excise it!

Grote works out his discovery thus, and in answering him we answer his contemporary followers. Achilles, in Book xi., sees the rout of the Achaeans, and sees Nestor conveying a wounded comrade to the rear. Achilles says to Patroclus (xi. 608), "Now methinks that the Achaeans will stand about my knees, praying to me, for need no longer endurable is coming upon them" That is, he will soon get the terms which he has from the first demanded, revenge, and, following perfect revenge, the humiliation of the Achaeans. Grote says that Heyne "not unnaturally asks, 'had Achilles repented of his previous harshness to the embassy,' in Book ix., 'or was he arrogant enough to expect a second embassy'? I answer, 'Neither one nor the other: the words imply that he had received no embassy at all.'" Therefore Book ix. is a later interpolation.

It follows that the great poet of Book ix., who so consistently maintains the attitude taken by Achilles in Book i. 408-410, where the hero demands the slaughter of the Achaeans among their ships,[429] now unscrupulously throws over and destroys the work of his still greater predecessor. Here is indeed a matchless discrepancy in human nature!

As I understand the words of Achilles (xi. 608, 610), he is joyously anticipating the moment when "need no longer endurable" will come on the host. In Book ix. their necessity, as we have demonstrated, had not reached the point which, in Books i. and ix.,

[429] Cf. Book ix. 650-655.

he had demanded. Hector has not yet reached the ships, not yet do the Achaeans know fully "what manner of king they have" in his enemy, Agamemnon. Doubtless they will again beseech Achilles: they have done that already, but they have not yet suffered as he will have them suffer. There is here extreme consistency, not impossible inconsistency. Achilles retains the position which he took up in Book i.

Grote pursues his theory to Book xvi., where Patroclus comes with news that the Trojans are slaying around the ships, and that Agamemnon, Diomedes, Odysseus, and Eurypylus are wounded and out of action. As Achilles (Book ix.) has vowed not to fight till Hector attacks his own ships, Patroclus asks to be permitted to lead the Myrmidons into fight. Achilles replies by rehearsing all his wrongs, and then says, "But let bygones be bygones ... verily I said that my wrath would not slacken one whit till the battle and the cry came to my own ships; but do thou put on my armour and lead the Myrmidons."[430]

He thus recalls his vow in Book ix., or rather, while keeping to the letter of it, he makes a concession in the spirit: he is sated: what he asked for in Book i. he has received in Book xvi. So the poet of Book xvi. had Book ix. before him. The Achaeans are dying around the ships, but till Hector approaches his own ships he will not fight in person. So he had vowed in Book ix. There is stern consistency, not discrepancy; but Grote finds inconsistency by agreeing with the Scholiast and Heyne in interpreting "ἔφην γε" (in its primary sense, "I said") "as equivalent to 'I thought' (διενοήθην), not as referring to any express antecedent declaration."[431] Mr. Leaf agrees, and thinks that the declaration of Achilles in Book ix. 650 "may well have been suggested by this very phrase." This very phrase may therefore, confessedly, mean that Achilles did make an express declaration; and we have every right so to understand it. If we do, the supposed discrepancy vanishes. If we do not, we must suppose the poet of Book ix. to have been at once most scrupulously attentive to the words of his predecessor,—the author of Book i., of Book viii., and of the opening of Book xvi.—and at the same time absolutely regardless of that minstrel in the most important point. We only shift the insane error from one great poet to another.

Meanwhile Grote says that the poet of Book xi. et seqq. "could not have had present to his mind the main event of the ninth Book, the embassy, and its offers of atonement."[432]

[430] Book xvi. 60-65.

[431] Grote, vol. ii. p. 179, note I on p. 180.

[432] Grote, vol. ii. pp. 179, 180.

Next, in xvi. lines 72, 73, Achilles says that the Achaeans would not be in such straits "if Agamemnon had been but kindly disposed to me." But, in Book ix., says Grote, Agamemnon was more than kindly, he offered to pay any price for reconciliation. So Achilles himself admitted in Book ix. Agamemnon would pay any price, but Achilles regarded this as mere hypocrisy: he would not believe that Agamemnon was "favourably disposed" in his heart. "He shall not deceive me, shall not persuade me." The poet has anticipated Grote's objection, but Grote does not understand.

Achilles is not really in heart reconciled to Agamemnon, even after he consents to take the gifts; is not reconciled till after the funeral games for Patroclus. At this moment (xvi. 77) Achilles speaks of Agamemnon as "hateful."

In xvi. 83-86, to copy Grote's paraphrase, Achilles says to Patroclus, "Obey my words, so that you may procure for me honour and glory from the body of the Greeks, and that they may send back to me the damsel, giving me ample presents besides...."

Grote has oddly misunderstood the whole story. He says, "The ninth Book has actually tendered to Achilles everything he demands and even more." Now Achilles had demanded only the massacre of the Greeks at the ships, and then recognition of what kind of king they have. In what passage does Achilles demand anything else? In none till, in Book xvi. 84, 85, he bids Patroclus fight, when he himself will receive Briseis and fair gifts: his revenge he has already enjoyed, but Phoenix had warned him that he would be dishonoured if he fought without receiving atonement.

Grote, in the spirit of his school, rejects later allusions to the offered atonement of Book ix. as interpolations thrust in for the sake of restoring harmony. Yet the cunning interpolators allowed the Great Discrepancy to stand! If we may reject whatever lines destroy our theory, criticism is an idle game of contradictory conjectures, each inquirer discerning interpolations in all passages that ruin his favourite hypothesis. After all Grote concludes, "The poem consists of a part original and other parts superadded; yet it is certainly not impossible that the author of the former may himself have composed the latter." If so, "the poet ... has not thought fit to recast the parts and events in such manner as to impart to the whole a pervading thread of consensus and organisation such as we see in the Odyssey."[433] Thus the poet did not mind a ghastly discrepancy.

I trust that all who have not invincible prepossessions will see that Book ix. is not only consistent with Books xi. and xvi., but is the very clou of the Iliad, without which Achilles is not himself, and the

433 Grote, vol. ii. p. 202.

Achilleid would have been a purposeless tragedy. This opinion is not based on aesthetic and literary criticism alone, but on the actual ideas about allegiance, the wrongs done by the Over Lord, the rights of the injured vassal, and the rules concerning atonement which pervade the Iliad. As in all such early societies, a man was dishonoured if he forgave a wrong without receiving atonement; and was blamed if, like Achilles, he refused atonement when it was offered with due ceremonial. Even if students, under the suggestion of Grote, fail to accept my view that Book ix. is no discrepancy, but contains the central moment, and, as Phoenix's words in that Book prove, the motif of the tragedy of Achilles—"he who refuses the prayers of the penitent may fall and pay the price" (ix. 512), I trust that, at least, I have proved that the discrepancy is not "flagrant" and "crying," and an infallible proof of late interpolation.

It is not necessary for me to repeat my unanswered criticisms, in Homer and the Epic, of many alleged discrepancies. If I have succeeded in showing that the three most flagrant inconsistencies are not inconsistent, it is easy to imagine how innocent are most of the other inculpated passages.

One may be noted. In Iliad, xviii. 446-452, Thetis, who has gone to ask Hephaestus to make armour for her son, explains the causes of his mutiny. "And the princes (γέροντες) of the Argives entreated him, and told over many noble gifts. Then albeit he refused to ward destruction from them, he put his armour on Patroclus and sent him to the war." The gifts were offered "while Achilles in grief wasted his heart, while the men of Troy were driving the Achaeans on their ships, nor suffered them to come forth."

The gifts were offered, in fact, when the Greeks had found it necessary to fortify their camp, purposing to act on the defensive; and Achilles did not send out Patroclus in consequence of the offer of gifts. Absorbed in her own grief for her son, whom she will never welcome home ("excited," as Miss Stawell says), Thetis has avoided the point of the question of Hephaestus, "Why hast thou come hither?" and poured forth her own lament (430-441). "Homer," says the Scholiast, "renders the nature of woman, she does not answer the question put to her, but dilates on her own sorrow." Then she hurriedly and confusedly describes the past events, hastening to her request that the god will make arms for her Achilles. As Mr. Leaf writes, "Though the reference (450, 451) does not give the whole course of events, it is near enough—there is only omission, not misstatement." To myself the speech of Thetis seems exactly what a distraught mother in a hurry would be apt to make.

But Mr. Verrall takes it as proof positive that "a new hand" is at work, the new hand who invented "The Making of the Armour." He—the new hand—is in even a greater hurry, and is much more distraught than poor Thetis, it seems to me; but then Mr. Verrall observes he did not mean his story of the armour "for a continuation of the other's, otherwise he would have told the previous incident as he found it." Finally, some one, some time, for some reason—person, time, and reason being all equally unknown—"takes the "Sending of Patroclus" from one version and the "Making of the Armour" from another, and combines without reconciling them."[434]

Here Mr. Verrall differs from Mr. Leaf, while we take it that Homer makes a grief-distraught mother in a hurry speak like a grief-distraught and hurried mother.

But Homer, where there is a doubt, never gets the benefit of the doubt.

CHAPTER XX

CONCLUSIONS

As much of this treatise is occupied with criticism of the views of the most modern representatives of the Wolfian school, I ought, in fairness, to state my own general conclusions. I am led to suppose that the Iliad is a work of one brief period, because, as has been shown, it bears all the notes of one age; and is absolutely free from the most marked traits of religion, rites, society, and superstition that characterise the preceding Aegean, and the later "Dipylon," Ionian, Archaic, and historic periods in Greek life and art.

Again, I believe that the Iliad is, in the main, the work of a single poet. To that conclusion I am led partly by the unity of the thought, temper, character, and ethos of both epics; partly by the perfect consistency in the drawing, throughout, of multitudes of characters, all conceived with as much delicacy as firmness. It is to me inconceivable that a number of poets should have developed, with such perfect consistency and with such fine nuances, the

[434] Quarterly Review, July 1908, pp. 64-66.

character, for example, of Achilles, who has been called "a splendid savage!"

If our critics studied him as Shakespearian students examine Hamlet or Macbeth, it is improbable that they could think the wrath of Achilles "a second-rate subject." It does not appear to me that his wrath about "a personal slight"—the loss of Briseis, is a fit of the sulks; that Achilles, as was said of Byron in one of his portraits, looks like "a great sulky schoolboy whom somebody has deprived of a plum-cake."

Consider what Achilles is; the son of a goddess: himself, in extreme youth, the recognised hero and nonpareil of the whole Achaean array. His one over-mastering passion is desire of renown:

"One crowded hour of glorious life
Is worth an age without a name."

He might live long, happy, and honoured at home with the father whom he so tenderly loves and pities, but he sets forth to Ilios, knowing surely that there he must inevitably perish in the flower of his youth. He chooses to pay with his life for immortal renown. In Hades he says that he would liefer be on earth the hind of a landless man, than king over the Dead, so fast is the hold of this earth upon his heart. But he could not love his life so much

"Loved he not honour more."

Now, in the opening of the Iliad he is to lose life and the sunlight, and also to lose honour. This is no mere personal slight; loss of the honour which he is buying with his life is no unworthy cause of anger in such a hero. He complains, again and again, that Agamemnon has, on every occasion, dishonoured him. The seizure of Briseis, his special "mead of honour," is only the last straw, the culminating insult. "In like honour," he says, "are held both the coward and the brave." He has toiled most hardly of all. "Even as a bird bringeth her unfledged chickens each morsel as she winneth it, and with herself it goeth hard, even so was I wont to watch out many a sleepless night, and pass through many days of battle, warring with folk for their women's sake." There is here, in Book ix., that tenderness of reference to the devotion of the maternal instinct which characterises Achilles in his relations with his own mother, a goddess of many sorrows, for the sake of him who has chosen his doom. To her, in the first Book, as on the death of Patroclus, he cries, in the spirit of the little child of whom he speaks so touchingly in Book xvi.: "a fond little maid that runs by her mother's side, and bids her mother take her up, snatching at her skirts, and tearfully looks at her." Homer puts such words in the mouth of none but the slayer of men, Achilles.

"Mother," he cries by the grey sea, in Book i., "seeing thou didst of a truth bear me to so brief a span of life, honour at least ought the Olympian to have granted me."

Is it not plain that "the personal slight" to Achilles—being what he is, saying, like the great Montrose in a note scribbled on his pocket Bible, "Honour is my life," is it not plain that the insult is deadly both to life and honour?

In this sense Homer understands the wrath of Achilles. He had fond of tenderness,—he ransomed his captives, while Agamemnon slew the prisoners to whom Menelaus was giving quarter. Again, as we shall see ("The Supposed Expurgation of Homer"), it was far from unusual, in Homeric warfare, for the slayer to mutilate the slain, cutting off his head, putting it on a stake, or even carrying it home as a trophy. But Achilles did not even, as usual, despoil Eetion of his armour, "for his soul had shame of that; but he buried him in his inlaid armour, and raised a barrow over him." In contrast with his natural clemency, the wrath of Achilles for Patroclus's sake is all the more monstrous; he far transcends the customary ferocities of dishonour to the dead. Achilles says (xxi. pp. 100-105): "Until Patroclus met his day of destiny, dearer was it to my heart to spare the Trojans; and many I took alive and sold over sea." But when once his honour, his life-price, is taken from him, his wrath will be sated by nothing—not by prayers or gifts of atonement, but by the slaughter of his comrades among their ships—then, indeed, they will know his worth. It is this moral tragedy, corruptio optimi, that inspires Homer in the Iliad.

Achilles is, of all the men in Homer, the most passionately affectionate. His love of Patroclus, like that of Jonathan for David, "passeth the love of women"; an affection for his elder, the playmate of his childhood, so pure and so strong that poets of historic Greece could not understand it. But when he is smitten to the heart by the loss of Patroclus his wrath again breaks, as in the ninth Book of the Iliad, through all measure; and he does cruel and evil deeds, his revenge is hateful to Gods and men. This is the moral tragedy of the Iliad; and that which wrecks the heart and soul of Hamlet, or that which brings to shame the honour and courage of Macbeth, does not go deeper.

Having fashioned such a character as Achilles, no poet equal to the task could leave him in the course of cruelty and shame which is his in the opening of the last Book of the Iliad. No hand but that which created the Achilles of the first Book could so restore him to himself that the Achaeans might again "see the great Achilles whom they knew." Only that one genius could conceive and achieve the immortal scene wherein Priam kisses "the hands of Achilles, terrible, manslaying, that slew so many of his sons."

"Fear thou the gods, Achilles, and have compassion on me, even me, bethinking thee of thy father. Lo, I am more piteous yet than he, and have braved what none other man on earth hath braved before, to stretch forth my hand toward the face of the slayer of my sons." There follows the lament of Achilles, for the father whom he, in search of honour, "may not tend as he groweth old, since very far from my own country I am dwelling in Troyland, to vex thee and thy children."

Even here, Achilles feels that he dares hardly trust himself, so strong is the wild beast of passion within him. So consistent, so delicate, so strong a delineation of character, I cannot conceive to be the work of more hands than one, it is the work of the hand of Homer. Throughout the whole poem every person is drawn with equal firmness, delicacy, and consistency. The study of Agamemnon is the most complex (see Homer and his Age, pp. 50-81). The foil to Agamemnon, the good Menelaus, the kindest and most chivalrously honourable of men, always conscious of his debt to the Achaeans, always eager to dare beyond his strength, is a worthy pendant. Odysseus throughout the poem is the poet's most admired hero; the wisest and most steadfast, here as in the Odyssey. It is so with the rest, with all of them; and this with the unity of ethos, of temper, of thought on human destinies, is the great argument for the unity and single authorship of the Iliad in the main. To others, probably, as to Wolf, this consistency is apparent when they read the Iliad, as alone it was meant to be read or heard, "for human pleasure," without constantly dwelling on "oppositions of science falsely so called," and hunting for discrepancies which often are not discrepant.

It is not an article of my faith that there is no non-original matter in the Iliad. In another book, Homer and the Epic, I mentioned the passages which, to me, seem probably alien, for one reason or another. About the authorship of the Catalogue I do not know enough to be able to form an opinion. In the dream of Agamemnon and what follows, in Book ii., I might guess that two or three lines have been omitted, though on the whole the waverings of Agamemnon are thoroughly consistent with his character, and are meant to throw into light the steadfastness of Odysseus. I think that Phoenix is not properly introduced in Book ix., but there he is a necessary character; his warning to Achilles, not to fight before receiving atonement, has an influence throughout, backed as it is later by the counsels of Odysseus. The battles between Troy and the Ships, in Books xii.-xv., might be more lucid; but so might Napier's account of the battle of Salamanca, and Lord Roberts's of the Siege of Delhi. I understand Homer better than I do either of these military historians; but I have taken more pains to understand him. I would rather believe the Aristeia of Idomeneus to be by another hand; it is perfunctory; and the proceedings of Poseidon are perplexing, like the doings of Ares and Athene in the first fifty lines of Book v. The Gods always, by the infinite inconsistencies of mythology, cause confusion, but the text itself has an air of dislocation. The arming of Agamemnon in the opening of Book xi., seems to me non-authentic, as far as our knowledge of Homeric armature goes. The whole passage about the destruction of the Achaean wall by the Gods, in the after time, reads to me like a pedantic later explanation of the absence of traces of the works.

The meeting of Aeneas and Achilles in Book xx. would seem more suspicious than, to me, it does, if Aeneas were not, throughout, a special sort of person, the son of a goddess, and not a good Trojan, because of Priam's suspicion of "the Orleans branch." I am inclined to think that the poet knows, all through, a "saga" of Aeneas as preserving the seed of the Royal House of Troy. In Book v., and elsewhere, he is always under divine protection, that of Apollo or of Aphrodite, "only Zeus shielded thee, and other gods," says Achilles. "It is appointed for him to escape that the race of Dardanus perish not," says Poseidon in Book xx.; and were the passage solitary, I should think it all an interpolation. But the poet always, probably for traditional reasons, takes very good care of Aeneas. The last bouts in the Funeral Games seem unlike Homer.

In the Odyssey, the passages about the concealing of the arms (xvi., xix.) are dislocated, to say the least; and all the close of the poem, especially the second Nekyia, has always lain under suspicion in critical times. Sainte-Beuve would not abandon, but admired it; I only feel that, if all this be later, it has taken the place of lost earlier material, for the poem could not conceivably close till the blood feud of Odysseus and the kin of the Wooers was appeased. An Achaean like a Scandinavian audience understood the rules, and insisted that the settlement of the blood-feud must be explained.

These are the main points at which, as far as I can judge, something has gone wrong. There are others: the interchange of shields between Nestor and Thrasymedes in the opening of Book xiv. had probably some lines of explanation given to it, though, as Mr. She wan was the first to perceive, the exchange was the necessary consequence of the manoeuvres in Book x. Here Thrasymedes lent his shield to Diomede for his night reconnaissance, Thrasymedes would then send for and use Nestor's shield, while Nestor would obtain the shield of Thrasymedes next morning from Diomede.[435]

Nothing can be more simple and natural; but the thing was so obvious as to escape attention till Mr. She wan read Homer in a Homeric spirit. No doubt there are other passages with which I am dissatisfied, but the curious may refer for them to my earlier book, Homer and the Epic.

It is not so strange that there are dislocations ill patched up, as that far more of extraneous matter, especially of Ionian matter, has not found an entry into the Epics. How the text has been so well guarded I cannot explain; Mr. Murray's theory of expurgation of certain beliefs, ways and manners, is examined in Appendix B.

As to how the Epic was evolved, I am unable to say anything precise for want of evidence. Analogy from other early national epic poetry fails us here, because nowhere is there any early national poetry of the same scope and the same consistency. Again, in such epics as the Chanson de Roland, and even in Beowulf, mythical as it is, there are actual traces of historic events. We know that, because we have chronicles and official annals corroborating parts of the Chanson de Roland, or proving the historic existence of a few characters in the Volsunga Saga, and Beowulf; but in the case of the Homeric poems we have no evidence of the actual existence of any personage.

As for the chansons de geste, we know, or at least the most eminent French scholars believe, that these, or the earliest of them, are the final poetic results of actual reminiscences, recorded in lays or ballads, popular or military, of the reign of Charlemagne. But Homer is far in advance of the age of ballads on actual events in the remote past.

M. Gaston Paris says: "The Chanson de Roland is not a work composed d'un seul jet à un moment donné, it contains elements of very different dates and different sources"—there is a basis of popular or military ballads; there are additions invented by professional poets to increase the interest. "The author of the Chanson is Legion."[436] I entirely agree, and Legion is the author of Paradise Lost, and the author of King Lear, or Hamlet, or Macbeth. Legion is the name of the myth-makers from an age of savagery onwards; of the Greek and Roman and Celtic poets and historians, of the Christian theologians, and Anglo-Saxon minstrels and low Latin versifiers, and heavy Dutch poets, and gay Italian poets, who have contributed the ideas and material to Paradise Lost. But the

[435] Homer and his Age, pp. 276-278.

[436] Légendes du Moyen Age, pp. 46-47.

Epic is Milton's though Homer and Virgil are among the authors: without their lives it had not been what it is. The form is Milton's, and the form of the Iliad is Homer's.

These things are manifest. All poetry, down to a lyric like "Bonnie Dundee," has, in one sense, a multiplicity of authors. The poet selects, combines, and gives form to a mass of pre-existing materials.

In Lear, Shakespeare works on a Märchen still current in rural England. That Märchen he takes in the pseudo-historic form given to it by the chroniclers. Shakespeare combines with it—for Gloucester and Edmund—a French story which he finds in Sidney's Arcadia. He has before him an earlier drama on King Lear; he selects, arranges, composes, he adds what is his own, the poetry, and the fatal conclusion; and even so the author of our Iliad treated his materials. Of all poetry, and especially of all epic poetry, the author's name is Legion. Legion supplies the materials, and examples of different methods of dealing with them, and the stock of ballad or epic formulae. The final poet makes his selections, his combinations, and fuses all into a new form.

It may be said that I mean by "Legion" something which M. Gaston Paris did not mean. But what did he mean? Did he mean that a different laisses, or strings of verses on one assonance in the Chanson de Roland, were by different poets, and were tacked together by one man, who, perhaps, made omissions and additions? If this was what M. Gaston Paris meant, I do not agree with him, nor with any one who may hold the same opinion about the evolution of our Iliad. I know perfectly well what I mean, when I say that Legion provided Homer's materials, and showed various methods of treating them.

What these materials were we cannot exactly know. There must have been much heroic poetry in hexameter verse; in Homer the form has reached perfection. The style retains some peculiarities of popular poetry, of ballads, as in stereotyped formulae descriptive of habitual actions of every kind. Like our ballads, the poet never avoids a formula, if he can find one current; if he invents a new one, he clings to it. This recurrence of formulae is no less marked in Iliad viii. than in Child's four hundred English and Scottish Popular Ballads, or in La Chancun de Willame, one of the oldest chansons de geste.

Homer's chief heroes need no introduction to his audience, as Roland and Oliver, Ganelon and Naismes needed none. All his characters were familiar figures in an ancient legend of an expedition against the Northern shore of Asia. About that we have no historic knowledge, and it is rare indeed that chronicles record any "facts" given in early chansons de geste. The rear-guard action at Roncevaux is an exception; it is a historical fact.

Homer surveyed the whole, selected some situations, invented others, combined and fused all in the furnace of his genius, just as did Milton and Shakespeare. But how Legion made the Iliad, with no Homer, no one great genius, but in some incomprehensible manner of combination, I have never understood. I have never seen any description of the processes which was clear, coherent, intelligible, and corroborated by an example historically known. Theories of "redactors," "editors," literary committees, are all in the air; we cannot say, with Mrs. Quickly, "You, or any man, knows where to have them." No theory shows us "where to have" the Dichter, where, or when, or in what circumstances he did whatever he is supposed to have done.

APPENDIX A

THE CATALOGUE

The date, purpose, and historical value of the Catalogue are matters vigorously disputed, and critics not only vary among themselves, but change their own minds, as is natural, when new facts accrue. Topographical study of the Greek mainland, and new discoveries of prehistoric sites that had been overlooked, necessarily throw new light on Homer's conception of prehistoric Greece. Thus M. Bérard appears to have found again what learned late Greek geographers had lost, the site of Nestor's city of Pylos.

Nestor, in Iliad, xi. 664-762,[437] telling a long story about his early prowess, gives many topographical details. But he "is clearly ignorant of the geography of the western Peloponnesus," says a critic. Here the theory is that Nestor's story is by a late editor of the Iliad, who had read the Catalogue, picked out some places named at random, and thrown them in anywhere.[438] But M. Bérard studies the topography on the spot, and finds sites which, he thinks, coincide perfectly with the topography of Nestor, and also, with that

437 Leaf, Iliad, vol. i. pp. 465, 466.

438 Leaf, Note to Iliad, xi. 756; Iliad, ii. 615, 617.

of the journey of Telemachus, in the Odyssey, to Pylos, the home of Nestor, and on to Menelaus in Sparta. It is strong corroboration that M. Bérard's location of Pherae, where Telemachus passes the night on his way to Sparta, and of Pylos itself, makes the topography of Homer intelligible.[439]

But we must remember that people who deem the Iliad a thing of rags and patches, stitched on, in this case, by some ignoramus of about 540 B.C., are eager to find discrepancies everywhere; while the learned and minute French geographer was equally anxious to find proofs of Homer's accuracy. At all events, if he is right, Nestor does not talk ignorant nonsense.

Geographical and archaeological research produce modifications of opinion, but the critical weathercock veers, less necessarily, with every wind of theory that blows from Germany. Thus Mr. Leaf, in the first edition of his Iliad (vol. i. p. 73), found nothing to prove that the Catalogue "is of late origin." "It was considered a classical work—The Doomsday Book of Greece, at a very early date.... There seems to be no valid reason for doubting that it, like the bulk of the Iliad and Odyssey, was composed in Achaean times, and carried with the emigrants to the coast of Asia Minor."

Nothing new has been discovered since Mr. Leaf wrote in this orthodox fashion, nothing new has arisen except the studies of M. Bérard, which, if we accept his view, confirm the accuracy of the Catalogue. But, in 1900, Mr. Leaf abandoned his earlier position.

"The whole perspective of the Catalogue," he says, "is entirely different from that of the Iliad." Heroes, as Niese remarks, appear in the Iliad who do nothing in that poem; but play their parts "in other portions of the Epic Cycle." The conclusion is that "the Catalogue originally formed an introduction to the whole cycle, and was composed for that portion of it which, as worked up into a separate poem, was called the Cypria, and relates the beginning of the tale of Troy, and the mustering of the fleet at Aulis." This contains much debatable matter. What the cycle [440]was before it was "worked up into" separate poems, or whether such a nebulous cycle existed at all, we know not. I must refer the reader to Mr. Allen's essay on the whole subject, which is too condensed to be summarised in briefer space.[441] "The Catalogue was taken by Homer from its time and place in saga to his second Book and to the Troad." I do not quite understand how a long passage in hexameters could be taken from

---

439 Bérard, Les Phéniciens et l'Odyssée, pp. 108-113.

440 Leaf, vol. i. p. 86.

441 Classical Quarterly, April 1909.

"saga." Mr. Allen's critical remarks on prehistoric Greek topography and territorial divisions, are most valuable; and so is his account of the Dorian and other pretensions which wrought confusion in topographical designations. He has proved, I think, that the Catalogue is a very archaic document, which no later persons were interested in inventing, or would have been able to invent. Beyond that I am unable to go, and we must await the results of excavation on prehistoric sites in Greece. Our information as to the Cypria credits it with no Catalogue of the Achaean ships and men; but it is easy to reply that our accounts are wrong, that the authors spoke of a Cypria made up after the Catalogue was placed in the Iliad.

APPENDIX B

The argument of my book is that the Iliad and Odyssey represent the usages and ideas of a prehistoric society. They are not the ideas and usages of proto-historic and historic Hellas, but of the Achaean invaders, or, at least, of the high-born men and women to whom Homer sang. On the other hand, Mr. Murray, if I succeed in understanding his position, holds that the ideas and usages of the Iliad and Odyssey are a kind of mosaic, the result of a long process of "expurgation of Homer." If this view be correct, my whole argument, of course, is builded on the sand. Homer does not represent the ethical and religious beliefs and usages of a moment in the past.

It is therefore necessary to state, with textual citations as full as possible, Mr. Murray's presentation of his case, given, first, in his Rise of the Greek Epic, and, later, in one of the Oxford Lectures by several authors, published in Anthropology and the Classics. Mr. Murray has very kindly assisted me by explaining points in which I was unable to follow his reasoning. But these explanations prove that we start from assumptions so opposed in their nature that community in conclusions is impossible. Perhaps even mutual intelligence cannot be perfect. Thus my reading of the Epics leads me to the conviction that they were composed in an age which knew nothing of coined money; an age when cattle were the standard of values:—this or that object was worth so many cows. But in Mr. Murray's opinion this standard was preserved in the epics, after it was obsolete in practice, for reasons of stylistic convention. While I suppose our two epics to have been epics at a period very remote, when Achaean society was in its bloom; he holds that there were no epics till the Achaeans and the conquered peoples were intermingled. Earlier, there were only lays, and the silence of our epics as to coined money, for example, is a convention derived from the lays of a time when cows were the measure of value. Each of us, it seems to me, has to assume a kind of miracle. I have to think, and do think, that our epics were composed by a poet to amuse the leisure of an Achaean Court, and also that they were miraculously preserved, whether by writing or in memory, through several changeful centuries. I believe that this occurred because the poems are great harmonious structures, such as only a poet could produce; and because the many changes in society, costume, law, belief, and usage which the successive ages evolved, do not appear in the poems.

Mr. Murray, I think, has also to postulate another kind of miracle. Evolution, in some way which I do not understand, produced our epics out of a mass of floating poetical material. It appears that men are born to hold one view or the other, to believe in one or the other prodigy.

However, in the view which is not mine, stylistic conventions in the later poetry were based on a following of what was no convention in the older poetry, say as to the use of coined money or of cavalry. Now I know no other early national poetry, and no literary epics of the critical ages of Greek and Roman literature, where such convention is employed. Virgil was learned; Virgil knew Homer intimately; yet his Greeks and Trojans use iron weapons, not weapons of bronze; and the Roman buckler, not the Homeric shield.

To take another case, as soon as armorial bearings came into mediaeval Europe, the singers of the chansons de geste introduced them,—regardless of their absence in the earlier lays, which knew no such blazons. No convention of silence arose.

There is only one mention of writing in Homer. The Greek tragedians knew well that writing was, as far as Homer shows, very rare in the heroic age. But some of the heroes and heroines write whenever they have occasion. There is no archaistic convention. As I have shown in Homer and his Age, ancient poets and artists had, no more than Shakespeare, our modern habit of attending to "local colour" as historically known to us by research.

Perhaps it may be urged in reply, that early mediaeval epic poets were much less conservative than early Greeks. They altered, for example, the assonant laisses of the early chansons, and did them into rhyme, while Greece for epic purposes never deserted the hexameter. But I can give a fair parallel to the Greek non-observance of a convention in the Irish epic cycles.

The poets of the ancient Irish cycle of Fian ought, by the theory of convention, to have made their heroes use war-chariots like the heroes of the elder saga of Cuchullin. But they follow no such convention; their heroes ride or fight on foot, because such was the nature of war in their own later time.

The same reasoning applies throughout. I cannot believe that the makers of our epics, working in the early historic age, omitted mention of cavalry, coined money, periodical games, or anything else known to them, because they found no such matter in more ancient lays concerning and composed in a previous age. We have seen that the old "non-Homeric" epics were, as their fragments prove, full of non-Homeric usages. No "stylistic convention" forbade mention of these usages.

Thus no such stylistic convention—maintained in our Iliad and Odyssey, neglected in the Cypria, Aethiopis, and the rest—can be accepted. In fact, another and a special cause for many of Homer's silences has to be suggested, as we shall see. Once more it is my assumption that our epics were made in the main as we have them, for a peculiar audience, a courtly and knightly audience, known to themselves and their poet as "Achaeans." That they were of unmixed race I do not suppose; these Northern invaders, their chiefs at least, would marry the daughters of the princes of the land. But I assume that our epics were made for them, while they retained their Northern ideas; on many points very like the ideas, usages, and beliefs of the heathen Scandinavian settlers in Iceland. It is maintained by Mr. Murray that the ideas of "the conquered races" were very different, and that, as the two peoples mingled, the ideas of the conquered races re-emerged. This is manifestly true. But my view is that Achaean society, courtly society at least, had not adopted the beliefs and usages of the conquered races at the time when our epics, which ignore them, were composed. But these usages and ideas are usual in the fragments of the Cyclic epics on Trojan affairs. No stylistic convention interfered and kept them out. Mr. Murray has to discover a special cause for the presence in the "Cyclic" of much that is absent from our two epics.

The ideas of Mr. Murray, in some passages of his work, appear to be precisely the opposite of my own. In other passages we seem to be on the very point of agreement.

When we are told, in passages to be quoted, that there was in the formation of the Iliad, and to a less extent in that of the Odyssey, a strong element of reform and expurgation, we ask ourselves—who, in what age, and from what motives, were the reformers and purgers of what pre-existing poetic and legendary materials? Were those materials the property of the "Achaean or Northern" conquerors, or of the pre-existing "conquered races" (to use Mr. Murray's terms); or were the materials a medley derived from both sources? Were the purgers Achaean poets working on materials, at least in part the property of the conquered races? Or was the purgation mainly done by Ionians, that is, by the mixed Greek peoples settled in Asia; peoples certainly retaining many of the ideas of the conquered races which our Homer ignores? Or did "the Achaean or Northern spirit" purge away some things distasteful to that spirit, while the Ionians purged away other things? What the elements more or less purged away are supposed to be, we shall see later. In the passage to which I have referred[442] we find the following statements:—

"The epic tradition of Greece, vast and tangled in its wealth of varied beauty and ugliness, was left by the Homeric poets a much cleaner and colder thing than they found it. In the result, two influences were mainly at work. First, a general humanising of the imagination, the progress of a spirit which, as it loved beauty, hated cruelty and uncleanness. Secondly, a race prejudice. The relation of the Northern and the aboriginal elements in the Homeric poems are involved, when you come to details, in inextricable confusion, but in general the 'Homeric' tone of mind represents more of the Achaean or Northern spirit; the spirit of those scattered strong men who in their various settlements were leading and shaping the Aegean world. The special myths, beliefs, and rites that were characteristic of the conquered races are pruned away or ignored; the hero-worship, the oracles, the magic and witchcraft, the hocus-pocus of purification, all that savours of 'the monstrous regiment of women, the uncanny prowess of dead men, and the baleful confusion between man and God.'

Here I should absolutely agree with Mr. Murray, if I were convinced that "the Northern or Achaean spirit" of Achaean poets was dealing mainly with "the epic tradition" of præ-Achaean Greece. If they were, they would certainly "ignore or prune away" manners and beliefs which were not their own. But I have shown, I think, that between Achaean and Athenian early "Saga" a great gulf was fixed in Homeric times. The Homeric poet dealt with Achaean legend, which could not contain ghost-worship, "hocus-pocus of purification," and so on. Let me here remark that no known later Greek taste objected to the märchenhaft, the preposterous element

[442] R. G. E. p. 134.

in "Saga." Pindar and the dramatists do not reject it, I have shown, but Homer does in the Iliad. Had Homer revelled in it, later Greek taste saw nothing out of keeping here; had no temptation to expurgate Pegasus, or the soul-box of Meleager, or the magical invulnerability of Achilles, or his medicinal spear, or that magical property, the Luck of Troy, the palladium, and so forth. The genius of Homer, not later expurgation, accounts for his reticence.

Next, I seem to discern that "the progress of a spirit which hated cruelty and uncleanness" refers to a period when "Achaeans" and "Pelasgians," long intermingled, were becoming what is called "Hellenic," the people of early historic Greece in the sixth century. What this Hellenic spirit might, if it could, purge away is just the ferocity which is not purged away; the ferocity which mutilates, and, when the deed is not executed, has threatened to mutilate foes slain in open fight; and which denies, or wishes to deny, honourable burial to the dead. On the dead "unseemly things" are wrought, with little or no rebuke from the poet, except in the case of the extreme ferocities of Achilles against Hector and the twelve Trojan captives. Thus Agamemnon "smote Hippolochus to earth, and cut off his arms and neck with the sword, then tossed him like a ball of stone to roll through the throng"; or rather "like the trunk of a tree."[443] In the same way the minor Aias cuts off the head of Imbrios, and throws it like a football "into the scrum."[444] Hector is keen to cut off the head of Patroclus, and stick it on a stake, like the head of the great Montrose.[445] Peneleus decapitates Ilioneus, and waves the head at the Trojans.[446]

Manifestly these ferocities were de bonne guerre in the society to which Homer sang. I conceive that they were hateful to the taste of the historic Hellenic spirit. Could it have expurgated these ferocities it would have done so. But it could not. Other examples might be given. Thus Euphorbus,[447] who dealt the first wound to Patroclus, threatens to cut off and carry home the head of Menelaus. Euphorbus was avenging his brother, slain by Menelaus. Peneleus was avenging Antimachus, his friend. The ferocities are sometimes prompted by personal vengeance. Euphorbus would have kept his word, but the spear of Menelaus pierced his throat. We cannot find expurgation in failure to accomplish a purpose. Hector meant to fix

---

443 Iliad, xi. 145-147.

444 xiii. 202-204.

445 xviii. 176-177.

446 xiv. 496-505.

447 xvii. 39.

the head of Patroclus on a stake, so Iris tells Achilles,[448] and to give his body to the dogs to devour. Such was warfare as known to Homer; and the intellect of later Greece, which probably abhorred such deeds, expurgated nothing.

Mr. Murray writes[449] that "no other corpse" (except Hector's) "is maltreated in the Iliad." Such treatment was quite deliberately planned by men of both armies, and was also executed in hot blood. I have given examples enough of such maltreatment.

To cruelty we return, and to refusal of burial. It seems to have been quite usual. The notable exception in clemency is Achilles; before his passion came on him he ransomed his captives, and "his soul had shame to despoil the dead Eëtion"; but he burned him in his inlaid armour, and raised a barrow over him.[450]

In the Iliad ferocity runs high, in these particulars; the historic hatred of such doings is growing but slowly. "The spirit that hated cruelty" has left the facts where it found them; there is no expurgation of them. As to the Hellenic historic spirit and its hatred of "uncleanness"—autres temps, autres moeurs! Homer has no allusions to the survival of savage vices detested by "the Northern spirit." But, granting that the waxing spirit of Hellenism expurgated atrocities committed on the dead (though they stand staring upon us in the Iliad), "the Northern or Achaean spirit" is credited by Mr. Murray with "pruning away or ignoring" the characteristic rites, beliefs, and usages of the conquered races.

The earlier the period, the more drastic would be the purification. Achaeans, not yet leavened with "Pelasgian" blood and beliefs, could not celebrate what they confessedly did not practise. In their work no later expurgation could cleanse away that which their work could not contain.

Hero-worship; propitiation of the dead; purification of homicides by blood; initiatory ceremonies, mysteries, witchcraft, and so forth, these are practices with which we are familiar in savagery, in barbarism, and, by way of survival, in the rites and customs of the most highly civilised races. They exist in various degrees in different races and societies. In Northern society, as we know it in the sagas, most of these superstitions are comparatively rare. Ghosts were believed in by Gunnar and Grettir; very able-bodied ghosts they were, a kind of vampires. But they were not propitiated, they were met with the steel axe and short sword, or with muscular force in the wrestling match. Their bodies were

---

[448] xviii. 175-177, xvii. 126.

[449] R. G. E. p. 131.

[450] Iliad, vi. 416-419.

mutilated and then burned, as in the case of the vampire Glam in the Grettir saga.

There are few, if any, traces of hero-worship in early Teutonic and Scandinavian literature. Of purification from homicide in baths or by aspersions of swine's blood I can remember no Northern example.

The original purpose of this nasty practice is, apparently, to throw the pursuing ghost of the slain man off the trail of the slayer; but the heroes of the Icelandic sagas recked not a fig for the feud of the ghost. "Soul and body, on the whole, are odds against a disembodied soul," in their opinion, hence the absence of the Greek rite of purification by blood.

The Northerners had, doubtless, their various rustic rites and revels, originally intended to promote the fertility of nature. But if they once had initiatory ceremonies and mysteries like savages, these appear to have been forgotten by the time of the heroes of the Icelandic sagas. Witchcraft was an article of belief, but was held in great disesteem. There are legends of sacrifices of kings, but these are somewhat shadowy and remote.

As a consequence, if the Teutonic and Scandinavian people had possessed a great epic poet, working in accordance with the ideas of his people as they existed at the time of the occupation of Iceland, his poem would, I conceive, be as silent as the Homeric epics about hero-worship, ghost-feeding, purification of homicides by blood, sacrifices of girls, initiatory ceremonies, and mysteries like those of Demeter and Dionysus. Of second-sight we would hear, as we do in the Odyssey. The magic would be worked by mortals, not by a fair goddess, Circe. Ravening monsters like Grendel and his mother, in Beowulf, with their refraction in the Grettir saga, and vampires like Glam, would afford sport to the heroes; whereas in the Iliad we have only the Chimaera to represent such monsters, and the Chimaera is alluded to but slightly.

Thus, as regards the whole chapter of the superstitions "characteristic of the conquered races" in Greece[451] (and characteristic of the historical Hellenes and of Athens in her lustre), the supposed Scandinavian epic would be as pure as the Iliad. The absence of mention of hero-worship, ghost-propitiation, divinised mortals, purification by blood, sacrifices of girls, initiations and mysteries, would be quite natural and unaffected.

The poet could not speak of beliefs and rites which were not in the manners of his people. In the same way, and for the same reason, Homer scarcely hints at anything in this chapter of

---

451 R. G. E. p. 134.

superstitions and usages. Like the Scandinavians of the heroic age, his people had not these things in their manners.

As the oldest Achaean poetry must necessarily have been pure from the usages and beliefs of the conquered races, as the Achaean or Northern spirit ignored what, according to Mr. Murray, it actually persecuted,[452] we need not attribute this ignoring of such beliefs and practices to expurgation in a later age. The Ionians, as soon as we meet them in the dawn of actual history and in the "Cyclic" poems, are believers in ghosts, worshippers of heroes, and they practise purification by blood. People do not expurgate from older poetry the things consecrated by their own law and religion and celebrated in their own poems: things which could not be present, too, in the old poems of the uncontaminated Achaeans. Yet Mr. Murray appears, if I understand him, to incline to a theory that hero-worship, for example, was distasteful to the Ionian cult of the Delian Apollo, and perhaps for that reason was, in early historic times, expurgated from the Iliad. But certainly, given Homeric ideas about the dead, who could not help or hinder, hero-worship did not and could not exist in Homeric society and poetry. Moreover, if the Achaean spirit did "prune away or ignore" such ghostly matters, the Delian expurgators could find nothing here to expurgate. As to blood-purification, Apollo himself was purified, and, in art, holds the purifying pig above the homicide. So purification was "Apolline," and what was Apolline was safe from Apolline expurgation.

I now collect passages on the expurgators from Mr. Murray's writings.

EXPURGATION

"The middle and later generations of the Homeric poets ... were mainly responsible for the work of expurgation."

"Homer has cut out" certain stories of human sacrifice, cannibalism, and "mutilations of the Hesiodic gods" "for their revoltingness" (p. 122).

"Homer, if we may use that name to denote the authors of the prevailing tone of the Iliad" (p. 131).

So far the "expurgations" appear to have been done mainly by the Homeric poets themselves "in the middle and later generations." Yet, as to superstitions, the first uncontaminated Achaean poets must have been the purest of all.

---

452 R. G. E. pp. 245-246.

It is admitted that the poets did not in the same way "expurgate" the "Cyclic" epics.

"If the educational use of the Iliad began in Ionia as early as the eighth century, which is likely enough, we can hardly help supposing that it had some share in these processes of purification with which we have been dealing" (p. 133).

Here it appears that, probably by the eighth century, the Iliad was a distinct poem, recognised as such, and subject to processes of purification from which the Cypria, for example, and other "Cyclic" poems escaped.

"The Epos" has "its prevailing Achaean tone," owing to "the prestige of the Achaean chiefs, the convenience of the Achaean institutions of the Saga and the Bard," and "the partial return to the migratory life" (p. 245). If, then, it is really the austerity, and freedom from low superstitions, of the conquering Achaean race that our epics represent, the "Cyclic" poems, if equally old, should be equally austere, and equally free from superstition. But they, notoriously, were full of the superstitions of the conquered races. Why did the middle generations of Homeric poems leave them alone? Because already selected for recitation?

If the Achaean or Northern spirit, "the clean and lordly Northern spirit," made our epics so pure, what was left for the spirit of historic Greece (by no means Northern, or specially clean or lordly) to do in the way of purification?

It is plain enough that the clean and lordly Northern people became mixed with the pre-existing populations in Greece, like the Normans and the Cromwellian English settlers with the Irish. "As the population became more mixed, which was the case everywhere on the mainland, the result was that the old pre-Hellenic stratum of beliefs and emotion, re-emerged" (p. 246), for example, in worship of the dead, which is un-Homeric and un-Achaean.

Are we to suppose, then, that while the Achaeans were sinking to the pre-Hellenic level in such matters, all the superstitions of the conquered races found their way into the Homeric poems, and had to be purged out again, in Delos, or at Athens, where these superstitions were in full force? If so, the descendants of the pre-Hellenic populations inserted the superstitions into the Iliad where they had not been previously, and then cut them out again.

It is not easy to understand how stories "far too primitive and monstrous for Homer" "had been expurgated from Homer centuries back" (p. 247), centuries before Aeschylus, who introduced Io, once the mistress of Zeus, later a cow, in his Prometheus. If Homer or the Homeric poets were clean and lordly Achaeans, they never would have dealt at all in a story "far too primitive and monstrous for

Homer," or for any one but Major Weir. It does not appear to me that this theory of expurgation, all important as it is, can be easily understood. If later Greece expurgated the Homeric ferocities to the dead, why are they left standing? If the Achaean spirit got rid of the superstitions, why need we invoke later influences, Delian, Ionian, Athenian?

Then the old questions re-arise, why were the "Cyclic" poems of the heroic times left unexpurgated; why is the Attic drama tinged with what is too monstrous for Homer, if Homer was purged a generation, or two or three, earlier than the generation of Aeschylus? To account for the expurgations, we are to consider the establishment by law of Homeric recitations at Athens (see "The Alleged Athenian Recension of Homer"). Concerning the date of this event, and everything else connected with it, all is vague. Mr. Murray writes: "The recitation was established about the end of the sixth century ... so much seems historically clear." (I wish anything were historically clear in this business!) "It matters little that, in attributing the institution of this recitation to a definite founder, our authorities waver between three almost contemporaneous names, Solon, Pisistratus, Hipparchus. Whichever it was, the main fact remains the same. General considerations tell somewhat against Solon, and in favour of the tyrants." Now, as our authorities, all late, differ totally as to the name (and so, as to the date) of the man who instituted the recitations of Homer, it is plain that they had no good authority. "The Solonian laws and constitution were promulgated in 594 B.C.," says Grote; that was at least eighty years before a date "about the end of the sixth century." The men are far from being contemporaneous. Hipparchus was murdered in 514, in the thirteenth year of the tyranny of Hipparchus, and Hippias, if anybody, not Hipparchus, should have made a law regulating Homeric recitations.

All is vague; but if Thucydides correctly says that Hipparchus was slain in consequence of a quarrel arising out of an odious non-Homeric vice; and if, as Thucydides says, Aristogeiton died "not easily," if he was tortured to death, as later authors tell, then the society of Athens was little likely to expurgate either uncleanness or cruelty, if they found such matter in Homer.

Political and personal history being so vague and dim in the sixth century, literary history cannot be in better case; practically we know nothing beyond the fact that a law regulated the recitation of Homer at the Panathenaic festival.

How these recitations and hypothetical earlier Ionian recitations contributed to the expurgation of the Iliad and Odyssey, must be stated in Mr. Murray's own words. I may first observe that, in his opinion, "the body of the poem" (the Iliad), "even in the latest parts, is clearly Ionian; the ultimate nucleus something else, something older and more Northern."[453] How, if this be true, the Ionians are only once named in the poems, while the Athenians are but perfunctorily mentioned, is what always puzzles me!

A long extract in which Mr. Murray gives his views must now be quoted:

"In the remains of the earliest Greek poetry we are met by a striking contrast. As Mr. Lang has told us, 'Homer presents to the anthropologist the spectacle of a society which will have nothing to do with anthropology.' By Homer, of course, Mr. Lang means the Iliad and the Odyssey; and we may add to those poems a stream of heroic tradition which runs more or less clearly through most of our later literature, and whose spirit is what we call classic, Homeric, or Olympian.

"But there is also in the earliest epic tradition another stratum, of which this Olympian character does not hold. A stratum full of the remains, and at times even betraying the actuality, of those 'beastly devices of the heathen' which are dear to the heart of us anthropologists—if a mere Greek scholar may venture to class himself among even amateur anthropologists; ceremonies of magic and purification, beast-worship, stone-xvorship, ghosts, and anthropomorphic (theriomorphic?) gods, traces of the peculiar powers of women both as 'good medicine' and as titular heads of the family, and especially a most pervading and almost ubiquitous memory of Human Sacrifice.

"This stratum is represented by Hesiod and the Rejected Epics,—I mean those products of the primitive saga-poetry which were not selected for recitation at the Panathenaea (or the unknown Ionian archetype of the Panathenaea), and which consequently fell into neglect,—by the Orphic literature, by a large element in tragedy, most richly, perhaps, by the antiquarian traditions preserved in Pausanias, and in the hostile comments of certain Christian writers, such as Clement and Eusebius.

"Now the first thing for the historian to observe about this non-Homeric stratum is this: that non-Homeric is by no means the same thing as post-Homeric. We used to be taught that it was. We used to be taught that Homer was, practically speaking, primitive: that we started from a pure epic atmosphere and then passed into an age of romantic degradation. The extant remains of the non-Homeric poems frequently show in their form, and sometimes even in their content, definite signs of presupposing the Iliad, just as the

---

[453] R. G. E. p. 173.

Iliad here and there shows signs of presupposing them; and it is not until recently that we have been able to understand properly the nature and the method of composition of an ancient Traditional Book. I will not go into that point in detail here. Even supposing that the Cypria, as a poem, could definitely be called 'later' than the Iliad, it is enough to say that a later literary whole may often contain an older kernel or a more primitive mass of material, and in the case of the non-Homeric saga-poems it is fairly clear that they do so.

"Two arguments will suffice: First, the argument from analogy. Few anthropologists, with the knowledge now at our command, will regard the high, austere, knightly atmosphere of the Iliad as primitive when compared with that of Hesiod. In the second place, a great proportion of our anthropological material is already to be found in prehistoric Crete. The an-iconic worship, the stones, the beasts, the pillars, and the ouranian birds; the great mother goddess of Anatolia, the human sacrifices, and the royal and divine bull. I speak under correction from those who know the Cretan finds better than I; but to me it seems that there are many bridges visible from Crete to Hesiod or Eumelus or even Pausanias; but the gulf between Crete and Homer seems, in certain places, to have no bridge.

"Thus the later literary whole contains the more primitive modes of thought, the earlier religion.

"Now this fact in itself, though it may be stated in different ways, is not much disputed among scholars. But the explanations of the fact are various. That which seems to me much the most probable is the theory of Expurgation. As Mr. Lang seems not quite to have understood what I tried to say about this in my Rise of the Greek Epic, I will restate it in this way: We know that the great mass of saga-poetry began to be left on one side and neglected from about the eighth century on; and we find, to judge from our fragments, that it remained in its semi-savage state. Two poems, on the contrary, were selected at some early time for public recitation at the solemn four-yearly meeting of "all Ionians,"[454] and afterwards of "all Athenians." The poems were demonstrably still in a fluid condition; and the intellect of Greece was focussed upon them. This process lasted on through the period of that great movement which raised the shores of the Aegean from a land of semi-savages to the Hellas of Thales, of Aeschylus, and of Euripides. And we find, naturally, that amid all the colour of an ideal past, in which these two epics, like all other epics, have steeped their story, there has been a gradual but drastic rejection of all the uglier and uncleaner

---

454 This archetype, Mr. Murray has just said, is "unknown."

elements. That is a very broad statement; it omits both the evidence and the additional causes and qualifications. But it serves to explain why I treat the non-Homeric sagas as representing more faithfully the primitive pre-Hellenic habits of thought, the mere slough out of which Hellas rose."

I agree that the "non-Homeric sagas" represent more faithfully the primitive pre-Hellenic habits of thought. Homer was not concerned with pre-Hellenic habits of thought; he represents the Hellenes who "possessed Hellas, the land of fair women, and followed Achilles."

I also entirely agree that "the later literary whole" (by which I at least mean Hesiod, the "Cyclic" fragment, and much of Greek tragedy, not to speak of antiquarian learning) "contains the more primitive modes of thought, the earlier religion." But the theory that these things were once in, but were purged out of, the Iliad and Odyssey, still baffles me. If they were usages peculiar to the conquered races, how could they appear in the poetry of the uncontaminated Northern or Achaean conquerors?

How, again, can we say that "the great mass of saga poetry began to be left on one side and neglected from about the eighth century"? Notoriously the "Cyclic" poems, or the legends which were given in those poems, were greatly preferred as subjects of art by the Athenian vase-painters of the sixth century, and by Polygnotus when he decorated the Lesche at Delphi. The stories, I have shown, reached the Middle Ages through Rome and through Graeco-Roman literature, and eclipsed our Homer. To them we owe the unhappy Troilus and Cressida of Shakespeare.

We have no evidence known to me that proves the selection, "at some early time for public recitation," of "two poems," at the solemn four-yearly meeting of "All Ionians" and afterwards of "all Athenians." Mr. Verrall supposes the "Cyclic" poems, as well as our Homer, to have been recited at the Panathenaea. I know no evidence that they were, and none proving that they were not. I am unaware of any reason for which our Iliad should have been specially selected for education in the Ionia of the eighth century, and for public recitation. The reason is the further to seek if the Iliad and Odyssey, when thus selected, "were demonstrably still in a fluid condition"; indeed, while they were still in a fluid condition, I do not know how they could have been deemed so much more choiceworthy than other poems still (I presume) fluidic.

If "the intellect of Greece was focussed upon" Iliad and Odyssey while they were still fluidic, but already selected, then the expurgation was due, not to Achaean poets who ignored and pruned away the usages and beliefs of the conquered races, but to les intellectuels of Greece, who (whatever their private opinions might be) saw hero-worship in daily practice; and if they killed any one, were purified by pigs' blood. Hesiod stood high in universal knowledge, was a consecrated authority; if he could be purged, why was he not purged? Because he was not recited? Yet he was part of education, and needed a Bowdler much more than Homer.

The practices and beliefs expurgated from Homer were not "done in a corner" in historic Greece.

So "primitive," so barbaric was the intellect of historic Greece even in the sixth century and in the age of Pericles, and later, in regard to heroic tombs, for example, that the heroic ghosts were supposed to inhabit their sepulchres in the shape of rather harmless snakes, like the Idhlozi of the Zulus. "In Snake form the hero dwelt in his tomb," says Miss Harrison.[455]

Miss Harrison publishes reproductions of works of Greek art from the sixth century (when all ugly things of this kind, we are told, were drastically rejected from the Odyssey and Iliad) to the fourth century. We see the dead, a male and a female ghost, receiving offerings. The artist is determined to make his meaning clear. Behind the chairs of the holy heroes is a huge snake with a man's beard. He is a human snake, the incarnation of the dead man's ghost. This is the belief of the Baronga of Delagoa and of the Zulus.[456]

In a vase, a lecythus, of the fifth century, the worshippers surround a tumulus with a phallus-shaped pillar on top. A huge snake occupies the tumulus; he is the ghost's incarnation.[457]

Not in glens of mountainous Arcadia, or in recesses of rural chapels alone, were these things done. The theatre showed sacred tombs; each place of periodical games had its presiding hero; relics were in high request, living men, conquerors or athletes, came to be divinised; at the Eleusinia the initiates saw rites of savage origin; oracles of the dead were publicly consulted; the purification rites went on as law demanded—all publicly, all unrebuked.

Does any one suppose that priapic images like those of the Admiralty Islands were features in Homer's conception of a street in Mycenae or Ilios? These images were sacred in the Athens of Pericles, the Hermae were not like Homer's Hermes. Is it likely that, if the managers of Delian or Athenian recitations found such things as these in Homer, they would cut them out as too naughty to be mentioned, or for some other reason not to be mentioned, at a

455 Prolegg. to Study of Greek Religion, 1903, p. 329.
456 Ibid. pp. 327, 328.
457 Ibid. p. 329.

public festival of men and women familiar with all these things, and seeing in them nothing but good?

It seems unlikely. Moreover, if the Northern or Achaean spirit had ignored or pruned away these things, they could give no trouble to the managers of Delian or Athenian recitations.

When we come to consider examples of expurgation, we may prefer to pass by the odious vices reprobated by the code of Australian savages, but highly popular in historic Greece. They do not occur in our Homer, and I know but one allusion to them in the Icelandic sagas, and that is in a mere impossible taunt about a Bogle. But no one can say that Homer never heard of such things; we might as well say that, because nobody coughs in Homer, no Achaean ever condescended to cough. The profession of Rahab cannot have been unknown, though Homer never mentions it. In short, a high ideal tone is preserved, Homer is not Monsieur Zola; an epic is not a "naturalistic" novel.

When the Greeks did entertain a moral objection to anything, to adelphic marriage, for example: if Homer mentioned such an union, among the Phaeacians, I can easily believe that a palliative explanation might be later inserted. Thus, in Odyssey, vii. 54, Alcinous and Arete are "of the self-same parents." Later, a genealogy makes them uncle and niece. This, for what I know, may be a later palliative interpolation. But it is all one to Homer. He follows a well-known Märchen, a tale of No Man's Land, as in his mention of the adelphic marriages of the sons and daughters of Aeolus. Adelphic unions are capital offences in savage customary law; one has no reason to suppose that the Homeric Achaeans were more lax than savages, or no less depraved by Egyptian influences than the Ptolemy and Berenice of Theocritus.[458]

I am following Mr. Murray's examples of expurgation. The spirit of the battles in the Iliad "is chivalrous," he says. "No enemy is ever tortured" (as Sinon is in Quintus Smyrnaeus). Yet mediæval professors of chivalry never mutilated, I think, foes (not being rebels) slain in fair field. Homer's men did, I have shown; and nobody expurgated the melancholy facts. As to cruelty to living foes, Euripides and Sophocles make Achilles drag the living Hector behind his chariot, while Homer makes it plain that Hector is stone dead.[459]

One can only say that Homer shows better taste than the tragedians. If this good taste is due to late expurgators, if, in a Homeric lay, Achilles did drag the living Hector, one can only wish

---

[458] R. G. E. pp. 116, 117.

[459] Ajax, 1031. Andromache, 399.

that Sophocles and Euripides had been on the moral level of the expurgators. Whoever they were, their taste was vastly superior to that of the tragedians. I would attribute the better taste to Homer. The odious tale may be of Ionian invention: the Ionian poet makes Odysseus a child murderer. In the Tain Bo Cualgne, Ferdiad drags a very odious dead man at his chariot wheels, not a living man. Homer was probably, indeed certainly, on a higher level of taste than the ancient Irish epic-makers: on this point they are at one with him. The great tragedians preferred a more horrible story—not, of course, because they approved of such proceedings. In King Lear, Shakespeare has horrors undreamed of in his sources, in Märchen and chronicles. He followed a French story in Sidney's Arcadia, and pleased "the groundlings." To "groundlings" Homer did not sing: Sophocles and Euripides wrote for the cultured Pit of Athens. For that reason, or because they found their story in some unknown source, and liked the horrible, they made Achilles torture a living enemy.

There is a passage in the Iliad (xiii. 573) in which a man, speared from behind through the bowels, "where a wound is most baneful to wretched mortals, writhes about the spear ... for a moment, not for long"; his life follows the spear withdrawn. This is not a pleasant picture; but war, in fact, is not pleasant. Mr. Murray conceives the line which he renders "he struggled quite a little while, not at all long," to be a later palliative or expurgative addition; like the same formula in Odyssey, xxii. 473, where it is applied to the dying struggles of the hanged women-servants of Odysseus. This may be so, or may not; the fact that the line is a formula, like those of our ballads, makes me incline to think it ancient. The point is not of much importance, and cannot be decided. The horrible death inflicted on the treacherous thrall, Melanthius, in the Odyssey, is a proof that Homer's men could be very cruel to a treacherous thrall; but so could the Norsemen be, as in the scarcely quotable parallel case of Wolf the Unwashed. In the sagas generally we hear of few such cases, though many must have occurred, abroad, in Viking raids. In the Iliad there is no treacherous thrall; if such an one there were, he would have been treated like Melanthius.

I understand Mr. Murray to argue that the Iliad has been expurgated, but not quite successfully, of traces of poisoned arrows; while the Odyssey (l. 257-264) has the story of Odysseus seeking for arrow-poison at Ephyre, where poison was, we elsewhere learn, a marketable commodity. Ilus would not give it, for he feared the gods; another man gave it, as he dearly loved Odysseus. The story is not a true story, but a fable told by Athene. All it proves is that arrow-poison was known, but was hateful to the gods. As to Mr.

Murray's arguments that such words as ἄφυκτος, not "to be escaped," applied to arrows in the Iliad, and "bitter" (πικρός) and "groanful" and "not long to be supported" as proofs of the practice of poisoning arrows, I can only say that I do not think the inference necessary. Πικρός means "sharp," according to Liddell and Scott; unpoisoned arrows cause groans enough; the heroes "do not long support" flesh-wounds from spears, but "retire hurt." That Agamemnon expects Menelaus to die (iv. 134) when arrow—smitten in the belly, is very natural. Menelaus would have died had the arrow bitten deep, but it merely grazed him through several interstices of his armour. Pandarus shot with a fresh arrow, "unused before," "whose poison has not been rubbed off." I reply that in meditating an important shot, any archer would use a fresh arrow if he could, because the feathers would have been in better trim and the shaft unstrained, the point unblunted, exactly as a man would use a new spear in a tournament.

In the Iliad, men have strong bows, with iron or bronze points. People with these advantages do not use arrow-poison, the resort of races with blow-pipes, or with weak bows and arrow-points of bone, corrupt human bones by preference.

As to human sacrifice, a frequent topic in the Cyclic poems and the Greek dramatists, I have treated the subject elsewhere. I do not think that it was expurgated from the Iliad by men who let it stand in the Cyclic poems and the drama, but that it was not in Achaean manners. In the legends told of human sacrifice by Pausanias, the peoples concerned are usually Ionian or Athenian. The timid Calchas of Iliad, i. 74-83, who dare not name the cause of Apollo's wrath unless Achilles will guarantee his safety, could never have bidden Agamemnon to sacrifice his daughter Iphigeneia, who is not one of the Over Lord's three daughters, in the Iliad.

Mr. Murray suspects that stories of sacrifices of maidens "would have been rejected from the Iliad, not only because human sacrifice was a barbarity, but also because the stories involved too intense an interest in women."[460] As I am intensely interested in Helen, Hecuba and Andromache, in the Iliad, the argument seems to me strange. As to Mr. Murray's theory that the Cretan king was done to death at stated intervals,[461] the topic cannot be treated satisfactorily here. I do not believe that anything of the sort described occurred anywhere, and I am surprised at the remark, "We have no tradition of Minos's death."[462]

---

[460] R. G. E. p. 123.

[461] Ibid. p. 127.

[462] See Roscher's Lexikon, s.v. Minos.

The Minyan story of the intended sacrifice of Phryxus and Helle is a world-wide Märchen, with sacrifice substituted for endophagous cannibalism.

Finally, I do not suppose that the ferocities of Achilles towards Hector, and at the funeral of Patroclus, are an expurgated version of a lay in which they were narrated with pride and pleasure.[463] It was customary, in Homeric warfare, to maltreat the dead; but Achilles went too far, and persevered too long. He is, as Mr. Murray says, "a man mad with grief, a man starving and sleepless," a man who knows that Hector intended to mutilate his friend and give his body to the dogs. But these excuses do not palliate the perseverance of Achilles in outrage, or his slaying of the twelve Trojan captives. Sacrificed they were not. There was no ritual for such a slaughter, 'and, as a matter of fact, it is crowded into a shamefaced line and a half.' You would expect this sacrifice to have at the very least twenty."[464]

You might expect that, if you believed that the Achaeans had a ritual for human sacrifice! If they had, which I deem inconceivable, we may readily believe that the spirit of historic Hellas would have expurgated eighteen and a half of the twenty lines.

Much of this theory of expurgation of the Iliad and Odyssey seems to me to rest on the assumption of εὐφημία. This means abstention from ill-omened words in poems recited at a great public festival. It is impossible for me to understand why words referring, for example, to the habitual and legal purification of homicides, or to the established cult of heroes, should be deemed "ill-omened" at the recitations, in no way religious, at a public holiday, and yet be deemed "well-omened" in the performances of Athenian tragedy.

If the superstitions of the conquered races were not those of the conquerors, they could not be in the epics of the conquerors. If they were not there, les intellectuels of Athens could not expurgate them.

THE ALLEGED ATHENIAN RECENSION OF HOMER

Wolf could not but confess that the Iliad, as we possess it, is an unity, better or worse; is a literary structure. How, then, did it come to be what it is, if it were the work of several authors in several ages? Wolf replies, "History speaks! The voice of all antiquity, and,

---

463 R. G. E. pp. 130, 131.
464 R. G. E. p. 131.

on the whole, the consent of all report bears witness that Pisistratus was the first who had the Homeric poems committed to writing, and brought into that order in which we now possess them."[465]

This amazing statement shows that there are classical scholars who mean, when they speak of "History," something that no historical student means when he uses the same term. About any dealings by Pisistratus with Homer, history is mute as the grave. Not only is there no record—that is, no contemporary public inscription—testifying that Pisistratus or any other person "first had the Homeric poems arranged and committed to writing," there is not even a hint of a reference to any tradition of this event, in the great Historians of the following century, Herodotus and Thucydides, none in Aristotle, none in Ephorus (in the fourth century B.C.), none in the remains of Aristarchus and other famous Alexandrian grammarians. History is silent even as to a rumour. We know that Dieuchidas, a Megarian historian of the fourth century, said something about its being Solon rather than Pisistratus who did something in connection with Homer. We know this from a mutilated passage in an author of the third century, Diogenes Laertius. That is all.[466] Tradition from the time of Pisistratus himself to that of Cicero speaks no articulate and intelligible word as to what, according to Wolf, the voice of all antiquity declares. When we come after five centuries of historic silence to Cicero, we do not find him agreeing with Wolf that Pisistratus first had the poems of Homer committed to writing, but saying that "he is said" (by whom?) "to have been the first to have arranged, in their present order, the books of Homer, previously in disarray?"[467]

Cicero speaks only of what "is said." The unvouched for report mentioned by Cicero half a milennium after the date of Pisistratus is not history, of course; is not evidence. Long before Cicero, in the fourth century, Ephorus and Heraclides Ponticus told other stories about the coming of Homer to Sparta, stories equally unhistorical. The author of the pseudo-Platonic dialogue, Hipparchus, represented the second son of Pisistratus as the first to bring Homer to Attica, and to regulate Homeric recitations. None of these writers stands for History, none of them agrees with another; they had no historical knowledge of whatever facts there may have been.

We are in presence (1) of variants of a tradition doubtless founded on fact, namely, that at an unknown date an Act was passed in Athens regulating the recitations of Homeric poetry at the

---

465 Prolegomena, 2nd edition, 1859, p. 85.

466 See Homer and his Age, pp. 44-50.

467 De Oratore, iii. 34.

Panathenaic festival; by some accounts an Act limiting the recitations to "Homeric" poetry alone; and (2) of a legend that Pisistratus, or his second son, collected and arranged in a certain order the Homeric poems. The earliest and only good evidence, says Mr. Monro, with regard to the recitation of Homer at Athens, is that of two orators two centuries later than Pisistratus, Lycurgus and Isocrates. The former said in a speech "Our fathers thought Homer such a good poet that they made a law for him alone among poets that his poems should be recited by rhapsodists at every quinquennial holding of the Panathenaea."[468] No date is given, but Lycurgus must apparently be thinking of a date prior to Tyrtaeus, as we shall see later. When Lycurgus says that the poems of Homer alone were to be recited at the festival, he is of so late a date that he probably means the Iliad and Odyssey. If the Act were made in Solon's time, "Homer" may conceivably include all heroic epic poetry. We know nothing about it.

Isocrates[469] says that the ancestors of the Athenians "desired to make Homer's art honoured, both in contests of music (i.e. of the reciters) and in the education of the young" (Monro, Iliad, vol. i. p. 15). Still later, in a passage with an important lacuna, Diogenes Laertius says that Solon passed a law regulating the recitations,[470] the very law which is attributed to Hipparchus by the author of the Dialogue of that name.[471] In Sicyon also, in the sixth century, there were recitations of Homer by competing rhapsodists; they were put down by the tyrant Cleisthenes.[472]

Mr. Monro says that for the existence of an Athenian law about Homeric recitations, whatever the date of that law may have been, we have historical testimony. Indeed, if there were no such law, even rhetoricans of the fourth century could scarcely tell the Athenians that such a law existed. But as to its date and scope, and the name of the statesman who passed it, if any exact information had existed, perhaps there might have been some agreement among the persons who speak of it. If nothing like a History of Literature existed before the fourth century, we can expect no information. If it did exist, it was of no value to Ephorus, Heracleides, and the author of the Hipparchus. They are all at odds.

Mr. Monro says, as every man trained in historical criticism must say, "modern scholars have tried to harmonise these notices,

---

468 Leocr. p. 209.

469 Panegyr. c. 42.

470 Diog. Laert. Solon, i. 57.

471 See Monro, Odyssey, vol. ii. pp. 393. 397.

472 Herodotus, v. 67.

and to assign to (the Spartan) Lycurgus (named by Ephorus), Solon (named by Diogenes Laertius)," Pisistratus, and Hipparchus their several shares in the service done to Homer. "This would be legitimate if there were reason to regard any of the notices as historical. But, in fact, they are merely mythical anecdotes, supplemented by the guesses of scholars."[473] Whatever Homeric critics may think, they will find no trained historian to dissent from Mr. Munro on those points.

Historia silet! History is mute. We only know that from an uncertain period there were quinquennial recitations of "Homer," and Homer alone, at Athens, and that "Homer" was used in education. Beyond that all is "guesses of scholars." These guesses vary according to the taste and fancy of the learned.

In this conclusion every one who is accustomed to historical criticism will agree with Mr. Monro. Nothing can be made out of late and contradictory statements; nothing beyond the fact that "Homer" (whatever may be meant by "Homer") was quinquennially recited, under regulations, at Athens, and entered into public education.

Mr. A. W. Verrall, however, says: "In general, the very last thing that we get from disputants on either side is an exact construction and estimation of what, truly or falsely, is recorded about the history of Homer." Mr. Verrall writes thus in a Quarterly review of Mr. Murray's Rise of the Greek Epic, and of my Homer and his Age.

The questions as to what is "recorded" about "the history of Homer," I had treated in my Homer and the Epic (pp. 35, 38, 67-70), examining the evidence, such as it is, and the opinions of Wolf, Ritschl, and others; and siding with Mr. Monro (I may add, with Blass, Meyer, Nutzhorn, Mr. T. W. Allen, and many others). In Homer and his Age (pp. 46-50), I again went over the old ground, in reference to Mr. Leaf's changes of opinion.

Mr. Verrall writes:[474] "The texts, as we have said, are not treated fairly." Now really the texts are treated as the historian treats all texts that come into his province. The dates of the alleged events are set beside the dates of the texts concerning them; the texts are remote, contradictory, and unevidential; the best historians, and the historian who most carefully examined the popular traditions concerning Pisistratus and his sons, namely, Thucydides, say nothing about the alleged events.

Mr. Verrall also writes: "The record, such as it is, is hardly

[473] Iliad, vol. i. p. 27

[474] Quarterly Review, July 1908, p. 76.

ever correctly represented. The most punctilious of scholars (Grote, for example) are in this matter not to be trusted."[475]

These are severe reproaches! Mr. Monro is not mentioned: are any of his remarks unfair and untrust-worthy?

Mr. Verrall says: "We cannot but think that the ancient record about the origin of Homer suffers unfairly from certain prepossessions which all would disclaim, but which are more easily disclaimed than abandoned."

For me, I frankly confess my own prepossessions, but consciousness of his bias is the safeguard of the historian; it compels him to make certain that he adds nothing to and takes nothing from what Mr. Verrall calls "the ancient record," and I call "the various ancient legends." Mr. Verrall insists that "internal evidence about the history of a book, if not controlled by record, is liable to infinitely elastic interpretation." Certainly, but there is no possibility of "control by record" in the case of the history of the Homeric poems.

No historian can agree with Mr. Verrall that "as a matter of record and apart from inference or hypothesis, this Homer of ours ... appears as an artificial product of scholarship, the result of a critical process."[476] It is he who insists on the technical term "record"; it is not pedantic, therefore, to reply that "record" there is none. By "record" Mr. Verrall seems to mean, as regards the "artificial product of scholarship," a statement of opinion made five centuries after the alleged events.

The first testimony, or "record," cited by Mr. Verrall has nothing to say about our Homer as "an artificial product of scholarship." It deals merely with the legalised recitation of Homeric poetry, and of that poetry alone, at the Panathenaea. The text is that which Mr. Monro calls "the earliest evidence," "that of the orators Lycurgus and Isocrates," in the fourth century.

That is good evidence. Lycurgus could not speak to the Athenians of a law which, to their knowledge, did not exist. Lycurgus, in fact, had been cajoling his Athenian audience with a set of fables about their ancestors, whose patriotism and valour in pre-Homeric times he applauds. Did not Erechtheus in a war with Thrace sacrifice his own daughter in obedience to an oracle, and then defeat the invaders! For this noble action Lycurgus cites a play by Euripides, The Erechtheus!

Lycurgus next says that Athens made a law that the poems of Homer alone should be recited at the Panathenaea; and that,

---

475 Ibid. p. 53.

476 Quarterly Review, July 1908, p. 54.

encouraged by the patriotism ascribed by the poet to Hector, the Athenians, in the Persian affair, were ready to die, not for their city only, but for all Hellas. Such men were the Athenians, in public and private life: then comes the story of the Spartans borrowing Tyrtaeus from Athens, and their approval of a Tyrtaean poem adapted in part from Iliad, xxii. 71 ff.

That is all. Mr. Verrall writes: "By Lycurgus this whole educational movement, and the adoption of Homer as the basis of it, is attributed to the Athenians as a people...." What Mr. Verrall says about "a revolution in the method of education not less momentous than any movement in history,"[477] has, I think, but scanty warrant in the actual words of Lycurgus. It is Mr. Verrall, not Lycurgus, who compares the effect of Homer on Athens with the effect ("notorious," as he too truly says) of the Bible upon Scotland. All this about an educational movement, however true it may be, is, I fear, "inference and hypothesis" of Mr. Verrall's own. Lycurgus speaks of learning courageous patriotism from Homer, all the rest we have to assume; at least I cannot find it in Lycurgus.

Mr. Verrall has next to meet the charge of contradictions among the late writers who attribute to Solon, Pisistratus, and Hipparchus the law about recitations at the Panathenaea. But these texts, except the pseudo-Platonic Hipparchus, say nothing about Homer as "an artificial product of scholarship." Mr. Verrall declares that Lycurgus and the Hipparchus say nothing about the "arrangement" of the poems, "they speak merely of adoption and compilation."[478] But Lycurgus says nothing about compilation, the Hipparchus says nothing about compilation.

The Hipparchus says, what Lycurgus does not say, "that Hipparchus, son of Pisistratus, first brought the poems of Homer to Attica, and that he obliged the rhapsodists at the Panathenaic festival to recite consecutively, so that the people might hear entire poems, and not merely passages chosen at the will of the reciter."[479]

Not a word about "compilation." The Hipparchus falls into all the errors regarding the history of the Pisistradae that are pointed out by Thucydides.[480] Mr. Verrall is not lucky, he chooses a very erroneous anonymous author, and makes him speak of "compilation," which I do not see that he mentions, and calls his "no late or dubious authority."[481]

---

477 Quarterly Review, July 1908, p. 55.

478 Ibid. p. 60.

479 Hipparch, p. 228 B.

480 Thucydides, vi. 57-59; Monro, Odyssey, vol. ii. p. 393.

481 Quarterly Review, p. 58.

Next, the Hipparchus attributes to a man who might have been Solon's great-grandson the law which Diogenes Laertius attributes to Solon. Mr. Verrall palliates the contradictions in a curious way. "These ascriptions have presumably the same measure of truth as the connecting of the Reformation now with one and now writh another of the princes or statesmen of the sixteenth century."[482]

I do not know what historian connects the Reformation with one statesman or prince and with one only. But the texts of Mr. Verrall attribute not a religious and political movement dating, in England, from about 1370 to—?, but a single legislative Act, to several statesmen of about four generations. They are not speaking of a prolonged "educational movement," but of one legislative Act,—about which they really know no particulars.

The correct analogy to this Act is the authorisation of a translation of the Bible in England. No historian attributes that feat to any prince but gentle King Jamie: none says that it was due to Henry VIII., Edward VI., or Elizabeth. The historian cannot assume that when Diogenes Laertius attributes the law on recitations to Solon, and the Hipparchus attributes it to the son of Pisistratus, both authorities mean only that a whole educational movement occurred in the sixth century. The existence of primary education in the Athens of the seventh and sixth centuries is proved by the multitude of inscribed vases with paintings of Homeric, Cyclic, and Attic legends; but Diogenes and the Hipparchus are speaking variously about a single legislative enactment.

Mr. Verrall next supposes that the "Homer" then recited and taught at Athens was probably the whole "Cycle" of Cyclic poems.[483] This question he must settle with Mr. Murray, who, we have seen, says that the poetry selected for recitation at the Panathenaea was none but the still fluid lays of which, as I understand, our two epics are the final result; while the Cyclic poems were rejected.

---

482 Ibid. p. 58.

483 Quarterly Review, p. 60.

APPENDIX D

THE LOST EPICS AND THE HOMERIC EPICS (WIEDERHOLUNGEN)

In Chapter XVIII., on Homer and the "Cyclic" Poems, I fear that I have not succeeded in understanding Mr. Murray's view of the subject. The fault of misapprehension is not perhaps entirely without excuse. Generally speaking, I give the erroneous impression that Mr. Murray thinks the Iliad later than what are usually called the "Cyclic" poems on the themes connected with Troy. He certainly says that passages in the Iliad "seem to be derived from the Cypria, the Little Iliad, and the Sack of Ilion, the so-called Aethiopis...."[484]

He also says: "In its actual working up, however, our Iliad has reached a further stage of development than the ordinary run of poetic chronicles, if I may use the term." Moreover, "we happen to know that there was an old chronicle poem which both contained a catalogue of the ships[485] and also narrated at length the assembling of the fleet at Aulis—the so-called Cypria or Cyprian verses. Our Catalogue has in all probability been taken from there."[486] Here we are told that our Iliad derives some passages and the Catalogue from an old chronicle poem, the Cypria, and from several other named epics, "the Little Iliad, and the Sack of Ilion, the so-called Aethiopis," while, "in actual working up, our Iliad has reached a further stage of development than the ordinary run of poetic chronicles...." It was natural that, on hearing how the Iliad borrowed from an old chronicle poem, the Cypria, I should think that the Cypria was regarded as an old chronicle poem complete in itself before it was borrowed from by the Iliad. The chronicle poem of events so mythical and remote could not resemble a monastic chronicle in receiving additions from contemporary history. This remark also applies to the other poems with names, Sack of Ilion, and so on, and with contents which must be definitely known, if it be known that the Iliad borrowed from them, or seems to have borrowed from them. One could not but be convinced, then, that these old books which lent, were supposed to be earlier finished than the book, the Iliad, which borrowed from them. But Mr. Murray also said, and here the prospect wavers: "The truth is that

---

484 R. G. E. p. 165.

485 As has been said, I am aware of no evidence for this statement.

486 R. G. E. p. 164.

these various books or masses of tradition were growing up side by side for centuries. All the great books were growing up together, and passages could be repeated from any one to any other."[487]

Now a book is one thing—a book with a name, such as Cypria, is not equivalent to "a mass of tradition," which is another thing. To take an example, we have The Wallace of Blind Harry (circ. 1460), a book about as long as the Odyssey. Harry's materials were "a mass of tradition," including, it is believed, popular ballads, concerning events then remote by a century and a half. We cannot call the mass of tradition "a book which was growing up"; nor can we call the mass of tradition about the Graeco-Trojan affairs before the tenth year of the siege, a book. There is no book till the Cypria is made, and the Cypria cannot be borrowed from before it is made. A poet who relies on the mass of tradition is not borrowing from a book, any more than Harry was borrowing from a book (his use of an alleged book by Wallace's chaplain, John Blair, is another question). Manifestly incidents from a mass of tradition about Thebes, about the Greek and Trojan affairs before the war, and so on, may be introduced into an epic about the actual siege of Troy. That is all very natural and probable. But if a poem, with a definite name and a definite scope, the Iliad, borrow passages from another poem with a definite scope and name, the Cypria or others, then the poem that lends is the earlier, and the poem that borrows is the later. It was the use by Mr. Murray of these definite names of poems, Cypria, Little Iliad, Aethiopis, and so on, with his assertion that another book, the Iliad, borrows passages from them, which led me to suppose that the lending poems were, in his opinion, complete (in one form or another) when the Iliad borrowed from them. Here I misinterpreted him.

Had Mr. Murray written: "Other passages," in the Iliad, "seem to be derived from the masses of tradition about matters previous to and later than the opening and end of the Iliad—masses of tradition which in time became the topics of the Cypria, the Little Iliad, the Aethiopis," then I should have understood and agreed with him. The true view of the case, Mr. Murray's own view, seems to be this: there might be actual Greek books (probably not definitely named till a later age), and these books might, like the Chanson de Roland, be remaniés; might be modernised, and might receive additions; and another book, that which we call the Iliad, might exist, and, like the Chanson de Roland (in the Roncevaux poem) might receive additions, the facts, in some cases, being taken from the other books, which were undergoing similar vicissitudes.

[487] R. G. E. p. 163.

This is not my own view of what occurred, but it is a thinkable state of things, and I regret that I did not understand Mr. Murray's position.

At the same time, if one found in a chanson of the thirteenth century matter borrowed from the conclusion of Roncevaux (the remaniement of the Chanson de Roland), one could not say that it was borrowed from Roland, a substantive earlier poem, in a metre not that of Roncevaux.

There is a sense in which all early Greek epics might be said to borrow passages from each other. The statement would, however, I think, be misleading. The fact would be more correctly expressed by saying that the epics probably (like our own traditional ballads certainly) employ a common set of formulae to express habitual and often repeated actions and events—dawn, night-fall, feasts, preparations of food, arming, arraying a host, greeting a guest, falling in battle, and other constantly recurring circumstances.

"They hadna sailed a league, a league,
A league but barely three."

"They hadna walked in the bonny greenwood,
Na an hour but barely are."

The formula for the death of lovers—

"The one was buried in Mary kirk,
The other in Mary quire," etc.,

is of constant recurrence.
The murderer always

"takes out a little penknife
That hung low by his gare,"

or—

"Lifts up a gilt dagger
Hung low down by his knee."

The mother or lady, awaiting her son or lover, always

"Looks over tower and town,"

or—

"Looks over Castle Doune."

After a death it is always

"Bells were rung and mass was sung."

"'A grave, a grave,' Lord Bernard cryd,
'To put these lovers in.'"

"'A bed, a bed,' Clark Saunders cried,
'A bed for you and me.'"

Motherwell, who wrote without Homer in his mind, seems to state the case of the ballads very clearly. "There is not an action, not an occurrence of any sort, but what has its appropriate phraseology; and to enumerate all these would, in effect, be to give the principal portion of all our ancient ballads. For in all cases where there is an identity of interest, of circumstance, of action, each ballad varies not from the established mode of clothing these in language.... They were the general outlines of every class of human incidents...."

Motherwell adds that "something of the same sort, though in a less marked degree, may be discovered in the construction of the longer metrical romances."[488] When we look at Book viii. of the Iliad, we see that, in Mr. Leaf's words, "it has undoubtedly great spirit and movement," though "nearly one-third" of the lines "are found again in the Iliad and Odyssey—sometimes with a slight difference."

For reasons connected with the study of ballad poetry I have made some imitations of the traditional ballads, and find that, though the stories I tell are new, yet they abound in ballad formulae: indeed, a ballad, if it is to resemble the traditional sort, cannot be made on other principles. Ancient Greek epic poetry, intended, like the ballads, to be recited, not to be read, preserved the old popular and traditional convention. Critics quarrel as to the parts of the epic in which the lines are "original" and the parts in which they are "borrowed." Of many of them we may say that they are neither borrowed nor original, but are parcels of the common epic stock.

I lately met with a curious example of the critical method of treating Homer applied in certain criticisms of Scottish ballads. One ballad, "Auld Maitland," was distributed, by the critic, between Hogg and Scott. In certain stanzas he found Wiederholungen of lines in the English ballad of "Chevy Chase," and of others in Herd's version of "Otterburne" (1776). The verses in "Auld Maitland" which presented these Wiederholungen were speculatively assigned to the Ettrick Shepherd; because, in a confessed interpolation by him of two lines, where only half a stanza was received from the recitation of "Auld Maitland," the words "Remember Percy" occur. In "Chevy

---

488 See Motherwell's essay on "The Origin and History of Scottish Ballad Literature," in his Ancient and Modern Minstrelsy.

Chase" we have "But trust me, Percy." Hogg was following "Chevy Chase." But in "Auld Maitland" we read, "King Edward rode, King Edward ran"; while in "Jamie Telfer" we have "The Scotts they rode, the Scotts they ran." Now that line occurs in Scott's, and did not occur in Hogg's version of "Jamie Telfer." Moreover, Scott himself, the critic believes, wrote the part of "Jamie Telfer" where the Scotts ride and run. "If Hogg is responsible for the insertion of this line" ("King Edward rode, King Edward ran"), "he must have borrowed it from "Edom of Gordon," where we have "Sum they rode, and sum they ran."

He must have borrowed it! How like is all this to the higher criticism of Homeric Wiederholungen! In fact, ballad poetry and Homeric poetry have stocks of formulae open to every maker. Not to use them would be not to play the game.

Thus the criticism went on, and Scott's hand was detected exactly as Hogg's had been, by the occurrence, in "Auld Maitland," of ballad-formulae which also appear in ballads edited by Scott.

Enfin, "Auld Maitland" was declared to be, in the critic's opinion, in origin a composition of Hogg's, which he tried to palm off on Scott as traditional. Scott detected Hogg, entered into the plot, wrote stanzas and lines into the ballad, and palmed it off on the public.[489]

The critic happened not to know (or did not mention) the history of how the ballad was first heard by Laidlaw in the mouth of a servant girl; and how Laidlaw got a version in manuscript from Hogg, who heard a recitation by his uncle, Will o' Phawhope. The critic had never seen the extant original MS. sent by Hogg to Laidlaw, and given by Laidlaw to Scott. He had never, of course, collated that manuscript with the copy published by Scott. When we make the collation, we find that Scott neither rejected nor added a single stanza; that he made a necessary and successful emendation in one line; and that the few small verbal differences between Hogg's MS. and Scott's printed ballad may be accounted for by the fact that the copy printed from was that received from a recitation by Hogg's mother.

Thus the higher criticism, working on lines recognised as orthodox in Homeric circles, was absolutely erroneous from beginning to end. The critic was acute, ingenious, even brilliant, but he had scanty knowledge of the facts in the case. He had not consulted certain printed books germane to the matter; he had not

---

489 Further Essays on the Border Ballads. By Lieut.-Colonel the Hon. Fitzwilliam Elliot. 1910.

consulted the ballad-manuscripts at Abbotsford, and the manuscript letters.

In Homeric criticism, alas! we have not the letters and manuscripts of the poet. But it is clear from the case of "Auld Maitland" that, in the absence of facts, our motto, in conjecture, should be—Gang warily!

www.ingramcontent.com/pod-product-compliance
Lightning Source LLC
LaVergne TN
LVHW030633080426
835509LV00022B/3455

* 9 7 8 1 6 4 7 9 9 6 1 5 4 *